Downsizing
the
Federal
Government

Bureaucracies, Public Administration, and Public Policy

Kenneth J. Meier
Series Editor

Downsizing
the
Federal
Government

The Management of Public Sector Workforce Reductions

Vernon Dale Jones

M.E. Sharpe
Armonk, New York
London, England

Library of Congress Cataloging-in-Publication Data

Jones, Vernon Dale.
Downsizing the federal government : the management of public sector
workforce reductions / by Vernon Dale Jones.
p.   cm. — (Bureaucracies, public administration, and public policy)
Includes bibliography references and index.
ISBN 0-7656-0118-4 (c : alk. paper)
ISBN 0-7656-0119-2 (p : alk. paper)
1. Layoff systems—United States.
2. Downsizing of organizations—United States.
3. United States—Official and employees—Dismissal of.
I. Title.
II. Series.
JK744.J66   1998
352.3′67—dc21
97-35188
CIP

Printed in the United States of America

The paper used in this publication meets the minimum requirements of
American National Standard for Information Sciences—
Permanence of Paper for Printed Library Materials,
ANSI Z 39.48-1984.

BM (c)   10   9   8   7   6   5   4   3   2   1
BM (p)   10   9   8   7   6   5   4   3   2   1

About the Author

Vernon Dale Jones received his B.S. degree (1979) in aeronautical engineering from the United States Air Force Academy, his M.B.A. degree (1982) with a concentration in management from the College of Business and Administration of Wright State University, his M.A. degree (1990) in science, technology, and public policy from the Elliott School of International Affairs of George Washington University, and his Ph.D. degree (1995) in public administration from the Maxwell School of Citizenship and Public Affairs of Syracuse University. Additionally, he graduated from the Defense Systems Management College, where he completed the Program Manager's Course.

He is a Lieutenant Colonel in the United States Air Force. He serves as an Associate Professor and Chief of the American and Policy Studies Division in the Department of Political Science on the faculty at the United States Air Force Academy. Additionally, he served as adjunct faculty member at Syracuse University for the Maxwell School's Department of Public Administration. During his career, he worked at the field level, headquarters level, and the Pentagon. He held positions as a flight test engineer, advanced technology aircraft development engineer, special assistant to the director of engineering, program staff officer, and manager of defense systems acquisition policies. Additionally, he was a White House aide to President Ronald Reagan and an intern at the Organization of the Joint Chiefs of Staff at the Pentagon, where he was a strategic analyst.

Jones is a 1997–1998 Fellow in the Council for Excellence in Government Fellows Program.

To all the dedicated public employees
at all levels of government who
serve the people

and

For Lisa

Contents

List of Tables and Figures

Tables

Figures

List of Appendices

List of Acronyms

BOR	Bureau of Reclamation
BPR	Best practice research
BRAC	Base Realignment and Closure
CBER	Center for Biologics Evaluation and Research
CDER	Center for Drug Evaluation and Research
CDRH	Center for Devices and Radiological Health
CFSAN	Center for Food Safety and Applied Nutrition
CIM	Corporate Information Management
CPORT	Commissioner's Program and Organization Review Team
DBOF	Defense Business Operations Fund
DCAS	Defense Contract Administration Services
DFAS	Defense Finance and Accounting Service
DLA	Defense Logistics Agency
DMR	Defense Management Review
DOD	Department of Defense
DOI	Department of the Interior
DPSC	Defense Personnel Support Center
DSA	Defense Supply Agency
ECQ	Executive Core Qualification
EDI	Electronic Data Interchange
FDA	Food and Drug Administration
FOA	Field-Operating Activities
FTE	Full-time-equivalent
FY	Fiscal Year
GAO	General Accounting Office
GPRA	Government Performance and Results Act
GM	General Management
GS	General Schedule
HACCP	Hazard Analysis Critical Control Point

HEW	Department of Health, Education, and Welfare
HHS	Department of Health and Human Services
HQ	Headquarters
JCA	Job competence assessment
LEF	Leadership Effectiveness Framework
MQSA	Mammography Quality Standards Act
MSA	Management Support Activities
NAPA	National Academy of Public Administration
NASA	National Aeronautics and Space Administration
NPR	National Performance Review
OMB	Office of Management and Budget
OPM	Office of Personnel Management
ORA	Office of Regulatory Affairs
PDUFA	Prescription Drug User Fee Act
PROCAS	Process-Oriented Contract Administration Services
QDR	Quadrennial Defense Review
RAMP	Reinventing Administrative Management Program
RIF	Reduction-in-force
RSC	Reclamation Service Center
SES	Senior Executive Service
TSC	Technical Services Center
USDA	U.S. Department of Agriculture
VERA	Voluntary Early Retirement Authority
VSIP	Voluntary Separation Incentive Payment
WG	Wage Grade

Preface

Over the years, I developed a strong interest in the complexities and dynamics of public sector organizations. My career in the federal government took me to many locations and organizational levels—at the field level outside Washington, D.C., and at headquarters levels in the nation's capital—and intensified my desire to one day formally study government operations. My opportunity to conduct research on the federal bureaucracy came when I entered my doctoral program in public administration at the Maxwell School of Citizenship and Public Affairs of Syracuse University in New York. This excellent program elevated my commitment to government agencies and their devoted employees and prepared me to investigate government activities. In particular, I wanted to conduct research on organizational change and management practices within federal government agencies.

During my time at the Maxwell School, the Clinton Administration introduced its 1993 "reinventing government" reforms championed by the National Performance Review (NPR). The NPR initiated tremendous change in the federal government aimed at improving the government's performance and reducing its costs. Consequently, a fortuitous opportunity existed to investigate organizational change, its effects on agencies, and the management of that change.

Of all the change pervading federal agencies, from the NPR as well as other sources, what stood out for me was the component of reinventing government to reduce the size of the federal workforce. I spent several weeks in Washington, D.C., in late 1993 and early 1994 interviewing numerous scholars at universities, the Brookings Institution, the Congressional Research Service, and the National Academy of Public Administration; government officials at the United States General Accounting Office, the United States Office of Personnel Management, and elsewhere; leaders at the Senior Executives Association and the Federal Managers Association; NPR leaders and staff officers; and directors of NPR implementation programs in the Departments of Agriculture, Defense, Education, Housing and Urban Development, Labor, and State. From my discussions, I became acutely aware of the key role executives and middle managers have in change efforts as well as the dissatisfaction of middle managers over the plans to downsize the workforce. Thus, I decided to focus my research on organizational and managerial aspects of the downsizing process intended to remove 272,900 positions from the federal government between 1993 and 1999.

This study concentrates on how members of the Senior Executive Service manage downsizing. These senior federal career executives have the most responsibility and managerial experience in the federal workforce. They face the tremendous challenge of implementing many changes simultaneously in their organizations while they undergo downsizing. Furthermore, these executive professionals must manage the loss of middle managers and others in the workforce while keeping up morale and improving the performance of their organizations. Perhaps managing the workforce has never been more demanding. The research is intended to make a contribution to the development of downsizing theory and to the understanding of downsizing change processes and management in federal agencies.

Most citizens, elected officials, government employees, and political observers agree that improving government performance should be a priority. The Clinton Administration's reinventing and reforming efforts are aimed in the right direction. Reinvention has brought numerous forms of organizational change with it: customer service orientation, downsizing, employee empowerment, performance-based management, privatization, redesigning, reengineering, restructuring, streamlining, teaming, and more. No doubt, there have been some accomplishments and advances. However, change rarely occurs without some degree of difficulty and sometimes with unintended costs, too. It is a reality that reinventing the federal government comes with turmoil during this period of transformation. It is not an easy time for federal employees and their organizations. That is why I have written this book. This book communicates the difficulties of downsizing workforces in agencies—a central component of reinventing government. It is important that the experiences and perspectives ascertained by this research be made known. No one should interpret the contents of this book as a criticism of the National Performance Review and reinventing government. The intent is to explicate the challenging and painful conditions associated with downsizing. Through my discussions with and observations of federal civil servants for this project, it was obvious to me that they are highly committed to the missions of their agencies. The middle managers and executives I had the privilege of interacting with deeply believe in the value of their work and its contributions to the welfare of American society. Thus, they endure this turbulent period because they do want our government to work better and cost less. They are working hard, under stressful conditions, in a climate of uncertainty with great change, to achieve agency mission accomplishment. I have the utmost respect for their devotion to duty and government service.

The Defense Logistics Agency, Bureau of Reclamation, and Food and Drug Administration are the three agencies selected as case studies. Each of these vitally important agencies was extremely cooperative as a subject of investigation. Indeed, the executives and middle managers interviewed talked about downsizing with great passion and seriousness. Each agency has a different set of downsizing circumstances, but all faced arduous conditions associated with downsizing. The Defense Logistics Agency is operating worldwide in the throes of a long-term downsizing process. The Bureau of Reclamation is adjusting to a new mission of water resources management with a downsized workforce. And the Food and Drug Administration is protecting the public's health with a staff that contended with requirements to reduce and increase personnel simultaneously. The three agencies are fitting examples for a study of downsizing, and much can be learned from their experiences.

In March 1996, the first conference on "Reinvention Revolution: Reports from the Federal Front Lines" was hosted by the National Performance Review, the Maxwell School of Syracuse University, *Government Executive* magazine, and the Council for Excellence in Government. The following year, in April 1997, the second "Reinvention Revolution: Strategies and Tactics for the Twenty-First Century" conference was hosted by NPR, the George Washington University School of Business and Public Management, *Government Executive,* the Council for Excellence in Government, the Brookings Institution, and the Innovations in American Government program. The purpose of these events was to bring together hundreds of federal managers who are "in the trenches" as change agents leading innovations across the government. Many of the conference attendees work in "reinvention laboratories," places where work process reengineering, regulation waiving, customer focus, and cultural change are encouraged. I attended both to measure the temper of middle managers. As I sat in on the speakers' sessions, panel discussions, and "learning laboratory" group meetings, listened carefully to the feedback and concerns of middle managers, talked with middle managers about life in their agencies, and read the extensive middle manager comments on the "reinvention town hall wall," I learned again and again about the difficulties of downsizing. Government executives and middle managers continue to struggle with the management of downsizing and the management of their organizations after downsizing. This book is dedicated to the thousands of professional men and women in the ranks of leadership and management who keep the agencies and bureaus functioning in congenial times and in demanding times such as downsizing.

Audience

Anyone interested in organizational change and management principles will find this book beneficial. The book is intended for scholars, graduate students, and practicing leaders and managers who are interested in organization theory and downsizing theory. Most of all, the book should be valuable to those who are inspired toward research on public sector organizations. I hope that the scholarship presented will appeal to a broad audience of researchers, students, and practitioners interested in fields associated with organizational change, such as bureaucracy, business administration, political science, public administration, public policy, and psychology. Additionally, persons affected by downsizing—and there are many—will discover that the book is useful for gaining a greater understanding of the organizational and managerial aspects of the process.

Overview of the Contents

Research was conducted on executive management of downsizing in three federal agencies to investigate multidimensional aspects of downsizing. The book reports the results of the study and is organized into seven chapters.

Chapter 1 introduces downsizing as the subject of study. The chapter provides a background of the federal government's earlier experience with cutting back and its new mandate to downsize. Furthermore, a literature review and definitions prepare the reader for the focus of the research: executive management of government downsizing.

Chapter 2 discusses a theoretical framework to guide the research. The framework draws upon organizational change theory, organizational downsizing theory, and managerial competence models. From this, an initial theoretical model and the research theory building approach are described. Moreover, research questions and research propositions give direction to the research. Additionally, the chapter explains the methodology of the research. Agency sites were selected based on a set of criteria that preserved consistency among the agencies in some respects and allowed variability in other respects. Case study methodology was used with primary reliance on interviews and documentation reviews. Qualitative data analysis techniques were used to develop theory from the data.

Chapters 3 through 5 are the case study chapters that present the results and analysis of the Defense Logistics Agency, the Bureau of Reclamation, and the Food and Drug Administration, respectively. Each chapter contains sections on agency background, recent organizational changes, and downsizing activities, which provide the context for downsizing in the case. Then, the downsizing interviews are reviewed. Following the interviews, results are presented in a section on downsizing conditions, which contains numerous quotations from executives and middle managers to support findings in ten different areas. After a summary of major findings, conclusions are made for executive management of downsizing with the use of a causal network.

Chapter 6 presents a comparative analysis of downsizing for the three case studies, identifies lessons learned, proposes a theoretical model for executive management of downsizing, and generates hypotheses related to executive management during downsizing.

In Chapter 7, the book is concluded with several components. First, downsizing's greatest challenges are identified, and then steps for overcoming the challenges are presented. Next, management actions are recommended for managing in a downsizing environment or conditions of extensive change. Then, policy implications and theoretical implications are discussed. Finally, conclusions are made by addressing the contributions of the study and suggesting areas for future research on downsizing.

Vernon Dale Jones
Syracuse, New York, and
Colorado Springs, Colorado
July 1997

Acknowledgments

I have many people to thank for their support and assistance in enabling me to reach a new milestone with the publication of this book. First, I thank the many federal government employees who helped me as I went about exploring and researching activities in the Defense Logistics Agency, the Bureau of Reclamation, and the Food and Drug Administration. Next, this research could not have been completed without the involvement and cooperation of the Senior Executive Service and middle manager professionals I interviewed. I extend my sincerest thanks to each of these dedicated public leaders and administrators. I greatly appreciate their willingness to share their valuable time with me during the interviews. Moreover, I thank them for being candid and for imparting to me their personal thoughts about organizational change, reinventing government, downsizing, and management. I learned much about public management and leadership by listening to them and observing them. I have the highest respect and appreciation for the following executive civil service leaders who granted me access to their organizations and personnel during a very difficult downsizing period: Gary Thurber, Deputy Director, Corporate Administration, Defense Logistics Agency; Jim Malila, Director, Reclamation Service Center; and Sharon Holston, Associate Commissioner for Management and Systems, Food and Drug Administration. A special thank you goes to Don Glaser, formerly of the Bureau of Reclamation, now serving as the Executive Director of the Western Water Policy Review Advisory Commission, for his superb insights and guidance for managing with excellence to meet the challenges of the public sector. Valuable assistance was given to me by the following agency history, human resources, public affairs, and reinventing government staff members: John Cutrone, Janet Hoffheins, Donna Quigley, Kathy Stephens, and Mike Trescak of the Defense Logistics Agency; Sonja DeNeale, Cynthia Hancock, Carmen Maymi, Brit Storey, and Don Titus of the Bureau of Reclamation; and George Calvert, Pat Foley, Robert Sauer,

Suzanne White, and Jeylene Wood of the Food and Drug Administration.

Additionally, I received outstanding assistance from the United States Office of Personnel Management. I give my thanks to Tierney Bates, Nancy Gauthier, Donna Gregory, Mary Ann Maloney, Ed McHugh, and Charlie Taylor, who provided quick turnarounds for my data requests. I am also indebted to the staff at Vice President Al Gore's National Performance Review Office who helped me, especially during the early stages of my research. John Kamensky, Doug Farbrother, and Wallace Keene provided important information about reinventing government initiatives occurring in departments across the federal government.

Next, I thank public administration professors at the Maxwell School of Citizenship and Public Affairs at Syracuse University for their guidance and recommendations for improving my scholarship. I especially thank Patricia Ingraham for her strategic direction and all I learned from her about the civil service system and the history of public administration. I am fortunate to have served as a research associate with her during my years in Syracuse. She is a superb director of the Maxwell School's Alan K. Campbell Public Affairs Institute. I am also deeply grateful for the perspectives of Henry Lambright, Marcia Meyers (now at Columbia University), and Jeffrey Straussman. They challenged me to think in new ways. Of great assistance to me were the "insider" perspectives from Ronald Sanders, who provided expert advice and ardent encouragement. At the time of my research, he was a member of the Senior Executive Service and Director of Civilian Personnel for the Department of Defense. Now, he is a professor at George Washington University serving as the director of the Center for Excellence in Municipal Management.

I am extremely appreciative and thankful to Ken Meier for accepting the book in his series on bureaucracies, public administration, and public policy. I give my thanks to the anonymous readers who were enthusiastic about publication, offered helpful criticism, and motivated me to make the necessary revisions for publication. Anita Shute at the United States Air Force Academy served as my assistant for manuscript preparation, and I am extremely thankful for her heroic service, which enabled deadlines to be met. For M.E. Sharpe, Inc., Elizabeth Granda was a superb program coordinator who kept me on track to ensure the manuscript was properly prepared. Patricia Kolb was equally an excellent executive editor who taught me what book writing is all about. Thanks to both and to all the staff for making this endeavor a reality. I hope my first book meets their expectations.

A special thanks goes to my doctoral student colleagues. Together we encouraged and learned from each other. James Thompson, now on the faculty at the University of Illinois—Chicago, and I had many common interests and benefited from sharing our knowledge and resources with each other. Sarah Laditka, now a member of the State University of New York Institute of Technology faculty, gave me valuable critiques for improving my work. Furthermore, I gained something from every other fellow doctoral student in our program during our many conversations about improving public administration.

Especially important was the funding made available to me to conduct the research. I am very grateful for financial assistance that enabled me to travel to Denver, Philadelphia, and Washington, D.C., to carry out my research. The Syracuse University Graduate School Research and Creative Project Grant program awarded me a grant that helped to get the research through its early phases. Additionally, the Air Force Institute of Technology, Dayton, Ohio, provided travel funds to sustain the research in its interview phase. Finally, the Joint United States Air Force Academy/Defense Systems Management College Acquisition Research Group made funds available during the later phases, which enabled research completion. I appreciate the financial support of all these generous organizations.

Above all, I give my warmest and most affectionate thanks to my patient wife, Lisa, for allowing me to vigorously pursue educational advancement during the years we have shared together. She somehow not only endured the solitude necessary for me to complete this project but also managed to get through record snowfall levels during the winters. Thank you for supporting me.

Downsizing
the
Federal
Government

1

Downsizing Strikes the Federal Government

American business and government organizations are downsizing. The downsizing trend is now in its second decade, and it is not slowing down. To the contrary, it has accelerated in the private sector, taken on a new life in the public sector, and is expected to continue into the late 1990s in both sectors.

Downsizing first started in the private sector in the early 1980s in response to the poor competitive position of many U.S. companies in relation to their global competitors. Early downsizing efforts were actually a "demassing" of the workforces of many manufacturers of industrial equipment and commodity-based industries (Tomasko 1990). By the late 1980s, downsizing became a common strategy for reducing costs in U.S. businesses. About 3.4 million workers were cut from their jobs in the 1980s.[1] Then, in the early 1990s, streamlining and restructuring began to occur in technology and consumer-oriented manufacturing companies and service-oriented companies. A 1993 survey of corporate restructuring by the Wyatt Company found that downsizing occurred in 62 percent of the surveyed companies in 1991 and 74 percent of them in 1992 (Wyatt 1993, 19). Additionally, the survey revealed that downsizing was more frequent than other restructuring actions such as reorganizations, mergers and acquisitions, and divestitures. Furthermore, half of the 531 surveyed companies reduced their workforces by more than 10 percent, cumulatively, in the early 1990s. Another trend in the last few years is the increasing reliance on reducing management jobs as a downsizing strategy. More than 85 percent of the Fortune-1,000 companies downsized their white-collar workforces between 1987 and 1991 (Cameron, Freeman, and Mishra 1991, 58). Furthermore, although middle managers constitute only 5 to 8 percent of the workforce, they accounted for 17 percent of all dismissals from 1989 to 1991 (Cascio 1993, 95).[2]

In the public sector, budget limitations caused fiscal stress that led to cutbacks and retrenchment from the late 1970s to the early 1980s. Then, in 1993, the Clinton Administration's "reinventing government" program, initiated through the National Performance Review (NPR), included downsizing as a significant part of its plan to produce $108 billion in savings during fiscal years 1995 through 1999 (National Performance Review 1993a, iii).[3] Thus, the NPR expanded throughout the federal government the downsizing that had already been under way in the Department of Defense (DOD) since the late 1980s. The NPR calls for downsizing the bureaucracy by 272,900 civilian positions by the close of fiscal year 1999 for a total savings of $40.4 billion (National Performance Review 1993a, iii). Additionally, over half of the job eliminations are planned to come from middle manager positions. According to the first report of the NPR:

> We also expect that the reinventions we propose will allow us to reduce the size of the civilian, non-postal workforce by 12 percent over the next 5 years. This will bring the federal workforce below two million employees for the first time since 1967. This reduction in the workforce will total 252,000 positions. . . . Most of the personnel reductions will be concentrated in the structures of overcontrol and micromanagement that now bind the federal government: supervisors, headquarters staffs, personnel specialists, budget analysts, procurement specialists, accountants, and auditors. . . . Additional personnel cuts will result as each agency reengineers its basic work processes to achieve higher productivity at lower costs—eliminating unnecessary layers of management and nonessential staff. (National Performance Review 1993a, iii-iv)

The federal government considers itself to be ahead of schedule with its downsizing accomplishments. The total number of executive branch, non–Postal Service, civilian employees was 2,188,647 in January 1993 and declined to 1,949,366 in January 1996 according to the U.S. Office of Personnel Management (OPM) (National Performance Review 1996). The federal workforce dropped by nearly 240,000 during that three-year period. And, the downsizing continues. The Department of Housing and Urban Development announced on 13 August 1997 that it plans to reduce its workforce from 10,500 to 7,500 employees by 2002. OPM reported that at the end of fiscal year 1996, total federal on-board employment totaled 1,933,823, representing a reduction of approximately 255,000 workers since January 1993.[4] The workforce is at its lowest level since fiscal year 1965. The fourth NPR report stated:

> Most of the reductions were in three categories: administrative staff (44 percent); blue-collar staff (33 percent); and engineers, scientists, or medical

personnel (22 percent). . . . Defense civilians comprised 154,000, or 64 percent, of the reductions. . . . The proposed reengineering efforts of the National Performance Review (NPR) have enabled the Defense Department to downsize without impairing readiness or service delivery. . . . Thousands of positions on the civilian side of the government have been eliminated because of reinvention's new ways of doing things better with less. (National Performance Review 1996, 208–9)

Downsizing the bureaucracy by such a large extent introduces enormous levels of organizational stress and presents numerous challenges for federal agencies. As a consequence, organizational change is widespread. For these reasons, it is important to study downsizing. We need to know more about the antecedent conditions, processes, effects, and management of downsizing. The more that is understood about downsizing, the better agencies can manage downsizing and enhance the prospects for successful downsizing. The study of organizational downsizing remains in its early stages. Also, the literature on downsizing contains a paucity of empirical work. More attention especially needs to be given to downsizing in the public sector.

This book describes federal career executive management of downsizing in three federal agencies: the Defense Logistics Agency (DLA), the Bureau of Reclamation (BOR), and the Food and Drug Administration (FDA). The study examines downsizing activities and management during the first three years, 1994 to 1996, of a multiyear strategy in the federal government to downsize. The research uses qualitative research methodology and employs a case study research strategy. The analysis follows an inductive approach in which data gathered lead to empirical generalizations that result in theory construction. The research intends to contribute to the development of downsizing theory and add to the understanding of downsizing change processes and the management of downsizing in public sector organizations.

The study was driven by several interests. First, the author was interested in downsizing as a change process for government agencies. What happens during downsizing? What is the downsizing process? How is downsizing different from earlier government experiences with cutbacks and retrenchment? Second, the author wanted to know how downsizing affects middle managers. What are the reactions and concerns of middle managers to downsizing? How do executives accommodate middle managers during downsizing? Third, explaining executive management of downsizing was central. What is the role of executives in managing downsizing? How do Senior Executive Service (SES) executives manage during downsizing? What are the primary executive competencies for managing downsizing? Together, these questions provide the foundation and purpose of conducting the research.

The remainder of chapter 1 introduces the reader to how downsizing has struck the federal government. First, past government experience with cutbacks and retrenchment is discussed. Then, the NPR's plan to downsize the federal government and tools used for downsizing are addressed. Next, a review of relevant literature is presented. Finally, the importance of the research is emphasized.

Government Cutbacks and Retrenchment

During the past two decades, the federal government first experienced a cycle of "cutting back" and then the current cycle of downsizing. In the late 1970s to early 1980s, limited budget resources caused fiscal stress that precipitated cutbacks and retrenchment. In the late 1980s, DOD began the still ongoing reduction of its military and civilian personnel due to the end of the Cold War. Additionally, a huge budget deficit from the 1980s drove the government in the early 1990s to look for ways to reduce government spending in all departments. The outcome is a reinventing government program born in 1993 with downsizing as a major component. Consequently, cutbacks, retrenchment, and downsizing derive from a common source: federal budget uncertainties and shortages. Figure 1.1 illustrates how fiscal matters are the overriding factor behind cutbacks, retrenchment, and downsizing. Downsizing should be viewed in the broader context of government expenditure reductions. Like cutbacks and retrenchment, downsizing is a response to the contraction of budgetary resources. By taking a broader perspective, we can examine how the current wave of downsizing is similar to or different from earlier cutbacks and retrenchment. Additionally, we can investigate what was learned from each experience and accumulate knowledge useful for theory and practice (Lawler, Mohrman, Mohrman, Ledford, and Cummings 1985).

At this point, definitions of terms are important to help clarify concepts. The following terms are defined to elucidate their differences: *decline, cutbacks, retrenchment,* and *downsizing.* It is important to define these terms because (1) confusion exists about their conceptual boundaries, (2) usage of the terms varies over time, (3) the terms are sometimes used synonymously, (4) defining terms helps in the understanding and comparison of different bodies of literature, and (5) it aids in developing models and theories.

Organizational *decline* is a two-stage phenomenon in which an organization first experiences a deterioration in adaptation to its microniche and then undergoes a reduction of resources within the organization (Greenhalgh 1983; Zammuto and Cameron 1985; Cameron, Sutton, and Whetten 1988). Decline is viewed as a negative consequence of maladaptation to a dysfunc-

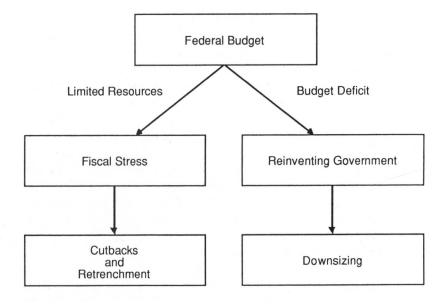

Figure 1.1 **The Federal Budget and Cutbacks, Retrenchment, and Downsizing**

tional environmental condition (Cameron, Freeman, and Mishra 1993). *Cutbacks* are a response to organizational decline. For government organizations, cutbacks are in response to the reduction of funds from budgets. Cutting back in government organizations can occur by making government agencies and subunits smaller, reducing funding resources, reducing the scope of work in bureaucracies, and reducing workforces. Cutback management refers to organizational leaders' managing the processes of cutbacks while addressing human resource management challenges and maintaining the ability of the organization to accomplish its mission. *Retrenchment* generally refers to the cutback actions associated with reduction in workforces and reduction in services provided. Retrenchment is often used synonymously with cutbacks. *Downsizing* is a particular organizational strategy used to increase organizational efficiency and productivity. It can be implemented when an organization is growing or declining. Most downsizing actions involve reductions in personnel. A more precise definition of downsizing appears later in this chapter.

The four terms defined above are often used interchangeably in the literature. In the public sector literature, *cutbacks* and *retrenchment* are the most commonly used terms for actions associated with government expenditure reductions from the late 1970s to early 1980s. *Downsizing* is the predominant term used during the current period of government reductions. A more detailed review of the downsizing literature appears later in this introduction in the "Literature Review" section. Scholarly interest in decline, cutbacks, retrenchment, and downsizing is relatively new, and most organizational research on the topics has been conducted since 1978. Most research and writing on organizational decline focuses heavily on the consequences from decreases in financial resources and decreases in the number of personnel (Sutton and D'Aunno 1989). The literature suffers from being noncumulative, widely dispersed, fragmented, confusing, and contradictory (Cameron, Sutton, and Whetten 1988). However, recent research on downsizing has advanced conceptual clarification, provided useful empirical research, and suggested important directions for future research (Cameron, Freeman, and Mishra 1993; Freeman and Cameron 1993; Kozlowski, Chao, Smith, and Hedlund 1993).

Cutback and Retrenchment Activities

The fiscal crisis of New York City in the mid-1970s focused attention on government responses to fiscal stress (Shefter 1977; Wolman 1980; Brecher and Horton 1985; Berne and Stiefel 1993). By the late 1970s, resource scarcity for federal government organizations was a reality. Literature appeared that addressed organizational decline, cutback management, and retrenchment behavior. Scholars and practitioners wanted to know more about strategies and tactics for managing cutbacks (Levine 1978, 1979; McTighe 1979; Lewis and Logalbo 1980; Behn 1988), resistance to cutbacks (Hardy 1985), managing retrenchment (Levine, Rubin, and Wolohojian 1981a, 1981b, 1982), leadership tactics for retrenchment (Behn 1980b; Biller 1980), retrenchment and political pressures (Rubin 1980a; Hardy 1989), retrenchment and budget flexibility (Rubin 1980b), termination of programs (Behn 1978a, 1980a; Brewer 1978), and strategies for workforce reductions (Greenhalgh and McKersie 1980; Feldt and Andersen 1982; Ketchum 1982; Hardy 1987). Much of the literature, especially in the earliest years, is prescriptive and not empirically based.

Cutback and retrenchment activities include reducing personnel through normal attrition, voluntary early retirements, across-the-board cuts, and reductions-in-force (RIFs); targeting cuts; reducing salaries and benefits; increasing workloads; conducting hiring and purchasing freezes; making trade-offs; stretching resources; rationing or cutting services; transferring functions and services to other levels of government; privatizing; reducing or terminating functions and programs; shifting incentives; increasing budgetary flexibility; increasing efficiencies; improving productivity; delaying expenses; and postponing maintenance and capital projects. Some of these activities are again being pursued by federal government agencies during downsizing.

President Ronald Reagan's Cutbacks

The Reagan Administration (1981–89) extended and strengthened cutback programs begun in the Carter Administration (1977–81). Reagan cutback strategies consisted of program budget and personnel cutbacks, tax reduction, deregulation, decentralization of control to state governments, and improved management. The improved management element centered on reducing fraud, waste, and abuse and improving productivity. Personnel reductions were targeted by political-level officials to specific agencies and programs. Deep budget and staffing cuts were aimed, in particular, at regulatory and social welfare agencies. Bitter political battles were fought among Congress, President Ronald Reagan, and interest groups over the extent of program cuts and reorganizations. In the end, Congress mitigated many of the President's proposed reductions; in other cases, agencies suffered painful and divisive personnel layoffs. In many cases, agencies regained their personnel levels by the late 1980s. Reductions were implemented largely by targeted layoffs; there were no incentive programs for voluntary attrition. Struggles over cutbacks, which stretched out over several budget years in some cases, resulted in a strong negative effect on the morale of federal employees and the appeal of federal employment. At the end of the decade, the National Commission on the Public Service reported that the public service was suffering from low pay, plummeting morale, recruitment rigidities, and attenuated career prospects (Volcker Commission Report 1990).

Agency Experiences

Throughout the cutback and retrenchment period of the late 1970s and early 1980s, some agencies were harder hit than others. DOD organizations were protected by the defense buildup. Regulatory agencies were specifically targeted. Additionally, interest groups and Congress were able to resist or slow cutbacks in some agencies. However, their influence and success varied from agency to agency. In some cases, agencies were able to recover from personnel losses later in the 1980s. Still, in other cases, the cutbacks exacerbated a downward trend already under way. Two agencies, the Department of Education and the National Aeronautics and Space Administration (NASA), are briefly highlighted here to illustrate the magnitude of cutbacks.

The Department of Education was established in 1979 and is the smallest cabinet-level department. During his campaign, President Ronald Reagan pledged to abolish the department. Although the threat never materialized, the department absorbed extensive personnel losses. In fact, the Education Department "was hit harder by the reductions-in-force of the 1980s than any other Cabinet department" (U.S. General Accounting Office 1993a, 4). Between 1981 and 1983, Education staff levels dropped from 7,256 to 5,226, the highest percentage of losses (28 percent) of all agencies (Stillman 1987, 10). Furthermore, its staffing levels were reduced 32 percent between 1982 and 1988, while its total appropriations for program growth increased from $14.8 billion to $28.8 billion between 1981 and 1992 (U.S. General Accounting Office 1993a, 100). During this period, the department experienced workforce composition, training, and recruiting problems. More recently, an NPR recommendation calls for the department to reduce its 230 programs by at least 40 (National Performance Review 1993a, 100). In 1994, before the implementation of its buyout program, the Education Department had 4,832 full-time-equivalent (FTE) employees.[5]

In 1958, NASA became the nation's civilian space agency. The "budgetary plenty" era of the Apollo project in the 1960s changed into the "budgetary squeeze" era of the 1970s and 1980s. According to Alex Roland, historian of NASA affairs, "The success that awaited NASA in the summer of 1969 was to be rewarded with retrenchment" (Roland 1989, 39). NASA's budget peaked around $5.25 billion in 1965 and then went through a steady cutback in real dollars for fifteen years, until 1980 (Roland 1983). Then, the budget gradually increased to $10.7 billion in 1989 (Bilstein 1989, 145). NASA staff levels decreased from 23,396 to 21,150 (9.6 percent) between 1981 and 1983, the thirteenth highest decline of all agencies (Stillman 1987, 10). The total NASA FTE workforce, including civil servants and contractor personnel, was approximately 60,000 in 1970, decreased to approximately 42,000 during 1975 to 1983, and then gradually grew to about 65,000 employees in 1990 (Augustine Report 1990, 41). In the mid-1990s, NASA underwent personnel reductions due to project curtailments and offered buyouts.

There are a few empirical studies of the effects of cutbacks and retrenchment on federal employees and agency performance. One study concluded that for cutback management, SES members should be recognized as part of solutions, trusted to work with political leaders, and granted financial rewards and incentives as motivators (Ingraham and Barrilleaux 1983). Abramson and Schmidt (1984) find that cutback environments make it difficult to implement management reforms, as was the case with civil service reform. Rubin's (1985) in-depth analysis of President Reagan's cutback programs offers a constructive account of the effects of cutbacks on five federal agencies. Her case studies are OPM and four agencies in the Departments of Health and Human Services, Housing and Urban Development, Labor, and Transportation. Her useful study analyzes the relationship between the political process of cutbacks and the impacts of cutbacks on agencies. The Rubin study provides an extensive set of management and strategic lessons learned for consideration in conducting research on downsizing. Table 1.1 contains findings extracted from the Rubin study that address phenomena worthy of attention in downsizing research.

Reinventing Government and Downsizing

Like cutbacks and retrenchment, downsizing is a response to the contraction of budgetary resources. The NPR is the cornerstone of the Clinton Administration's effort to lead the way by reinventing government.[6] The NPR initiative is intended to make historic, revolutionary transformational change to redesign, reinvent, and reinvigorate the federal government (Relyea 1993). More popularly known as "reinventing government," the NPR is intended to change and reform the federal bureaucracy's operations and culture to result in government's being more efficient and less expensive. Headed by Vice President Al Gore, the comprehensive reform strategy has the goal of creating a government that "works better and costs less" (National Performance Review 1993a, 1994, 1995, 1996, 1997).

The NPR initiative generally is considered to be a constructive endeavor. The U.S. General Accounting Office (GAO) (1993b, 1994b, 1996a) has assessed the NPR throughout its progress. The GAO "agree[s] with the thrust of most of the recommendations and support[s] their continued implementation" (U.S. General Accounting Office 1994b, 2); public management scholars call it a "reform movement in the right direction" (Kettl 1995, 74) and remind us that "the questions it raises are important and warrant continuing thought and work" (Carroll 1996, 246); and Congress considers it "a laudable initiative" (U.S. Congress, House 1996, v). However, there are also reservations and criticisms about reinventing government. Some flaws of NPR are highlighted in the "Literature Review" section later in this chapter, which addresses reinventing government.

Downsizing Plans

A central component of reinventing government is downsizing. Indeed, for many, downsizing *is* reinventing government. Downsizing 272,900 federal workers is described as the "centerpiece of the performance review" (Shoop 1994b, 19) and the "keystone of the cost savings" (Kettl 1995, 17). The

Table 1.1

Lessons Learned from Cutbacks During the Reagan Administration

1. Federal career employees implemented the cutback programs initiated by the president or required by legislation and did not delay, ignore, or sabotage the programs in their agencies.
2. Agencies with strong interest group support were able to reverse termination decisions, get programs reauthorized, and reverse cuts in funding levels.
3. The overall impact of cutbacks on federal agencies was a deterioration of management and productivity.
4. Impending cutbacks and struggles over cutbacks increased uncertainty in agencies which affected agency quality of decision making and action.
5. Cutbacks caused long-term disruptions in agencies because of employee-job mismatches, skills imbalances, and uncertainty about applicability of regulations.
6. Agency employees suffered lowered morale, lack of motivation, and reduced productivity due to fear of staffing cuts and adjustments to new jobs and demotions.
7. Relationships and communications among agency personnel deteriorated and became polarized.
8. The possibility of fraud, waste, and abuse in agency grants increased due to loss of personnel in oversight duties and decentralization of programs to the states.
9. The cutback period reduced the quality of work life for federal employees, reduced the appeal of federal employment, and hurt recruitment of new employees.
10. Employment levels of women and minorities decreased due to hiring freezes and RIFs; consequently, agency workforces became older and more homogeneous.
11. The possibility of increased political influence over the bureaucracy increased due to reduced OPM oversight and increased managerial discretion in agencies over personnel reductions.
12. Agency employees suffered from not knowing cutback levels and timetables and experiencing a sense of being punished.
13. The RIFs could have been implemented in ways to minimize damage to agencies and morale by using computerized personnel systems, updating position descriptions, communicating sympathy by personnel specialists, avoiding giving impressions of targeting individuals for dismissal, not using reorganization and personnel ceilings as purposes for RIFs, improving the timing of RIFs, reducing personnel by attrition instead of by demotions and bumping, and using outplacement programs.
14. Merging budget reduction and personnel reduction targets would have minimized damage to agencies and morale by coordinating budget and staffing levels.
15. Avoiding long battles over agency cutback and termination plans between the administration and Congress by taking quick and definitive action would have minimized agency uncertainty and improved agency productivity.
16. Clearly ending the cutbacks and reorganizations within agencies would have led to stability, reduced workforce alienation, and improved productivity.

Source: Irene S. Rubin, *Shrinking the Federal Government: The Effect of Cutbacks on Five Federal Agencies* (New York: Longman, 1985), 196–209.

272,900 figure was arrived at by a three-step process consisting of presidential Executive Order 12839 of 10 February 1993, which called for a reduction of 100,000 positions; a presidential memorandum dated 11 September 1993, which provided the official directive to cut 252,000 personnel as recommended in the NPR; and congressional legislation in March 1994, which increased the number to 272,900 employees. The first 100,000 are a part of the 272,900. A recommendation in the NPR report calls for reducing administrative and control staffs and supervisors concentrated in the structures of oversight and micromanagement. Of the total, "the Administration wants to get rid of roughly 140,000 supervisors, managers, and SESers" (Shoop 1994a, 11). Other personnel reductions are to be concentrated among headquarters staffs, personnel specialists, budget analysts, procurement specialists, accountants, and auditors. The presidential memorandum entitled "Streamlining the Bureaucracy" orders departments and agencies to carry out the personnel reductions and directs that agencies "will reduce the ratio of managers and supervisors to other personnel, with a goal of reducing the percentage who are supervisors or managers in halving the current ratio within 5 years." The NPR estimates that by 1999, the government will achieve a reduction of approximately 50 percent in the number of supervisors, 25 percent in the number of headquarters staff officials, and 21 percent in the number of management control positions (National Performance Review 1996, 218).

Additionally, Congress passed the Federal Workforce Restructuring Act of 1994 (Public Law 103-226) and Voluntary Separation Incentive Payment (VSIP) authority as part of the Fiscal Year 1997 Omnibus Spending Bill (Public Law 104-208). These laws authorize agencies to offer voluntary separation incentive payments, commonly known as "buyouts," of up to $25,000 to eligible employees who voluntarily resign. The buyouts are aimed at getting employees, especially middle managers, to leave the federal government and to avoid costly, cumbersome RIFs. RIFs are costly to agencies because they include severance payments, are highly disruptive in the short term to the remaining workforce by causing multiple employee reassignments, and lower morale and productivity.

Many federal career professional managers and executives have reacted with disillusionment. On the one hand, they support improving government and reducing its costs and accept their responsibility for implementing the changes. On the other hand, many are deeply concerned about the career civil service being faulted for ills of our government, a lack of sufficient participation by their professional associations in the reinvention effort, the justifications for an extremely high number of personnel reductions, a span-of-control ratio of fifteen employees per manager, the targeting of most of the personnel cuts at their ranks, and the consequences for the management of complex government programs in the future (Shoop 1993; Kam and Shaw 1994; Kettl 1994; McCarthy 1994).

Nevertheless, the federal government is undergoing a significant downsizing of its workforce. The government seems to be mimicking in the 1990s the extensive downsizng efforts that started in private sector organizations during the 1980s. A significant new trend within the federal government is greater targeting of middle managers. Also, individual government agencies are authorized to manage their own downsizing efforts. Therefore, approaches to downsizing vary. Very little is known about what management practices are effective for implementing downsizing and managing workforces experiencing downsizing.

Downsizing theory remains underdeveloped, few empirical studies of the downsizing phenomenon have been conducted, and not enough is known about the management and implementation of downsizing processes. Most of the research conducted focuses on the private sector. Consequently, even less is known about downsizing in the public sector. The research for this book responds to this condition by examining the management of downsizing in the public sector.

Tools for Downsizing

Table 1.2 presents the primary downsizing tools listed in order of preference used by agencies in the Clinton Administration. Unlike staffing reductions under the Reagan Administration, involuntary layoffs (RIFs) are considered to be an option of last resort in the Clinton Administration. Involuntary measures are only used when agencies fail to meet targets by voluntary means such as normal attrition, hiring freezes, transfers, outplacements, or buyouts. The emphasis has been to make cash payments to individuals to leave the public service and to offer early retirement incentives. The Federal Workforce Restructuring Act of 1994 with VSIP authority and the additional VSIP authority in 1996 make this strategy possible. Policy makers and union leaders recognized that, in most agencies, normal attrition would not achieve the necessary reductions. There was agreement that RIFs should be avoided as much as possible because of the high costs and morale problems such actions generate. In general, the policy framework promoted by the Clinton Administration is to minimize RIFs, maximize voluntary attrition, protect employment where possible by reorganizing work or facilitating transfers to other agencies, protect seniority in layoff situations, and minimize targeting of individuals in favor of targeting occupational categories. Thus, buyouts are considered a more effective, less expensive, and more humane way to reduce the workforce.

Table 1.2

Tools Used by Agencies for Clinton Administration Downsizing
(in descending order of preference)

1. Normal attrition
2. Hiring freezes
3. Transfers to other in-house positions or other agencies
4. Buyouts (voluntary separation pay incentives)
   a. Optional retirement
   b. Early retirement (early out)
   c. Resignation
5. Involuntary reductions-in-force (RIFs)

The preferred strategy for personnel reductions, other than natural attrition, is the use of separation pay incentives. The first VSIP authority for non-defense agency buyouts came with the 1994 Workforce Restructuring Act. DOD, in earlier legislation (Public Law 102-484), was authorized to offer buyouts starting in December 1992 and has approval to offer them until 30 September 1999. Civilian agencies received authorization to offer buyouts from 30 March 1994 to 31 March 1995. Agency heads could delay the separation of employees until as late as 31 March 1997 if continued employment was required to ensure performance of the agency mission. Agencies are required to cut one FTE position for every buyout paid.

Under the buyout provisions, eligible employees who resign voluntarily receive a payment equal to a severance allotment (based on a formula including salary and years of service) or $25,000, whichever is less. There are three possible categories for buyout eligibility. First, optional retirement refers to employees who are retirement eligible at age 55 or older and with thirty years of service, or age 60 with twenty years of service, or age 62 with five years of service. Second, early retirement or "early out" refers to those at age 50 with twenty years of service, or at any age with twenty-five years of service. OPM must grant Voluntary Early Retirement Authority (VERA) before an organization can offer this category. Third, an employee who does not have sufficient age and years of service for the first two categories can resign and take the buyout. Such payments had been in place for more than a year for civilians in defense agencies and were, by the act, extended to civilians in all federal agencies. However, each agency decided for itself if buyouts would be offered to employees depending on the agency's need to use the tool. In general, agencies may offer the buyouts to specific groups or categories, and employees within those groups may request a buyout. Additionally, agencies have the flexibility to offer buyouts

Table 1.3

Department of Defense and Non-DOD Buyouts
Fiscal Years 1993 to 1996

	FY 1993	FY 1994	FY 1995	FY 1996	Total
DOD	32,000	21,033	24,792	14,607	92,432
Non-DOD	0	14,531	18,203	3,301	36,035
Total for FY	32,000	35,564	42,995	17,908	128,467

Source: U.S. Office of Personnel Management.
Note: DOD buyout totals are as reported to OPM by DOD. Non-DOD buyout totals for FY 1994 and FY 1995 are from the OPM Central Personnel Data File. FY 1996 buyout totals are as reported to OPM in agency reports.

only to specific units within the agency or only during specific "windows" of time when necessary to induce employees to leave voluntarily.

Between January 1993 and September 1996, federal agencies paid 128,467 buyouts. Of the total, 92,432 were paid by DOD and 36,035 were paid by non-DOD agencies to downsize workforces. Table 1.3 shows DOD and non-DOD buyout statistics for fiscal years 1993 through 1996. Statistics by buyout category for the 3,301 non-DOD buyouts taken in fiscal year 1996 appear in Table 1.4, with the average grade expressed in terms of general schedule (GS) grade level. Furthermore, during the period from 1 October 1992 to 30 June 1996, approximately 27,000 employees across all departments were involuntarily separated by RIFs.

All agencies have an obligation to provide assistance to those who have lost or may lose their jobs involuntarily. President Bill Clinton issued an administrative directive to the heads of all departments and agencies to work in partnership with labor representatives to develop agency plans for methods of career transition assistance and policies for retraining workers for new career opportunities. In addition, the directive gives redundant workers a right to priority placement for vacant positions within their agencies and across the government. Agencies maintain their own internal priority placement lists, and a national vacancy database is maintained by OPM.

The second VSIP authority for non-defense agency buyouts resulted from Section 663 of the Fiscal Year 1997 Omnibus Spending Bill (U.S. Office of Personnel Management 1996). Signed on 30 September 1996, the law authorizes buyouts between 1 October 1996 and 30 December 1997. This new VSIP authority covers all executive branch agencies except those already with buyout authority for any part of fiscal year 1997. There are no delayed separations under this law. Again, agencies are required to cut one

Table 1.4

Buyout Statistics for Fiscal Year 1996
Non–Department of Defense

Buyout Category	Number of Buyouts	Percentage of Total Buyouts	Average Grade	Average Age	Average Payment
Optional retirement	1,736	52.6%	GS-11.8	61.3	$24,833
Early retirement	1,314	39.8%	GS-11.5	53.3	$24,949
Resignation	251	7.6%	GS- 9.7	43.9	$14,499
Total buyouts	3, 301				

Source: U.S. Office of Personnel Management, Central Personnel Data File.

FTE position for every buyout paid. Eligibility requirements are generally the same as for the earlier VSIP authority. Although the new legislation contains many of the same flexibilities and provisions of the previous legislation, there are some significant differences.

What Was Learned

There are some common threads between the earlier cutback and retrenchment programs and the current downsizing efforts. In both cases, budget constraints drive the reduction responses. Moreover, both cycles are targeted at reducing costs of operating government. Also, both rely heavily on reducing the number of employees in government service. However, the current round of staff reductions also differs from previous cutback efforts of the early 1980s. Although Reagan Administration cutbacks included personnel reductions, they differ from the current wave of downsizing in several respects. First, the Reagan personnel cuts were more unevenly applied across the government. Second, success in reducing personnel levels was mixed. Third, RIFs were relied upon as a primary tool. Fourth, RIFs were used in some places to downgrade middle managers away from policy positions and to help consolidate loyalty at the highest levels of agencies. And fifth, there was no buyout program. Table 1.5 compares the personnel reduction efforts in the Reagan and Clinton Administrations.

Literature Review

This research focuses on downsizing within the federal government. More specifically, it analyzes how federal career executives manage downsizing

Table 1.5

Comparison of Reagan Administration and Clinton Administration Personnel Reductions

	Reagan Administration	Clinton Administration
Strategies	Cutbacks; Retrenchment	Downsizing
Time period	Early 1980s	1993–99
Driven by	Budget constraints	Budget constraints
Purpose	Reduce operating costs; Reduce number of employees, particularly in regulatory and social welfare agencies	Reduce operating costs; Reduce number of employees in all agencies
Characteristics	Unevenly applied among agencies	Decentralized process; Flexible options
	Used to downgrade middle managers away from policy positions	Emphasis on streamlining middle management and oversight positions
	RIFs are a primary tool	Voluntary methods are primary; RIFs are limited and used as a last resort
	No buyout program used	Buyout program used
	Mixed success in reducing personnel	Greater success in reducing personnel

in DLA, BOR, and FDA. Figure 1.2 displays a map of the relevant research literature. The figure shows two sets of literature—reinventing government and downsizing—within the broader organizational change literature. The intersection of the two sets of literature contains the executive management and competencies literature. Thus, the center of the diagram represents the focus of the research: executive management of federal government downsizing. This literature review section contains five parts relating to the research conducted: organizational change, reorganization, reinventing government, downsizing, and executive management and competencies. Because reorganization is prevalent in many government agencies implementing the NPR and downsizing, the literature review includes reorganization as a particular type of organizational change.

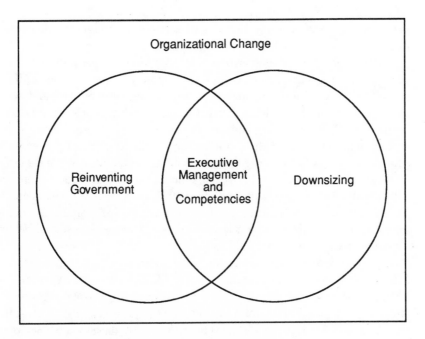

Figure 1.2 **Relevant Research Literature and Research Focus**

Organizational Change

The NPR is the latest effort to reform the government. The establishment of commissions by presidents and Congress to study the federal government and make recommendations for improvement have occurred regularly since the early 1900s. These commissions concentrated on increased authority for presidents, better management of the executive branch, and increased efficiency, streamlined activities, reorganized bureaucracy, and reduced costs in the federal government (March and Olsen 1983; Ingraham 1992; Moe 1992; DiIulio, Garvey, and Kettl 1993; Relyea and Galemore 1993). The 1989 National Commission on the Public Service, the most recent commission preceding the NPR, was an external body that advised the President and Congress on the issue of the quality of the public service (Volcker Commission Report 1990).

Organizational change must be viewed within a broader context of organizations' environments (Hall 1991). Much current research in organization theory concentrates on organizational environments in an effort to deepen the understanding and explanation of organizational phenomena. Theories of organizational change emphasize causes and processes of organizational change (Meyer 1979). Two schools of thought that undergird this book's research are briefly highlighted next.

Contingency theory emphasizes that appropriate organizational structures, processes, and changes will depend upon the contingencies of technology, size, environment, and strategic choice (Lawrence and Lorsch 1967; Thompson 1967; Pugh, Hickson, and Hinings 1969; Child 1972; Perrow 1973). Resource dependence theory emphasizes organizational decisions made in the context of internal and external political processes to acquire resources from an organization's environment (Aldrich and Pfeffer 1976; Pfeffer and Salancik 1978). This model posits that organizations are active with their environments and make strategic decisions about adapting to, manipulating, and managing the environment. The political economy model of organizational action is closely associated with resource dependence theory (Wamsley and Zald 1973).

Organizational change can result from internal or goal-directed forces (Thompson 1967) or from external forces (McKelvey 1982). Additionally, organizational change can occur as a transition in organizational strategy, structure, or process in the form of restructuring, repositioning, or revitalizing (Kimberly and Quinn 1984). There are a number of factors or "systemic obstacles" within organizations that resist change, such as investments in the status quo, constraints on behavior, and lack of resources and ability (Kaufman 1971). Other change resistance factors include stabilizing mechanisms, individual and group inertia, perceptions of threats (Katz and Kahn 1978), and inertia due to homogeneity of personnel (Hannan and Freeman 1984). Some case studies support the perspective that change in public agencies is impeded by the political and institutional context of government. Warwick (1975) describes the case of the State Department's failed attempt to reduce bureaucracy and change its personnel systems. Baxter's (1989) case study of the U.S. Postal Service finds that efforts to improve productivity and mail service were limited by political and institutional considerations. On the other hand, a study by Blau (1955) of two government organizations concluded that bureaucratic conditions generate favorable attitudes toward change. Recent case studies of successful strategic change in government organizations reveal that multiple elements must be present such as improved communications, participative management approaches, resources, and sufficient time (Poister 1988; Cole and Pace 1991; Epstein 1993). Garvey (1993) details the evolution of a major project within the Federal Regulatory Energy Commission. DiIulio, Garvey, and Kettl (1993) argue that constructive change in government performance is more likely to occur if it is evolutionary, selective, and experimental.

The literature on organization theory and organizational change has tended not to differentiate between public and private organizations. Of course, many important contributions about organizational change and innovation have come from literature focusing on the private sector (Kanter 1983; Hammer and Champy 1993; Champy 1995; Hammer 1996). This research does not investigate any differences in public and private organizational change or management practices. It does, however, extend to the public sector theories built largely upon the private sector.

What is missing from the literature on organizational change is a sufficient number of empirical, comparative case study analyses of the organizational change process internal to federal government departments and agencies. Each of the three agencies in this study is experiencing some common external environmental forces, faces some unique elements of the environment for that particular agency, is interactive with the environment, and is making strategic decisions about adapting to, manipulating, and managing the environment. These agencies are undergoing significant change processes intended to reform their structures, processes, and outcomes. The research undertaken performs an analysis of public organizations and public management that adds to the public dimension of organization theory and organizational change work.

One framework views organizational change from the perspective of organizational evolution. In this framework, models of organizational change make a distinction between revolutionary, metamorphic, or discontinuous change versus evolutionary, incremental, or convergent change (Miller and Friesen 1980; Pettigrew 1985; Tushman and Romanelli 1985). Tushman and Romanelli (1985) develop a punctuated equilibrium model in which organizations evolve through convergent periods punctuated by reorientations. The Tushman and Romanelli (1985) theory of organizational evolution appears to be applicable to the current effort to reinvent the federal government. According to the theory, organizations go through long periods of incremental change and adaptation (convergence) and eventually experience short periods of "frame-breaking" change (reorientation) (Tushman, Newman, and Romanelli 1986). The Clinton Administration's NPR program is an attempt to make significant, system-wide changes in the government. Reinventing government initiatives thus represent a reorientation for the way government and its employees operate. Viewed differently, the political environment for public organizations causes government agencies to experience reorientations quite frequently, such as when a new administration begins. Therefore, the applicability of the theory is called into question and may be in need of modification for public organizations.

Reorganization

One type of organizational change, which is a part of the reinvention of some agencies, is reorganization. Reorganization is implemented primarily to achieve goals of greater control, cost containment, economy, effectiveness, efficiency, and responsiveness. Szanton (1981) contends that all substantial reorganizations seek to shake up, streamline, reduce costs, symbolize priorities, improve effectiveness, or improve policy integration. Reorganizing the bureaucracy is a common occurrence (March and Olsen 1983; Gormley 1989). Seidman and Gilmour (1986) found that most studies of reorganization concentrate on the broad context of the executive branch with little reference to internal departmental organization. Reorganizations are associated with many of the downsizings being conducted by federal agencies. In this study, forms of reorganizations in DLA and BOR are fused with their downsizing activities.

The goals of reorganization are not always achieved. Conant (1986) concludes that reorganization for economy and efficiency has been largely discredited in the contemporary academic literature. Additionally, Maynard-Moody, Stull, and Mitchell (1986) report a consistent finding among many observers of reorganizations that visible improvements in efficiency, economy, and responsiveness are not produced. Furthermore, Szanton (1981) argues that unless reorganizers advance their reforms with persistence and skill, reorganizations will have little effect. Other literature shows that outcomes of reorganization sometimes include unanticipated negative effects and disarray and confusion (Kaufman 1971). Levine (1980) attributes organizational internal atrophy and declining performance to system and management failures from continuous reorganization. Finally, some scholars argue that reorganizations result in counterproductive behavior, bureaucratic pathologies, and internal managerial dysfunctions for organizations (Kaufman 1971; Hood 1974; Peters 1981; Caiden 1991). Despite the findings that reorganizations are not entirely successful in achieving their goals, they are useful as a symbolic and political tool (Salamon 1981; Conant 1986; Maynard-Moody, Stull, and Mitchell 1986). Gawthrop (1984) advocates redesign, not reorganization, and the integration of management, organizational designs and systems, and ethics for public organizations to deal with their complex environments.

According to Salamon (1981) and Conant (1986), serious empirically based studies on the real effects of reorganization are almost nonexistent. Therefore, this study includes consideration of reorganizations to the extent that they are a part of NPR and downsizing activities within the agencies.

Reinventing Government

Much of the literature on reinventing government addresses public management innovation. There has been a strong need for and a robust rise in
innovations in the public sector in the past few years. In fact, the Osborne
and Gaebler (1992) best-seller, *Reinventing Government: How the Entrepreneurial Spirit Is Transforming the Public Sector,* is dedicated to government innovations and provided a major impetus for the NPR. Moreover,
Barzelay's (1992) case study of Minnesota's government reforms supports
his view that new ideas and concepts are being developed for management
of government that constitute an emerging postbureaucratic paradigm (see
also Hale 1991 and Osborne 1993). Other recent works on public sector
management approaches are relevant to the innovation debate. DiIulio, Garvey, and Kettl (1993) make a case for rebuilding government capacity,
streamlining the bureaucracy, and changing the civil service system.
Denhardt (1993) addresses how public managers are transforming bureaucracies into organizations driven by commitment to values, concern for
serving the public, empowerment and shared leadership, pragmatic in-
crementalism, and dedication to public service. Kettl (1993) argues that the
government must have a smart-buyer capacity in the new environment of
increased privatization and public-private relationships.

Another area of the literature on reinventing government provides cri-
tiques of this reform movement. First, in recent years numerous publica-
tions have pointed out waste in government (Grace Commission 1984; U.S.
Congress, House 1992), problems with government efficiency (Downs and
Larkey 1986), the "quiet crisis" in the public service (Volcker Commission
Report 1990; Levine and Kleeman 1992), executive branch mismanagement
(Williams 1990), "hollow government" (Goldstein 1989, 1992, 1993; Gold-
stein and Clark 1992), the "hollow state" (Milward, Provan, and Else 1993;
Milward 1994), and the need to improve government administration
(DiIulio 1994). Of course, government bureaucracy has also been defended
(Goodsell 1994). Within the first year of reinventing government, critical
discussion appeared in the scholarly literature. The criticism states that real
administrative change requires political change also (Rosenbloom 1993);
the NPR rests on a set of faulty premises (Moe 1994); the NPR is atheoretical in nature (Thompson and Jones 1995); the NPR is based on faulty best
practice research (BPR) (Overman and Boyd 1994); many of the reinventing government ideas are not new but have been "rediscovered" (Goodsell
1993; Moe 1993); institutional reform requires incremental and evolutionary, not sweeping transformational, change (DiIulio, Garvey, and Kettl
1993); citizens are not the same as customers (Frederickson 1992); and

private sector models may not apply to public sector organizations (Kettl 1993; Ingraham and Romzek 1994).

The GAO believes the NPR's success depends on an executive-congressional partnership, attention to agencies' capacities, and sustained political and career leadership (U.S. General Accounting Office 1994b). In addition, Kettl (1995, 11), in a comprehensive Brookings Institution appraisal of the NPR, believes *"the NPR is not now sustainable"* (italics in original) because a foundation for lasting success was ignored. He argues that NPR success depends on resolving the problems of an unorganized focus ("tensions"), the requirement for a vision for the public service of the future ("capacity"), confusion over guiding principles ("ideas"), and the need to hold the movement together ("glue"). Still, others have charged that actions need to be taken to ensure the survival and institutionalization of government reform (Sanders 1996; Sperry 1996; Sanders and Thompson 1997). Furthermore, it is asserted that NPR's "pseudoreforms" have failed to remedy government's most serious problems and its purported savings are exaggerated (Hodge 1996). More recently, Light (1997a, 1997b) asserts that reinventing government compounds government mismanagement because there is too much management reform in government.

The literature contains a plethora of publications with multifarious views. NPR officials (Gore 1994; Kamensky 1996), public administration academics (Moe 1994; Arnold 1995; Thompson and Jones 1995; Van Wart 1995; Frederickson 1996; Peters and Savoie 1996; Thompson and Ingraham 1996), and public management scholars at research organizations (DiIulio, Garvey, and Kettl 1993; Kettl 1994, 1995; Ban 1995; DiIulio 1995; Foreman 1995a, 1995b; Garvey 1995; Radin 1995; Sundquist 1995; Hodge 1996; Pfiffner 1997) have explained and assessed the NPR. Also, witnesses before Congress and reports from Congress (U.S. Congress, House 1995, 1996) have appraised the NPR.[7] Each has contributed to an ongoing debate over the merits, flaws, progress, potential, successes, and failures of reinventing government. According to Carroll (1995), assessments of the strengths and weaknesses of the NPR depend upon the framework used. We know that "a government that works better and costs less" (National Performance Review 1993a) is where we want to go, but we do not know how well we are doing in that effort.

While all of this literature is an important response to reinventing government, some of it tends to be normative and lacks sufficient empirically based qualities. Indeed, some of the literature suffers from scholarship using maligned BPR (Overman and Boyd 1994). Some also reflects scholarship characterized by faulty emphases on principles of management and experiential and didactic approaches that disregard theory and are noncumulative in nature (Lynn 1994). More empirical studies should examine specific elements of the reform process. This research does so by conducting an empirical investigation of downsizing, which is a central part of reinventing government. The research for this study focuses attention where it is needed: on the innovation and management processes within federal agencies and on their responses to a specific kind of change—downsizing—brought on by internal and external forces.

Downsizing

The study of organizational downsizing has rarely been investigated by organization and management researchers. Not enough is known about downsizing implementation processes and downsizing effects on organizational performance. Because few empirical studies on downsizing exist, downsizing theory remains underdeveloped (Cameron, Freeman, and Mishra 1991, 1993; Freeman and Cameron 1993; Kozlowski, Chao, Smith, and Hedlund 1993). This literature review section discusses a definition of downsizing, a distinction between organizational downsizing and decline, an overview of some problems with literature dealing with downsizing, and ways this study fills some gaps in the literature.

This study uses the following definition of downsizing, which provides precise conceptual meaning to advance the development of models and theories:

> Downsizing is an intentional set of activities, usually involving reductions in personnel, to improve efficiency and productivity by affecting work processes. Downsizing often includes the intended reductions of personnel through the planned elimination of positions or groups of positions. Downsizing may occur by reducing employees or work; by eliminating functions, hierarchical levels, or organizational units; and by implementing cost-containment strategies that simplify and streamline activities. Downsizing strategies include normal attrition, voluntary severance programs, early retirements, buyouts, outplacements, and layoffs. (Cameron, Freeman, and Mishra 1993, 24–25; Freeman and Cameron 1993, 12–13)

Downsizing activities are often referred to by other terms in popular usage such as *building down, compressing, consolidating, contracting, cutbacks, decruitment, delayering, demassing, deorganization, dismantling, downshifting, growth-in-reverse, leaning up, rationalizing, reallocating, reassigning, rebalancing, redeploying, redesigning, reengineering, refocusing, restructuring, retrenchment, rightsizing, slimming down,* and *streamlining.* Some of these terms have meanings that are different from the meaning of *downsizing.*

Also, some of the terms refer to particular aspects of downsizing. Because some of these terms are used in the case study chapters later in the book, they are defined here now. *Redesigning* is the reduction or elimination of tasks, work, functions, hierarchical levels, or organizational units considered to be duplicative or unnecessary. *Restructuring* is the realignment of functional activities or change in work operations for an organization. *Streamlining* is the minimization of non-value-added steps and the maximization of value-added steps in a process, system, or organization. *Reengineering* is a management technique for achieving dramatic improvements in cost, quality, and customer service by making radical change or significant alteration in the way an organization defines its mission and organizes its work processes. Reengineering usually is accompanied by equally radical change in the shape and character of the organizational unit responsible for the work. It should be noted, however, that downsizing often does not achieve its intended goals of greater efficiency, improved productivity, and reduced costs (Cameron, Freeman, and Mishra 1991, 1993; Cascio 1993; Noer 1993; Wyatt 1993). A recent review of the literature on downsizing as well as on reengineering and total quality management reveals that none of these three change approaches has a consistently positive relationship with organizational effectiveness (Druckman, Singer, and Van Cott 1997).

There is a well-developed literature on organizational decline (Zammuto and Cameron 1985; Cameron, Sutton, and Whetten 1988). However, it is important to understand that downsizing and decline are distinct constructs. Decline is a negative consequence of maladaptation to a dysfunctional environmental condition, happens *to* an organization, is unintentional, may not necessarily produce a reduction in personnel, is not a targeted improvement strategy, is not aimed at improving efficiency, and may not necessarily affect work processes (Cameron, Freeman, and Mishra 1993). Organizations can downsize without declining or downsize in response to decline.

The literature on downsizing does address some aspects of the phenomenon. One area of the literature addresses determinants of downsizing targets and strategies. Models have been developed that predict which organizations are most likely to downsize (Sonnenfeld and Peiperl 1988), identify factors that affect the severity of organizations' downsizing actions (Greenhalgh, Lawrence, and Sutton 1988), identify external and internal factors that determine whether organizations pursue outplacement or inplacement strategies (Latack 1990), and explain organizations' choice of downsizing targets and practices as either proactive or reactive (Kozlowski, Chao, Smith, and Hedlund 1993). The problem is that none of these macrolevel models have been tested by empirical research (Taylor and Giannantonio 1993). A second area of research addresses the impact of downsizing strategies on organizational performance. Kozlowski, Chao, Smith, and Hedlund (1993) propose that the effects of downsizing on organizational performance is mediated through its effects on surviving and terminated employees. The Cameron, Freeman, and Mishra (1991) study of downsizing practices used for white-collar jobs in the automobile industry tends to support recommendations for proactive downsizing. Again, a gap in research is that there have been no attempts to test exactly how, or if, these relationships operate as proposed (Taylor and Giannantonio 1993). Finally, a third area contains much research on the effects of downsizing on people and the individual-level reactions of victims and survivors. Some studies look at aspects of a stress and coping model of job search by victims of downsizing (Harris, Heller, and Braddock 1988; Leana and Feldman 1991; Gowan and Gatewood 1992). Furthermore, there is a rich depth of research on survivors' reactions to downsizing (Brockner 1988, 1992; Brockner and Greenberg 1990; Brockner and Wiesenfeld 1993; Noer 1993).

Some of the public sector literature addresses downsizing and streamlining and identifies important issues concerning agency operations, management practices, and human resources for government organizations. The literature makes note of such issues as the morale of remaining employees, new challenges for management, and a concern about maintaining sufficient capacity to perform functions. However, very little of this literature is based upon empirical research in federal agencies to determine the conditions and effects of downsizing and streamlining. Those few examinations of agency activities have reported on various strategies for implementing the NPR (Radin 1995; Thompson and Jones 1995). The U.S. General Accounting Office (1995) issued a report on downsizing strategies based on the experiences of private sector companies, states, and foreign governments. Additionally, the National Academy of Public Administration (NAPA) (1995) published a guide to best practices for downsizing government organizations. Furthermore, some attention to downsizing is included in reports on the status of reinvention laboratory efforts (Sanders and Thompson 1996; U.S. General Accounting Office 1996a). Again, what is missing is an empirical investigation of agency downsizing and streamlining activities.

Other scholarly literature on downsizing contains gaps that provide opportunities for research. The study by Cameron, Freeman, and Mishra (1991, 1993) investigated how downsizing is implemented in organizations, what the impacts of downsizing are on organizations, and what are the best practices in downsizing. However, the study was done on firms in the automotive industry and, obviously, not on public sector organizations. Furthermore, a study by McCune, Beatty, and Montagno (1988) surveyed manufacturing firms for downsizing practices. The study for this book investigates issues related to downsizing management practices in the public sector rather than private sector. Additionally, some works are experience based, cite surveys of downsizing firms, and then generate prescriptions for implementing downsizing (Tomasko 1990; Cascio 1993). Kozlowski, Chao, Smith, and Hedlund (1993) emphasize how too much of the organizationally oriented literature is too strongly focused on descriptions of the normative mechanisms used to downsize and prescriptions regarding how to accomplish downsizing. The major contribution from this study is its empirical investigation of management practices during downsizing and the effects of downsizing management on public agencies and their employees.

Executive Management and Competencies

Executive leadership and management of downsizing forms the central focus of the research. The NPR calls for exerting leadership in and changing the culture of the federal bureaucracy to make it more conducive to better performance. Successfully changing the culture and implementing the many other changes from the NPR require leadership and management from the cadre of executives in the federal career SES. SES professionals are "essential to effective governance, particularly during a period of fundamental change in government's structure and operations" (Sanders 1994, 234–35). There is widespread agreement that successful change efforts require leadership involvement in their initiation, implementation, and sustainment (Selznick 1957; Greiner 1967; Kaufman 1981; Poister 1988; Kotter 1990, 1996; DiIulio, Garvey, and Kettl 1993; Rainey 1997). Additionally, studies of federal bureaucracies indicate that stable leadership leads to continuity, predictability, and operating effectiveness (Barnard 1938; Downs 1967; Gawthrop 1969; Meyer 1979). Furthermore, Schein's (1992) seminal work relating organizational culture to leadership is critical in helping to understand organizational change. Also, Behn's (1991) case study of the role of leadership and management in the success of a Massachusetts welfare program provides important lessons for public managers. Thus, executives, as the professional leaders of government agencies, are vital to change and downsizing processes. Because of the expected critical role of executive management in the organizational downsizing process, this dimension is central to the research.

The Tushman and Romanelli (1985) model of organizational convergence and reorientation emphasizes the role of executive leadership and management:

> Executive leadership is the primary agent capable of mediating between these contrasting forces for stability and change. While middle-level management

can sustain convergent periods, only executive leadership has the position and potential to initiate and implement a strategic reorientation. (Tushman and Romanelli 1985, 209)

The key role of executive leadership and management is required for initiating and managing organizational transformations (Tushman, Newman, and Romanelli 1986). Furthermore, executive managers must possess the necessary characteristics and competencies for leading organizational reorientations (Morgan 1988; Nadler and Tushman 1989, 1990; Schroder 1989; Spencer and Spencer 1993). Chapter 2 provides greater details about managerial competencies.

Middle managers, like the executives who are their superiors in their organizations, are integral to effective government operations and successful change implementation such as downsizing. Consequently, executive management of middle managers is an important dimension of the study. Middle manager roles of liaison, disseminator, disturbance handler, and negotiator are traditionally middle management functions and are central to successful management of change (Mintzberg 1973). Colvard explains:

> Connecting is the process of converting policy-level strategic decisions into executable tactics. This is the role of what is commonly called middle management. . . . Vertical middle management is the connecting link between broader conceptual levels and execution-specific levels in an organization. Horizontal middle management provides administrative expertise outside the main line of business. . . . Middle management in both forms is critically important. . . . Middle management, done properly, is much more. It involves translation and judgment. (Colvard 1994, 57)

Kettl adds:

> Middle managers play a critical role in the reinvention effort. They occupy the key positions throughout government that determine how well programs work. They are the project managers, branch chiefs, and section heads who shape programs and the behavior of their agencies. They model the behavior for their subordinates. (Kettl 1995, 28)

In summary, both government executives and middle managers perform pivotal functions in change affairs such as downsizing.

Importance of Downsizing Research

This study seeks to make an important contribution to understanding downsizing in the public sector. The research will help correct two conditions frequently complained about in the organization theory literature (Rainey 1991, 1997). One is the incomplete analysis of public organizations and public management and the influences of their political and institutional environments. The other is the anecdotal and descriptive nature of the public sector literature, which insufficiently addresses internal structure, behavior, and management in the bureaucracy. This study will add to a growing body of literature in the 1990s that analyzes effective management and organizational efforts to transform federal departments and agencies. This research is unique in that it is an empirical, comparative case study analysis of the downsizing process internal to federal agencies. The research is especially important at this time when a wide spectrum of support and high expectations exist for change in government. Moreover, the research is important because almost every federal government agency is experiencing downsizing and its effects. Furthermore, agencies can expect to downsize throughout the remainder of this decade.

It is hoped that this research helps improve our understanding of the management of downsizing in public organizations. There are many important aspects of downsizing management that can be explained by research on the topic. Some of the most salient aspects are exercising management tactics and strategies for ensuring mission accomplishment; managing downsizing programs with diverse elements; dealing with resistance to change; making decisions about changes related to the reduction or elimination of workloads, positions, functions, hierarchical levels, and organizational units; maintaining high morale, commitment, and motivation among remaining employees; and managing any unexpected outcomes and challenges.

Notes

1. See Jay Mathews, "Downsizing's Ups, Downs," *Washington Post*, 29 May 1994, H1. This article addressing corporate downsizing is representative of many appearing in the press since the late 1980s documenting the plight of American companies and employees.

2. Also, for a list of ten lessons learned from previous downsizing experiences, see Cascio (1993, 103).

3. For details of estimated savings, see the first NPR report's (National Performance Review 1993a) Appendix A, which contains a numbered list of major recommendations with fiscal impacts by agency on pages 133–53, and Appendix B, which shows savings according to major issue areas and fiscal years on pages 155–57.

4. According to OPM's Central Personnel Data File numbers that represent all executive branch civilian, non–Postal Service, employment of all work schedules (full-time, part-time, and intermittent) and all tenure groups (permanent and temporary).

5. The employment figure comes from a Department of Education internal document titled "Staff Levels" obtained during an interview with a department official in the Office of the Secretary on 2 June 1994.

6. For a brief overview of the NPR, including its Phase I and Phase II, see "A Brief History of the National Performance Review," February 1997, a paper updated periodically by John M. Kamensky, Deputy Director, National Performance Review Office.

7. The Subcommittee on Government Management, Information, and Technology of the House Committee on Government Reform and Oversight, 104th Congress, 1st Session, conducted hearings between 2 May 1995 and 27 June 1995. Witnesses at the hearings on 2 May 1995 testified on the NPR's role and mission and on whether NPR had met expectations and could attain its stated objectives. Witnesses included Alice M. Rivlin, Director, and John Koskinen, Deputy Director for Management, Office of Management and Budget; Charles A. Bowsher, Comptroller General of the United States, U.S. General Accounting Office; Tony Dale, Budget Manager of the New Zealand Treasury; Duncan Wyse, Executive Director, Oregon Benchmarking Project; Dwight Ink, President Emeritus, Institute of Public Administration; R. Scott Fosler, National Academy of Public Administration; Donald F. Kettl, Senior Nonresident Fellow, Brookings Institution; and Herbert N. Jasper, Senior Associate, McManis Associates. The Subcommittee on Civil Service of the House Committee on Government Reform and Oversight, 104th Congress, 2d Session, held hearings on 8 May 1996 to address downsizing "soft-landing" (buyout pay) legislation. Witnesses included G. Jerry Shaw, General Counsel, Senior Executives Association; Lisbeth Chandler, National Vice President, Region II, National Federation of Federal Employees; and Mark Gable, Federal Managers Association. Additionally, this same subcommittee on 23 May 1996 conducted a hearing on "Reinventing Downsizing or Downsizing Reinvention?" Witnesses at the 23 May hearing included Timothy P. Bowling, Associate Director, Workforce Management Issues, U.S. General Accounting Office; John A. Koskinen, Deputy Director for Management, U.S. Office of Management and Budget; James B. King, Director, U.S. Office of Personnel Management; John H. Luke, Deputy Assistant Comptroller General for Human Resources, U.S. General Accounting Office; and P. Patrick Leahy, Ph.D., Chief Geologist, U.S. Geological Survey.

2

Selecting Downsizing Agencies
for Study

The purpose of chapter 2 is to disclose the process followed and preparations made for the investigation into downsizing in three federal government agencies. This study uses a case study research design and benefits from the development of a theoretical framework prior to data collection in selected agencies. The study includes a theoretical framework composed of a theoretical model, research questions, and research propositions to help focus and guide the research. The approach aims to improve the quality of the research and its findings by making the theoretical framework explicit, fully codifying research questions and propositions, standardizing data collection procedures, and using systematic devices for analysis (Miles and Huberman 1994).

This chapter highlights organizational change theory, downsizing theory, and managerial competence models that lead to an initial theoretical model for the study. Following the theoretical background and model, the research theory building process is discussed. Then, research questions and research propositions are presented. Finally, the study's methodology is described for selecting the Defense Logistics Agency, the Bureau of Reclamation, and the Food and Drug Administration as case studies. Included are details of the qualitative research process and case study research methods.

Theoretical Background

Organizational Change Theory

The study of organizational change is not very advanced. The term *organizational change* is defined, in general, as change in how an organization is structured and operates. Ledford, Mohrman, Mohrman, and Lawler (1989) define large-scale organizational change as a lasting change in the character of an organization that significantly alters its performance. According to these researchers, a change in an organization's character requires changes in the organization's design and its processes. NPR's attempt to create lasting change that improves the government's performance can be classified as large-scale organizational change.

Organizational change triggered by organizations' environments is one kind of organizational change and is relevant in this study. Organizations are experiencing enormous change, greater in magnitude and speed than ever before. The extraordinary change affecting organizations derives in large part from organizations' dynamic, unpredictable, and turbulent external environments. The relationship between change and the environment is described as follows:

> Organizational change must be viewed within a broad context which includes the environment, which itself consists of other organizations as well as economic, political, and social patterns and changes, and the change efforts of organizations themselves. (Hall 1991, 193)

Huber, Sutcliffe, Miller, and Glick (1993) conducted several literature reviews and found that characteristics of an organization's environment constitute a major category of factors that lead to organizational change. Turbulence, competitiveness, and complexity are environmental characteristics identified as determinants of organizational change (Aldrich 1979; Huber 1984; Hrebiniak and Joyce 1985; Mohrman and Mohrman 1989). In the Huber, Sutcliffe, Miller, and Glick (1993) study of 119 heterogeneous organizations, the researchers found that environmental turbulence as well as environmental competitiveness interacting with organizational size are highly significant predictors of organizational change. In an important study with public sector implications, Meyer (1979) found in his study of U.S. state and local government finance agencies that the structure and behavior of public organizations are highly influenced by environmental forces. In another early study, McKelvey (1982) determined that the vast majority of changes in organizations are caused by external forces rather than internal forces.

The external environments of organizations are causing profound change in organizations. Global competition, information technology, scarce resources, and demographic changes are just some of the many external factors inducing organizational change. There is a recognition that a paradigm shift is occurring for the management of private and public organizations. The shift is away from hierarchical organization, bureaucratic structures, and centralized control to organizations characterized by flexibility, adaptivity, continual innovation, flatter hierarchies, decentralized decision making, delayered management levels, permeable boundaries, leadership without control, team processes, participatory approaches, empowerment of employees, self-organizing units, continuous learning, shared relationships, tolerance for ambiguity, and capacity for renewal (Daft and Lewin 1993; Huber and Glick 1993). The Burke-Litwin (1992) model of organizational performance and change specifies causal relationships among organizational variables and provides a useful framework. The model considers the external environment to be a key factor and distinguishes transformational and transactional dynamics in organizational behavior and change. In the public sector, organizational change is pervasive, and reinventing and reforming government are manifestations of it (Ingraham and Romzek 1994).

Management's attitude toward change is a beneficial way of viewing environment-organization relations (Whetten 1980b). Managers can negatively value change and respond to it by being reactive with defensive measures or by being proactive with preventive measures to avoid change. Conversely, managers can positively value change and respond to it by being reactive with steps to deal with the change or by being proactive with embracement of change.

Organizational Downsizing Theory

Distinctions already were made among decline, cutbacks, retrenchment, and downsizing in chapter 1. However, because some of the literature fails to clearly define or make distinctions among these constructs and because there is little agreement in the literature about definitions and distinctions, downsizing theory is inhibited. Nevertheless, we can extract some valuable insights and findings from the literature to provide a theoretical framework for this study.

Strategies

The manner in which organizations downsize is a basic aspect of the downsizing phenomenon. Downsizing strategies are linked to subsequent organizational performance and consequences. Downsizing strategies for reducing personnel vary: natural attrition, layoffs with or without assistance, voluntary departures through transfers or buyout programs, and involuntary separations such as demotions, position downgradings, furloughs, or RIFs. Assistance to employees may include advanced notification, benefits continuation, counseling, outplacement, retraining, or severance pay. Other alternatives often used in conjunction with the previously identified strategies include hiring freezes, job sharing, pay reductions, program terminations, service cutbacks, reorganizations, and unit mergers. Application targets are another element of downsizing. Downsizing may be applied to specific locations, organizational units, hierarchical levels, or work functions, and it may be applied uniformly across-the-board or selectively. Additionally, other downsizing strategies affect work processes and may include organizational reengineering, redesigning, restructuring, or streamlining,. which reduce or eliminate particular workloads, positions, functions, levels, or units.

In addition to the downsizing strategies, application targets, and alternatives described above, any other organizational actions, behaviors, and patterns used in downsizing should be examined. The Cameron, Freeman, and Mishra (1993) study of thirty automotive firms identified three major types of downsizing strategies: workforce reduction, organization redesign, and systemic culture change. The researchers grouped specific downsizing actions into the three broader downsizing categories. This study investigates how federal executives use various strategies to manage downsizing in their agencies.

Organizational Performance

A major gap in the literature is the dearth of empirical studies on the effectiveness of downsizing. Very little is known about whether or how downsizing affects organizational performance. Fortunately, Cameron, Freeman, and Mishra (1993) conducted a thorough empirical study of downsizing that provides some early findings on the topic of organizational performance. They found that firms with effective and improving performance were those that incrementally implemented downsizing, conducted a systematic analysis before downsizing, involved employees through participation, increased communication, and developed an advanced quality culture. This empirical study of three federal agencies will help identify factors that affect later organizational performance.

Consequences

There is a fundamental consensus in the literature that decline results in dysfunctional consequences for organizations and individuals within them (Cameron, Kim, and Whetten 1987; Whetten 1987). Dysfunctional consequences have also been observed in environments of cutbacks and retrenchment. A number of negative consequences are frequently cited. Conflict increases due to fewer resources (Levine 1978, 1979; Whetten 1980b).

Coalitions form among interest groups, Congress, and the bureaucracy to keep programs from being eliminated (Kaufman 1976; Behn 1978b). Non-prioritized cutbacks occur (Boulding 1975; Cyert 1978; Whetten 1980b).

Several dysfunctional consequences are related to how decline impedes adaptation (McKinley 1993). The threat-rigidity model of Staw, Sande-lands, and Dutton (1981) argues that threats to an organization lead to responses that reduce the organization's ability to adapt to environmental change. Thus, decline leads organizations to centralize control, resist change, decrease innovation, emphasize efficiency, increase conservatism, focus on the short term, consume slack resources, and avoid risks. These outcomes, in turn, lead to reduced employee participation, lowered morale, and restricted communication. A large body of theoretical and empirical research on decline and cutbacks, much of it centered on the public sector, supports the dysfunctional consequences identified above (Hall and Mans-field 1971; Starbuck, Greve, and Hedberg 1978; Bozeman and Slusher 1979; Rubin 1979; Whetten 1980a, 1981; Levine, Rubin, and Wolohojian 1981a, 1981b, 1982; Jick and Murray 1982; Cameron 1983; Petrie and Alpert 1983; Bourgeois 1985; Cameron, Kim, and Whetten 1987; Cameron, Whetten, and Kim 1987; D'Aveni 1989; D'Aunno and Sutton 1992).

Alternatively, research literature exists which supports the view that organizational decline stimulates adaptation. This view holds that external threats lead to adaptive responses (Meyer 1982; Miles and Cameron 1982; McKinley 1984; Koberg 1987) and risk-taking behavior at the individual and organizational levels (Singh 1986; Fiegenbaum and Thomas 1988; Bromiley 1991). Opportunities are sought amid conditions of decline. The literature further argues that firms which successfully downsized view downsizing as an opportunity to improve their performance (Cameron, Freeman, and Mishra 1991, 1993; Cascio 1993).

The downsizing literature also provides support for dysfunctional conse-quences of downsizing. According to this literature, downsizing results in deteriorated productivity; reduced employee morale, motivation, and trust of management; increased stress and challenges for managers; and lack of costs savings and efficiency improvements (Brockner 1988, 1992; Tomasko 1990; Cameron, Freeman, and Mishra 1991, 1993; Cascio 1993; Noer 1993; Wyatt 1993; Druckman, Singer, and Van Cott 1997).

The preceding discussion of consequences references the decline and downsizing, and to a lesser extent cutback and retrenchment, literatures. Because a plethora of literature addresses the possible consequences of decline, cutback, and retrenchment, it is reasonable to want to know if these same consequences occur from downsizing. Therefore, downsizing conse-quences are an important piece of the theoretical model.

Managerial Competence Models

For organizations to successfully achieve effective organizational performance in the midst of complex and changing environments, they must be managed by competent executives and managers. Research on job competencies has burgeoned since it began in 1973 (McClelland 1973, 1976). *Competency* is defined as "*an underlying characteristic* of an individual that is *causally related* to *criterion-referenced effective and/or superior performance* in a job or situation" (italics in original) (Spencer and Spencer 1993, 9). The five types of competency characteristics that indicate ways of behaving or thinking are motives, traits, self-concepts, bodies of knowledge, and skills.

In one study, Schroder (1989) identified, measured, and developed managerial competencies that were significantly related to superior organizational performance. He distinguished among three classes of managerial competencies: entry level, basic, and high performance. Entry-level competencies represent individual characteristics to function as a manager, such as communication skills. Basic competencies represent personal effectiveness skills to perform the more technical, functional, and specialized aspects of managing, such as planning, organizing, controlling, developing, and interacting. High-performance competencies are those that represent "a relatively stable set of behaviors which produces significantly superior workgroup performance in more complex organizational environments" (Schroder 1989, 22).

The high-performance competencies were derived from three previous comprehensive studies. The first is research by the Board of the Florida Council on Educational Management, which used behavioral event interview methodology to study the effectiveness of schools (Huff, Lake, and Schaalman 1982). The second is a set of studies that also relied on behavioral event interview techniques to determine twenty-one competencies of more than two thousand managers in forty-one different management jobs in twelve public and private organizations and is one of the most extensive sets of competency studies performed (Boyatzis 1982). The behavioral event or critical incident interview methodology is also used in this study and is explained in appendix D. Finally, a third set of studies over a twenty-year period used laboratory simulation methods and behavioral observation to identify cognitive competencies of individuals associated with superior group performance (Schroder, Driver, and Streufert 1967; Streufert and Swezey 1986).

Another more detailed set of competencies is found in a comprehensive summary of twenty years' worth of job competence assessment (JCA) methodology applications (Spencer and Spencer 1993). The researchers analyzed 286 studies that used the behavioral event interview methodology to distinguish competencies of superior performers in jobs in private and public organizations.[1] Superior performance was defined statistically as one standard deviation above average performance in most of the studies. From their analysis, the researchers identified twenty-one most common competencies.

To lead and manage organizations successfully through periods of downsizing or any kind of organizational change, executives need to possess and upgrade certain competencies. A government-wide occupational study of federal executives, managers, and supervisors was conducted by Corts and Gowing (1992) of OPM to establish an empirically based continuum of behaviors and competencies.[2] The Leadership Effectiveness Survey was sent to a stratified, random sample of 20,664 federal executives, managers, and supervisors in October 1991. A response rate of nearly 49 percent was achieved with the return of 10,061 completed surveys. The result is a new Leadership Effectiveness Framework (LEF) with twenty-two competencies. From this, five Executive Core Qualifications (ECQs) were identified that are considered necessary for effective performance in any SES position. Table 2.1 lists the twenty-two managerial competencies of federal SES executives in four categories. OPM later changed the names of two competencies: "Client Orientation" became "Customer Orientation" and "Internal Controls/Integrity" became "Management Controls/Integrity." Table 2.2 displays the ECQs with competencies from the LEF considered to be important for each core qualification. Appendices A and B contain the definitions for the competencies and ECQs, respectively. As of 31 January 1994, all announcements for career appointments to the SES include the ECQs. SES candidates do not need to have experience in each LEF competency to demonstrate possession of an ECQ. In this book, to avoid any confusion, OPM competencies are identified with upper- and lower-case letters ("Team Building") while the study's competencies are labeled in lower-case letters ("team orientation").

This study gathers data from federal SES executives about their management practices and competencies during downsizing. Collecting information about SES competencies presents an opportunity to compare the study's findings about downsizing competencies with the LEF's competencies. Therefore, an examination is made to determine which OPM competencies are being utilized for downsizing. Additionally, the study identifies any competencies for downsizing not listed in OPM's list of competencies.

Initial Theoretical Model

Figure 2.1 shows a theoretical model based upon the discussion of organizational change theory, organizational downsizing theory, and managerial

Table 2.1

Managerial Competencies of Senior Executive Service (SES) Executives

Basic Competencies
1. Decisiveness
2. Flexibility
3. Interpersonal Skills
4. Leadership
5. Oral Communication
6. Problem Solving
7. Self-Direction
8. Technical Competence
9. Written Communication

First-Level Competencies
10. Conflict Management
11. Human Resources Management
12. Influencing/Negotiating
13. Managing Diverse Workforce
14. Team Building

Mid-Level Competencies
15. Client Orientation (Customer Orientation)
16. Creative Thinking
17. Financial Management
18. Internal Controls/Integrity (Management Controls/Integrity)
19. Planning and Evaluating
20. Technology Management

Higher-Level Competencies
21. External Awareness
22. Vision

Source: U.S. Office of Personnel Management, *Occupational Study of Federal Executives, Managers, and Supervisors: An Application of the Multipurpose Occupational Systems Analysis Inventory—Closed Ended (MOSAIC),* PRD 92-21 (Washington, DC: U.S. Office of Personnel Management, 1992), 3, 4, 15.

competence models. The external environment of organizations often leads to organizational change. The reinventing government movement is one prodigious kind of organizational change occurring within federal agencies. Furthermore, downsizing is a particularly significant component of the reinventing government initiative. To manage organizational change, reinventing government, and downsizing, SES competencies are essential. The SES executives have specific managerial competencies for managing downsizing in their agencies. The management of downsizing, in turn, affects strategies, organizational performance, and consequences.

Figure 2.2 depicts the theory-building process for the study. The study

Table 2.2

Senior Executive Service (SES) Executive Core Qualifications (ECQ)

Core	Leadership Effectiveness Framework Competencies
1. Strategic Vision	Creative Thinking Customer Orientation External Awareness Leadership Oral Communication Planning and Evaluating Self-Direction Team Building Vision
2. Human Resources Management	Conflict Management Customer Orientation Decisiveness Flexibility Human Resources Management Influencing/Negotiating Interpersonal Skills Leadership Managing Diverse Workforce Oral Communication Planning and Evaluating Problem Solving Self-Direction Team Building Vision
3. Program Development and Evaluation	Creative Thinking Customer Orientation Decisiveness External Awareness Flexibility Human Resources Management Influencing/Negotiating Leadership Management Controls/Integrity Oral Communication Planning and Evaluating Problem Solving Self-Direction Team Building Technology Management Vision Written Communication
4. Resources Planning and Management	Conflict Management Decisiveness External Awareness Financial Management Flexibility

(Table 2.2 continued)

	Human Resources Management
	Influencing/Negotiating
	Leadership
	Management Controls/Integrity
	Oral Communication
	Planning and Evaluating
	Problem Solving
	Technology Management
	Written Communication
5. Organizational Representation	Conflict Management
and Liaison	Customer Orientation
	External Awareness
	Flexibility
	Influencing/Negotiating
	Interpersonal Skills
	Oral Communication
	Self-Direction
	Written Communication

Source: U.S. Office of Personnel Management, *Guide to SES Qualifications,* Office of Executive Resources, Human Resources Development Group, SES-94-01 (Washington, DC: U.S. Office of Personnel Management, August 1994), 10–18.

investigates how SES executives manage downsizing in three agencies. Of interest is how these executives "respond" to "downsizing" and how they "utilize" management competencies. Responses will be dependent on perceptions (Ford and Baucus 1987; Rosenblatt, Rogers, and Nord 1993). The research design allows the meaning of the data collected to be from the perspective of each executive. Thus, executives view "downsizing" in a variety of ways, such as its being positive or negative; good or bad for the organization, its employees, and its future; and cost saving or cost increasing. Likewise, variation occurs in how executives "respond" in terms of their actions, behaviors, decisions, processes, proactive measures, reactive measures, resistances, roles, strategies, and tactics. Similarly, "utilization" varies in terms of high or low frequency of occurrence of the OPM competencies. Or, some competencies may be absent or additional competencies present.

The research uses the method of comparative analysis to identify emergent patterns, themes, relationships, and dynamics of organizational downsizing (Glaser and Strauss 1967; Eisenhardt 1989; Agranoff and Radin 1991; Miles and Huberman 1994). From analysis of the data, downsizing theory is generated (see chapter 6).

Research Questions and Propositions

Several principal research questions guide the conduct of the research. These questions serve to provide the general direction for the study to

42

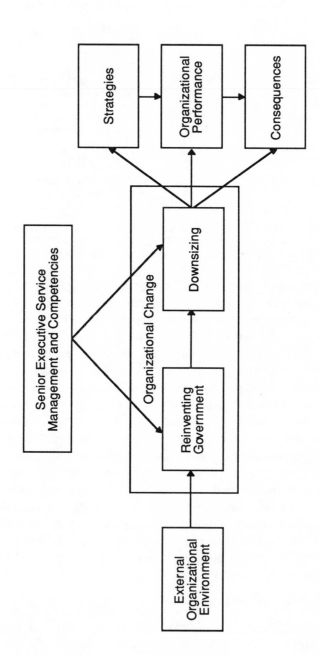

Figure 2.1 **Initial Theoretical Model**

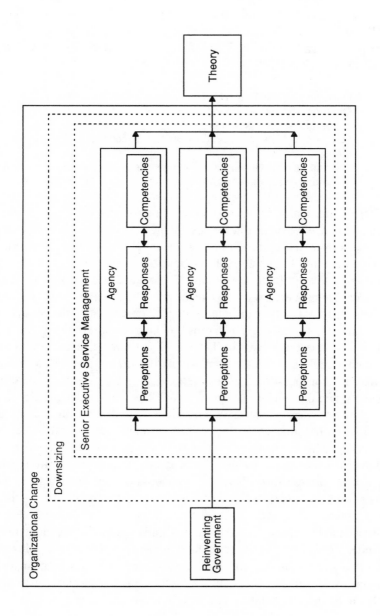

Figure 2.2 **Research Theory-Building Process**

pursue through systematic inquiry (Marshall and Rossman 1989). Like the conceptual framework introduced in the first part of this chapter, the research questions are stated explicitly in order to clarify the facets of the downsizing empirical domain of most interest (Miles and Huberman 1994). Four general questions represent the key areas to be investigated, narrow the focus of the study, and do not overly constrain the study (Creswell 1994). Furthermore, the questions define this research as having an explanatory purpose and nature, and they favor the use of case studies as a research strategy (Yin 1994).

> Question 1. How do agencies downsize?
> Question 2. How do federal career SES executives perceive downsizing for middle managers?
> Question 3. How are federal career SES executives managing downsizing?
> Question 4. What management competencies are federal career SES executives utilizing for downsizing?

Clearly, the major orientation of the questions is on the role of SES executives in downsizing activities in their agencies. By interviewing SES executives and gaining information about downsizing through their management of downsizing, it is possible to discover and generate downsizing theory. Interviews with middle managers enabled validation of results from interviews with executives. The research questions aid in focusing the data collection and analytical processes of the study. It is important to note that each of the overarching questions above implicitly contains subquestions (Creswell 1994). For example, a subquestion for Question 1 could be, "What organizational factors influence how agencies downsize?" For Question 2, a subquestion could be, "What are the effects of downsizing on middle managers?" For Question 3, a subquestion could be, "How do federal career SES executives view downsizing?" For Question 4, a subquestion could be, "What strategies are federal career SES executives using to manage downsizing?" The research questions are limited to four major questions in order to avoid question proliferation, which diminishes research flexibility. The broader and more open type of questions permit the concepts for theory generation to emerge during the research process.

Because this research takes a qualitative approach and generates grounded theory, there is no requirement for a priori propositions. However, Yin (1994) contends that for case studies, propositions are an important component of a research design. The following four propositions help to further point the study in the direction of relevant evidence.

Proposition 1. Agency downsizing processes depend on organizational environment factors.

Proposition 2. Federal career SES executives perceive downsizing to be difficult for middle managers.

Proposition 3. Federal career SES executives are managing downsizing with greater emphasis on particular practices.

Proposition 4. Federal career SES executives are utilizing particular management competencies during downsizing.

Research Methodology and Setting

This research uses qualitative research methodology (Glaser and Strauss 1967; Strauss and Corbin 1990; Bogdan and Biklen 1992; Miles and Huberman 1994). As such, this qualitative study uses the inductive form of analysis and method of theory construction. More specifically, case study research methods are employed (Yin 1994) because they are particularly suitable for public administration research (Agranoff and Radin 1991). Qualitative procedures used with the case study approach seek to understand human and organizational action at a greater richness and depth and to record the phenomena through a more complex, idiosyncratic, and subtle set of interpretive categories (Orum, Feagin, and Sjoberg 1991; Miles and Huberman 1994). The primary data collection methods relied upon are interviews and documentation reviews, and the secondary methods are archival records reviews and direct observations. Research was conducted at field sites in Denver, Colorado; Philadelphia, Pennsylvania; and the Washington, D.C., metropolitan area in the offices of DLA, BOR, and FDA.

The Federal Government

The executive branch of the federal government is comprised of a multitude of organizations. There are fourteen cabinet-level departments with numerous internal agencies, offices, and subunits and more than sixty primary independent agencies, regulatory commissions, corporations, and boards (Stillman 1996). Chapter 1 highlighted the number of employees now in federal service. As documented earlier, the downsized workforce is at its lowest level since the mid-1960s. The numbers of middle manager employees at the GS-13, GS-14, and GS-15 grades, the percentage of the total workforce for each grade, and the average length of service for each grade at the end of fiscal year 1996 appear in Table 2.3. For the civilian workforce in March 1996, 41.4 percent were employed by the DOD; 15.2 percent worked in the Washington, D.C., metropolitan area; 85.7

Table 2.3

Middle Manager Employees by Selected Grades
End of Fiscal Year 1996

Grade	Number of Employees	Percentage of Total Federal Employees	Average Length of Service in Years
GS-15	39,722	2.1	22.0
GS-14	82,332	4.3	20.0
GS-13	164,555	8.5	18.5
Total	286,609	14.9	19.4

Source: U.S. Office of Personnel Management, Central Personnel Data File.

percent were in white-collar occupations, and 14.3 percent were in blue-collar jobs; 11.4 percent were supervisors and managers; 55.5 percent were men and 44.5 percent were women; and 29.1 percent were minority group members.[3]

The Senior Executive Service

The Civil Service Reform Act of 1978 (Public Law 95-454) created the Senior Executive Service, which became effective 13 July 1979 (Ingraham and Ban 1984).[4] The SES is a separate personnel system for the federal government's top-level career program administrators who are its senior executives. The majority of SES positions are supervisory and managerial, although some are scientific and professional. The SES is a system in which, originally, salary and career status were to be based on the individual, but it has evolved to one based primarily on position. About half the SES positions are "Career-Reserved" and filled only by career appointees. The other half of SES positions are "General" and filled by career or noncareer appointees. Noncareer appointees do not have tenure, serve at the pleasure of the agency head, may not exceed 10 percent of the total number of SES positions government-wide, and may not exceed 25 percent of an agency's SES total. As of 31 March 1997, 6,821 total SES positions were filled out of an authorized allocation of 7,726. Of the total number of filled SES positions, 6,045 were career appointees. Just as for other grade levels, downsizing has occurred at the executive level, as reflected in Table 2.4. Traditionally, among SES members, approximately 38 percent serve in general administration and management occupations, and 75 percent work in the Washington, D.C., metropolitan area.

One of the stated objectives of the SES system is to ensure that executives have the necessary managerial competencies to provide the most ef-

Table 2.4

Senior Executive Service (SES) Downsizing
Fiscal Years 1994 to 1997

End of Fiscal Year	SES Allocation	SES Filled	Career Appointees	Average Length of Service in Years
1994	8,751	7,509	6,740	22.9
1995	8,302	7,294	6,473	22.6
1996	7,896	6,985	6,191	22.9
mid-1997[a]	7,726	6,821	6,045	NA

Source: U.S. Office of Personnel Management, Central Personnel Data File.
[a]As of 31 March 1997.

fective management of government programs. The "Managerial Competence Models" section earlier in this chapter discussed the twenty-two managerial competencies of the LEF developed by OPM.

Agency Site Selections

Criteria

The research uses a multiple-case design. A decision to use three sample cases was made in order to have a small enough sample for in-depth analysis of each case and a large enough sample for comparative analysis across cases. Eight criteria were used to select DLA, BOR, and FDA as the three agencies from the many possible federal agencies. The criteria relate to location within a cabinet-level department, number of employees, number of SES executives, downsizing activities, diversity among the selected agencies, missions, level of interest by outsiders, and accessibility. Table 2.5 identifies the criteria in greater detail. The table also shows how the three cases selected fit the criteria.

Stratification

The sampling for the study was theoretically driven by ensuring that all case agencies were experiencing downsizing. The objective was to select cases that were similar in ways bounded by the criteria and different in ways to ensure sufficient stratification. Therefore, theoretical sampling as shown in Table 2.6 was used to ensure sufficient variability among the selected agen-

Table 2.5

Criteria for Selection of Agencies for Case Studies

1. The agency is a separate organization within a cabinet-level department.
   DLA—Within the Department of Defense
   BOR—Within the Department of the Interior
   FDA—Within the Department of Health and Human Services
2. The number of agency employees exceeded 5,000 in January 1993.
   DLA—64,834 employees
   BOR—7,620 employees
   FDA—9,390 employees
3. The number of Senior Executive Service (SES) executives exceeded 20 in January 1993.
   DLA—23 executives
   BOR—23 executives
   FDA—68 executives
4. The agency is undergoing downsizing at the GS-14, GS-15, and SES management levels.
   Each agency is making a contribution to the federal government's downsizing process and:
   DLA—Experiencing decreasing defense budgets and the military and civilian personnel drawdown.
   BOR—Implementing a major reorganization and redesign to change its mission and reduce managerial layers.
   FDA—Undergoing personnel reductions and growth (due to user fee collections) in different units within the agency.
5. Diversity occurs across the three agencies in terms of:
   a. Small and large numbers of employees
   b. Military and nonmilitary organizations
   c. Small and large numbers of SES executives
   d. SES executives located at headquarters and field sites
   e. Organizational and workforce cultures:
   DLA—Military and logistics
   BOR—Engineering (dam construction) being replaced by water resources management
   FDA—Scientific and health
6. Agency missions vary in terms of roles, service delivery, interface with the public, and visibility to the public.
   DLA—Provide logistics support to the military services for national defense
   BOR—Manage water resources for diverse interests for the welfare of citizens
   FDA—Regulate foods and drugs to protect consumers and the health of citizens
7. The agency is of general interest to scholars, the National Performance Review community, and citizens.
   DLA—Designated as a pilot agency for the Government Performance and Results Act of 1993
   BOR—Recognized as a reinvented government agency
   FDA—Is expanding the collection of user fees
8. The agency agrees to participate and permits the necessary access required by the researcher.
   DLA—Volunteered to participate and permit access
   BOR—Volunteered to participate and permit access
   FDA—Volunteered to participate and permit access

Table 2.6

Theoretical Sampling of Agencies for Case Studies

	Type of Agency		Number of Executives		Location of Most Executives	
	Military	Civilian	Small	Large	Headquarters	Field
Number of Employees						
Small		BOR, FDA	BOR	FDA	FDA	BOR
Large	DLA		DLA		DLA	

Table 2.7

Agency Case Study Variables

Similarities among Case Study Agencies	Differences among Case Study Agencies
Public sector organizations	Unique missions
	Distinct cultures
Federal government	Separate agencies and departments
Undergoing downsizing	1 engaging in a long-term effort with a recently completed restructuring
	1 implementing a new mission and undergoing redesigning
	1 downsizing and growing simultaneously
More than 5,000 employees	2 small agencies
	1 large agency
More than 20 SES executives	2 small agencies
	1 large agency
SES management level	2 with most executives at headquarters
	1 with most executives in field
Civilian SES executives	2 civilian agencies
	1 military agency

cies (Glaser and Strauss 1967; Strauss and Corbin 1990; Miles and Huberman 1994). Table 2.7 summarizes the variables among the three selected agencies. Details about the agencies are included in case study chapters 3 through 5.

Research Sites

Table 2.8 provides an overview of the organizational change, reorganization, and downsizing activities occurring in DLA, BOR, and FDA. The data presented in Tables 2.5, 2.6, 2.7, and 2.8 show that variability exists among the three agencies selected for the study. Each agency is experiencing downsizing, but each has unique factors associated with its organization, structure, change experiences, and approach to downsizing. Each individual case is an embedded case study in that it involves more than one unit of analysis (Yin 1994). The focus is on individuals, programs, processes, and organizations within agencies that are involved with downsizing initiation, implementation, and management. The research sites for DLA were the headquarters in Alexandria, Virginia, for six executive and three middle manager interviews and field sites in Philadelphia, Pennsylvania, and Arlington, Virginia, with one executive interview each. For BOR, two executive interviews were conducted at the headquarters site in Washington, D.C., and five executive and four middle manager interviews took place at the Reclamation Service Center field site in Denver, Colorado. The research sites for FDA were the headquarters in Rockville, Maryland, for two executive interviews and center-level offices in Rockville, Maryland, and Washington, D.C., for six executive interviews.

Respondents

The respondents are the twenty-three SES executives and seven middle managers interviewed. After agency selection and agency agreement to participate in the study, eight executives per agency were selected to be interviewed (one interview was canceled). The intent was to interview at least 25 percent of the total number of executives in each agency with the exception of FDA, where it was not practical due to a large number of executives. Eight of twenty-nine executives (27.6 percent) were interviewed in DLA, seven of nineteen (36.8 percent) were interviewed in BOR, and eight of seventy-six (10.5 percent) were interviewed in FDA. The criteria for the selection of executives were that: (1) each executive be a federal career appointee and not a noncareer or political appointee, (2) each executive be in a supervisory and managerial position for an agency subunit experiencing downsizing, and (3) each agency be represented by a mix of executives from headquarters and the field (or center-level operations). Table 2.9 summarizes demographic and employment-related information for the executives interviewed. The data were obtained from a one-page form sent to the executives to be completed in advance of the interviews. Eighteen forms were completed before interviews and received from executives at the interviews, and five forms were completed after the interviews and mailed to the researcher. See appendix C, which contains the background information questionnaire as Part III of the interviews.

Table 2.8

Organizational Change, Reorganization, and Downsizing Activities in Agencies, at Time of Agency Selection for Study

DLA 1. Mission broadened by the Defense Management Review (DMR).

2. Experienced decreased defense budgets and the military and civilian personnel drawdown.

3. Field organizations strongly impacted by the Base Realignment and Closure (BRAC) process:
    a. Will merge 2 of 6 Inventory Control Points and be left with 5.
    b. Will close 5 of 33 Distribution Depots.
    c. Will consolidate 5 Contract Management Districts into 3.
    d. Will relocate 1 of 3 remaining Contract Management Districts.

4. Implemented reengineering business practices such as just-in-time fill capability, electronic procurement transactions, best-value contracting, performance-based contract management, and Process-Oriented Contract Administration Services (PROCAS).

5. Executed a headquarters restructuring on 6 March 1993.

6. Designated as one of the pilot project agencies for the Government Performance and Results Act (GPRA) of 1993.

BOR 1. A reorganization order from the Secretary of the Interior became effective on 13 April 1994. Major changes were as follows:
    a. Eliminated layers of management.
    b. Redesignated the Denver offices from the headquarters to a technical and administrative Reclamation Service Center.
    c. Consolidated functions in the Reclamation Service Center in Denver.
    d. Redesignated field project offices as field area offices.
    e. Flattened organizational structures.
    f. Reduced the number of personnel.

2. Reorganization and redesign changes made BOR one of the first and most prominent examples of a reinvented government agency. BOR received recognition when presented with Vice President Gore's Golden Hammer Award for its actions.

FDA 1. Required to downsize within the agency.

2. Authorized by Congress and OMB to grow by 600 personnel in FY 1994 due to collection of user fees in drug and biologics review programs within the agency.

3. On 15 March 1994, OMB agreed to support request for $890 million to fund FDA headquarters' consolidation of 2 sites in Maryland. Currently FDA operates from over 40 buildings at 16 sites in Maryland and Washington, D.C.

The research design focused primarily on the executive level because of the extensive experience and knowledge held by executives. Furthermore, the executives have the responsibility to lead and manage downsizing in their agencies and, therefore, have wider perspectives. However, to corroborate executive views of middle manager reactions, concerns, and behavior, middle managers were interviewed also in a follow-up phase.

Field Methodology

Case Study Methodology

The case study research method is appropriate for the research's purpose of understanding the complexities associated with organizational downsizing. This case study approach is explanatory in nature, focusing on questions related to the management of downsizing activities in federal agencies. Moreover, this case study approach is an empirical inquiry that investigates phenomenon within its real-life context (Miles and Huberman 1994; Yin 1994).

Multiple-Case Design

The cases for the multiple-case design were carefully and purposefully selected. Cases were selected to provide the widest range of similar and contrasting cases. Multiple cases produce a deeper understanding of the downsizing process and executive management of downsizing. The study uses the replication logic such that each case either predicts similar results (a literal replication) or generates contrasting results for predictable reasons (a theoretical replication) (Yin 1994). The primary advantage of the multiple-case design is that multiple-case evidence is considered more compelling and the design leads to greater confidence and robustness in the study and its findings (Eisenhardt 1989; Agranoff and Radin 1991; Miles and Huberman 1994; Yin 1994).

Time Period of the Study

The study was conducted in six phases beginning in October 1993 and concluding in July 1997. Preliminary research activities in Phase I started after the first NPR report was released and were completed between October 1993 and May 1994. Data collection from documentation and archival records reviews in Phase II took place at research sites from June to September 1994. Executive interviews at research sites in Phase III occurred in

Table 2.9

Demographic and Employment Data for SES Executives Interviewed

	DLA	BOR	FDA
Mean Age	50.3	51.1	51.3
Mean Years in SES	8.3	5.7	6.4
Mean Years in Present Position	2.6	1.3	3.4
Mean Years Worked in Present Agency	10.0	20.9	18.3
Mean Total Years of Federal Service	23.6	27.1	25.0
Mean Total Years of Federal Supervisory/ Managerial Job Experience	17.4	21.0	18.4
Occupational Group:			
200-Personnel Management	1	0	0
300-General Administration	3	4	3
400-Biological Sciences	0	0	1
600-Medical & Public Health	0	0	2
800-Engineering & Architecture	0	1	0
900-Legal	0	0	1
1100-Business and Industry	1	0	0
1300-Physical Sciences	0	1	1
2000-Supply	2	0	0
Unknown	1	1	0
Education Level Attained:			
B.A. or B.S.	2	4	3
M.A. or M.B.A.	6	2	2
Ph.D., M.D., or J.D.	0	1	3
Number of Males	7	6	7
Number of Females	1	1	1

September and October 1994. Direct observations were accomplished throughout Phases II and III. Data analysis of the executive interviews was conducted in Phase IV from November 1994 to April 1995. Follow-up interviews with middle managers in Phase V were accomplished in July 1995. Finally, further analysis of downsizing and book writing took place in Phase VI from late 1995 to mid-1997.

Interviews

The primary source of data collection was interviews. Phase I involved preliminary open-ended, informal, nondirective questioning interviews. Forty-two interviews were conducted with a diversity of academic, government, and private sector officials in Washington, D.C., to discuss the NPR, downsizing the government, and the research design. Additionally, nineteen interviews were conducted with agency key officials and staff personnel to obtain basic background information on each agency and seek approval to conduct case study research on the agencies. The interviews lasted from thirty minutes to two and a half hours, with most taking about one hour. Phase III executive interviews consisted of three parts (see appendix C). Part I followed the critical incident interview and behavioral event interview formats (Flanagan 1954; Spencer and Spencer 1993). Part II consisted of twenty in-depth, open-ended, semistructured interview questions. The researcher used probing to obtain additional information from respondents. Part III was the background information questionnaire. Appendix C shows the interview protocol, which includes the interview ground rules and the interview protocol packet used during the interviews. Appendix D lists the critical incident and behavior interview steps and techniques.

Phase III interviews were tape-recorded, and transcripts were prepared by two experienced transcribers. All executives granted permission to be tape-recorded. Field notes were additionally recorded as a precaution in case of tape recorder malfunctions. The interviews lasted from forty-eight minutes to four and a half hours, with the typical interview lasting about one and a half hours. Appendices E, F, and G summarize the executive interviews.

Phase V interviews of middle managers consisted of two parts. Part I was a background questionnaire. Part II consisted of five questions on job background and twenty-three questions about downsizing. Of the twenty-three downsizing questions, eight are identical to and six are worded similar to the twenty questions asked in executive interviews. The other nine downsizing questions for middle managers were aimed at getting responses to issues that surfaced during the earlier executive interviews. Appendix H contains the middle manager interview questions. Middle manager interviews were tape-recorded after permission was granted to do so. Field notes were recorded as a precaution in case of tape recorder malfunctions. The interviews lasted about one hour each.

Documentation Reviews

The researcher also relied heavily on reviews of documentary information. During Phase I, permission was obtained from each of the agencies for the researcher to return to the sites to review documentation related to downsizing initiation, strategies, and management. Intensive documentation reviews occurred in Phase II, and follow-up reviews occurred in Phases III and IV. Copies of documents were obtained, and field notes were recorded for those

SELECTING DOWNSIZING AGENCIES FOR STUDY 55

documents not permitted to be copied. The following documents were reviewed: agendas, announcements, articles in newspapers and the mass media, briefing charts, downsizing strategic and implementation plans, evaluations, human resources data, letters sent and received, memoranda, minutes of meetings, organizational charts, progress reports, proposals, public affairs materials, schedules, studies, talking papers, white papers, written reports, and other internal documents.

Archival Records Reviews

Archival records were a secondary source of evidence. However, the oldest of the records related to the current downsizing wave from the NPR is dated March 1993, when the NPR was initiated. Other archival records of relevance were reviewed also. Intensive archival records reviews took place in Phase II and follow-up reviews took place in Phases III and IV. Copies were made or field notes recorded. The following archival organizational records were reviewed: charts, chronologies, data, inputs from subordinate units, lists, personnel assignments, and project plans.

Direct Observations

Direct observations were a supplemental data-gathering technique. Direct observations were made every time the researcher made a field visit to any of the agency sites. Thus, direct observations occurred and the researcher recorded field notes from them in Phases I, II, III, and V. Most of the direct observations were conducted in Phases II and III, since the researcher spent extended time at the sites during those phases. The researcher paid close attention to attitudes and behaviors of personnel, especially as they related to downsizing and its strategies and management. Additionally, as much as possible, the researcher attempted to discern environmental conditions and factors. Other targets for observation included organizational communications, indicators of culture, efforts and resources, interpersonal dynamics, and routines.

Qualitative Data Analysis

The form of analysis is inductive: data gathered through multiple techniques lead to empirical generalizations that result in theory construction (Glaser and Strauss 1967; Mintzberg 1979; Eisenhardt 1989; Miles and Huberman 1994; Yin 1994). The process generates formal grounded theory defined as theory discovered from data systematically obtained and analyzed in social research (Glaser and Strauss 1967; Strauss 1987). Data analysis in earlier phases informs and guides data collection in later phases.

Central to data analysis is an ongoing process of coding field notes, interview transcripts, documents, and archival records. The coding process entails reading and summarizing the data; identifying concepts; establishing codes; and attaching codes to words, phrases, sentences, and paragraphs and other forms of data. The coding process follows an iterative sequence in which the codes are modified until the researcher is satisfied that the coding scheme can be fully applied to the data. The final coding scheme contains seventy-two codes. The codes with operational definitions are listed in appendix I. To maintain internal consistency, the researcher was the only person to code the interviews and documents. A coding scheme check was conducted to determine the reliability of the codes. The coding scheme was deemed reliable according to accepted standards (Miles and Huberman 1994).

Additionally, the researcher employed the practice of generating theoretical notes during the earlier phases. As the research progressed, the researcher integrated the theoretical notes into expanded analytical notes. This data analysis process continued during and after data collection until theory was developed that accounts for all the phenomena observed. The ultimate goal was to develop theory that accounts for how federal SES executives manage during downsizing in the three agencies.

Extensive within-case analysis was performed for the researcher to become intimately familiar with each case, generate insight, and identify themes. Furthermore, cross-case search for patterns was conducted. Together, these two techniques enhanced the recognition of themes, patterns, concepts, and relationships between variables (Eisenhardt 1989). The techniques set the foundation for a constant comparison between case data and emerging theory. The iterative process led ultimately to empirically valid theory. Chapter 6 presents the cross-case analysis results and lessons learned as well as a theoretical model of downsizing.

Construct validity is increased by the use of multiple sources of evidence, establishment of chains of evidence, and review of draft chapters by key officials and interviewees. Internal validity is increased through the explanation-building process within each case and then a cross-case analysis. External validity is increased through analytical generalization in which the researcher generalizes a set of case results to resultant theory. Reliability is increased by the use of a highly formalized set of procedures that included interview protocols and a case study database. The database consists of an organized and clearly labeled classification system of field notes, coded interview transcripts, documents, archival records, theoretical notes, and analytical notes. Finally, interpretation of results is strengthened through the combined data analysis techniques described for this research. Appendix J contains details of the within-case analysis and cross-case analysis procedures.

Notes

1. Spencer and Spencer (1993) summarize the research conducted by the McBer/ Hay Group, formerly McBer and Company and Hay Management Consultants, using the McClelland/McBer JCA methodology. The competencies identified by the Boyatzis (1982) studies are integrated into the Spencer competencies.

2. OPM finalized a set of twenty-two competencies after extensive research, which included a review of the management and psychological literature to identify work behaviors (tasks) performed by managers and the competencies needed to perform them. See the Corts and Gowing (1992) report, which integrates the behaviors and competencies with descriptions as they appear in the literature. Another step was to eliminate confusion of terminology that appeared in the literature for managerial behaviors and competency labels. A "crosswalk" identified common elements in various models and ensured that all major competencies were identified in the final set of OPM competencies. A *competency* is defined as a skill or ability, according to a subsequent OPM study (U.S. Office of Personnel Management 1992). OPM later defines the Leadership Effectiveness Framework (LEF) competencies as "attributes of an executive who successfully demonstrates the Key Characteristics," which are "behavioral activities" (U.S. Office of Personnel Management 1994).

3. For more statistics on demographic and job characteristics of the "typical" federal civilian employee as of 31 March 1996, see the *Federal Personnel Guide* (1997, 14). The data are obtained from the Central Personnel Data File of the U.S. Office of Personnel Management.

4. For details about the SES system and statistics on SES members, see U.S. Office of Personnel Management (1993, 1995). Additionally, for recent critiques of the SES system, see Huddleston (1991) and Harper (1992).

3

The Defense Logistics Agency: Downsizing and Downsizing and Downsizing

The Defense Logistics Agency is one of sixteen separate agencies within the Department of Defense that provide expertise, support, and services to DOD and the Army, Navy, and Air Force Departments. DLA is headquartered at Fort Belvoir, Virginia, near Washington, D.C., and has a worldwide logistics and contract management mission. As a joint-service DOD Combat Support Agency through the Goldwater-Nichols Reorganization Act of 1986, the agency purchases and provides supplies to the military services and supports their acquisition of weapons and other materiel. Additionally, DLA provides supply support, contract administration services, and technical and logistics services to several civilian agencies. Military life-cycle support includes joint planning with the military services for new weapon system parts, involvement in production and distribution of supplies and parts, and disposal of materiel that is obsolete, used, or no longer required. During fiscal years 1995 through 1997, DLA executed an annual program of approximately $14 billion. By the middle of fiscal year 1997, the employment level reached approximately 47,500 in its long-term downsizing running from the late 1980s to the early 2000s.

DLA provides significant worldwide logistics support and services that are vital to the nation's armed services through two main mission areas: materiel management, which encompasses supply, distribution, procurement, reutilization, and logistics information management; and acquisition, which includes contract administration and management. Facilities are dispersed around the United States and the world and include supply centers, distribution depots, property disposal offices, contract administration offices, in-plant offices in defense contractor facilities, and property reutilization offices. The following is DLA's mission statement:

The Defense Logistics Agency is a combat support agency responsible for worldwide logistics support throughout the Department of Defense. The primary focus of the Agency is to support the war fighter in time of war and in peace, and to provide relief efforts during times of national emergency. (Defense Logistics Agency 1994b, 2)

Agency Background

After World War II, the first Hoover Commission recommended management centralization of common military logistics support and use of uniform financial management practices. During the 1950s, DOD allowed each military service to purchase, store, manage, and distribute certain commodities of supplies and parts for all of DOD. Although DOD achieved increased efficiencies and economies of operation, it still lacked uniform procedures. In 1961, Secretary of Defense Robert McNamara ordered that the separate service "single managers" be consolidated into one central agency.[1] As a result, the Defense Supply Agency (DSA) was established and began operations on 1 January 1962. In 1977, DSA was renamed the Defense Logistics Agency to reflect more accurately its broadened role for the logistics of military systems. From 1962 to 1992, the agency experienced tremendous growth in its mission and organization. Table 3.1 lists some of the major expansions in the evolution of the agency.

DLA is an enormous business. If it were ranked in the Fortune 500, it would be approximately sixty-second (Defense Logistics Agency 1995b). Table 3.2 presents an overview with statistics of DLA and its component organizations as of November 1996. Most of the work and employees are in the supply management, distribution support, contract administration services, and logistics support services areas of the agency.

Recent Organizational Changes

The end of the Cold War and the nation's fiscal problems are generating immense changes for the Defense Department in the 1990s. Reductions of force and budget levels in turn lead to reductions in defense infrastructure and support functions. Because DLA's mission is central to military operations, defense reductions have contracted DLA. At least six major related events since 1988 have resulted in organizational changes for DLA. Some of the changes increased and some decreased the scope of DLA's mission. All these events have in common the objectives of reducing the size and cost of logistics support throughout DOD. The following six events since 1988 established a dynamic downsizing environment for DLA.

Table 3.1

Defense Logistics Agency Expansions

1962	Defense Supply Agency (DSA) created the Defense Logistics Services Center to manage the Federal Supply Catalog System.
1965	DSA created the Defense Contract Administration Services (DCAS) to consolidate some of the separate military department contract management and administration activities.
1965	The Defense Subsistence Supply Center, Defense Clothing Supply Center, and Defense Medical Supply Center were merged to form the Defense Personnel Support Center in DSA.
1972	DSA established the Defense Property Disposal Service, and in 1979 DLA changed its name to the Defense Reutilization and Marketing Service when its mission was expanded to include surplus materiel overseas.
1973	DSA supply operations were extended overseas for wholesale food and bulk fuel.
1988	DLA acquired the responsibility for the nation's stockpile of strategic materials from the General Services Administration and established the Defense National Stockpile Center.
1990	The Office of the Secretary of Defense established the Defense Contract Management Command to consolidate under DLA the existing DLA DCAS mission and the military departments' contract management and administration activities.
1992	DLA completed the consolidation of the military services' 30 distribution depots into a single, unified supply distribution system within DLA.

Sources: Defense Logistics Agency: Historical Summary (Defense Logistics Agency, Office of Public Affairs, 9 October 1992); and *DLA Reinvention Journal* (Fort Belvoir, VA: Defense Logistics Agency, October 1995).

Defense Management Review (DMR)

During the Bush Administration (1989–93), the Pentagon initiated the Defense Management Review (DMR) aimed at improving defense management practices to enhance operations and cope with forthcoming force and budget reductions. The report from the DMR was issued in July 1989. The purpose of DMR was to establish businesslike practices in DOD to achieve improved efficiencies, reduce infrastructure, and realize monetary savings.

Many of the DMR initiatives, particularly the most important ones, directly affect DLA.[2] First, numerous DOD finance and accounting centers and their 150 separate accounting systems were consolidated into a single Defense Finance and Accounting Service (DFAS) between 1990 and 1992. Parts of DLA were transferred out and made part of DFAS. Second, the $81 billion Defense Business Operations Fund (DBOF) was established in October 1991 as a centrally managed revolving fund to control DOD business operations. DBOF operates with financial management principles that pro-vide improved cost visibility and accountability to enhance business man-agement and improve decision-making processes. Since many of DLA's functions are business-type operations, over 90 percent of DLA's opera-tions are resourced through DBOF.[3] Instead of using the traditional budget practice of annual budget appropriations, these organizations operate on a reimbursable basis in which they receive revenues from charging customers for what they supply to them. In other words, if DLA is not providing what the military customers want and are willing to pay for, that part of the DLA organization would go out of business. Third, thirty separate DOD supply depots were consolidated into one DLA supply distribution system in 1992. And fourth, the new Corporate Information Management (CIM) program, which began development in 1991, is now central to helping DLA success-fully reengineer business functions (Corbin 1992a).

Defense Personnel Drawdown

Congress legislated the downsizing of U.S. military forces after the Cold War ended. Since the mid-1980s, DOD has reduced its personnel signifi-cantly. Between 1990 and 1995, over 100,000 military positions per year and about 45,000 civilian positions each year have been eliminated (Peters 1996, 20). In 1985, there were 2.2 million active duty military personnel, 1.1 million in the Reserve forces, and 1.1 million civilians serving DOD. In 1997, there are 1.45 million in the military, 900,000 in the Reserves, and 800,000 in civilian employment. Ultimately, according to the *Report of the Quadren-nial Defense Review* (QDR) (U.S. Department of Defense 1997, 31) released by Secretary of Defense William Cohen, those numbers are expected to shrink further to 1,360,000 (down 36 percent since fiscal year 1989), 835,000 (down 29 percent from fiscal year 1989), and 640,000 (down 42 percent since fiscal year 1989), respectively, in fiscal year 2003. QDR plans ensure that DLA personnel will continue to be downsized through at least 2003.[4]

Defense Base Realignment and Closure (BRAC) Process

The Base Closure and Realignment Act of 1988 (Public Law 100-526) and the Defense Base Closure and Realignment Act of 1990 (Public Law 101-510 as amended by Public Law 102-190 and Public Law 103-160) set requirements for DOD base and installation closures and realignments to go along with the personnel drawdown. The main steps in the Base Realign-ment and Closure (BRAC) process are the recommendations made by inde-pendent BRAC commissions and then the "all or nothing" votes by

Table 3.2

Defense Logistics Agency Organization

All of DLA
Statistics: 49,000 civilian and military employees
                                $14 billion budget in FY 1996

Supply Management
Statistics: 9,900 employees
                                Management of 3.9 million items
                                Management of 89 percent of DOD consumable items
                                $11.5 billion in sales each year
                                $9.3 billion in purchases each year

Commodity Areas:
Clothing, construction material, electronic supplies, food, fuel, general supplies,
    industrial supplies, and medical supplies

Inventory Control Points:
Defense Supply Center Columbus (Columbus, Ohio)
Defense Supply Center Richmond (Richmond, Virginia)
Defense Fuel Supply Center (Fort Belvoir, Virginia)
Defense Industrial Supply Center (Philadelphia, Pennsylvania)
Defense Personnel Support Center (Philadelphia, Pennsylvania)

Distribution Support
Statistics: 15,700 employees
                                5.1 million items stored
                                $99.4 billion inventory
                                30.1 million transactions each year

Distribution Depots:

Defense Distribution Region East (New Cumberland, Pennsylvania)
16 depots throughout eastern, midwestern, and southern United States and Europe

Defense Distribution Region West (Stockton, California)
11 depots throughout western and southwestern United States

Contract Administration Services
Statistics: 14,600 employees
                                24,400 contractors
                                378,000 prime contracts worth $955 billion

District Regions:
Defense Contract Management District East (Boston, Massachusetts)
Defense Contract Management District West (El Segundo, California)
Defense Contract Management District International (Fort Belvoir, Virginia)

(Table 3.2 continued)

Statistics:

Logistic Support Services
5,900 employees
$6.1 billion stockpile
$390.8 million in stockpile sales
$21 billion in property disposal

Service Centers:
Defense Logistics Services Center (Battle Creek, Michigan)
Defense National Stockpile Center (Fort Belvoir, Virginia)
Defense Reutilization and Marketing Service (Battle Creek, Michigan)
DLA Systems Design Center (Columbus, Ohio)
DLA Administrative Support Center (Fort Belvoir, Virginia)
Defense Automated Printing Service (Fort Belvoir, Virginia)

Source: "Facts about the Defense Logistics Agency" (Defense Logistics Agency, Public Affairs Office, 18 November 1996).

Congress to enact the recommendations. The acts established four commissions: BRAC 1988, BRAC 1991, BRAC 1993, and BRAC 1995. Altogether, 86 of 303 domestic major military installations were closed (Dering 1996). Additionally, numerous smaller military installations were closed or realigned. The QDR proposes two more rounds of BRAC, with the first in 1999 and the second in 2001. However, it is doubtful any more BRACs will occur before 2000 because of the realities of the political process. DLA organizations were affected by each of the completed BRAC decisions, and the agency actively participated in the BRAC 1993 and BRAC 1995 decision-making processes (Defense Logistics Agency 1993b). The BRAC process results in DLA operations at some locations being consolidated, transferred, or terminated. Consequently, some DLA personnel are required to retire, transfer, or undergo a RIF.

DLA Reengineering

The DMR, personnel and budget drawdowns, and BRAC process highlighted above were some of the drivers for many business, management, and systems changes throughout DLA beginning at least as far back as 1988. According to an internal DLA "Transition Book" document prepared for Secretary of Defense William Perry in January 1994, DLA reengineering was established well before the NPR was born:

> DLA began "process reengineering" or "reshaping the paradigm" before these terms became part of the everyday lexicon. DLA submitted to the National Performance Review (NPR) and the Defense Performance Review

(DMR) offices, descriptions of DLA programs which were already underway, innovative, and on the cutting edge of business reengineering. Some of these were included in the NPR. (Defense Logistics Agency 1994a, 12)

DLA has already realized major savings by utilizing the best business practices of the private sector. Numerous innovative business practices are in place to improve service and reduce costs. For example, the agency is the government leader in the use of electronic data interchange (EDI). EDI is the computer-to-computer exchange of business data through telephone lines.[5] Additionally, DLA is now emphasizing a "buy response vice inventory" philosophy. The Prime Vendor program permits a single vendor to provide a wide range of items for less total cost and at a higher customer satisfaction level. The Direct Vendor Delivery program, a form of just-in-time inventory management, enables materiel to be delivered from vendors to the customer when needed. This arrangement avoids costly storage of inventories. Furthermore, Process-Oriented Contract Administration Services (PROCAS) is a quality-oriented approach that encourages DLA contract management personnel to work with industry to identify process changes that will add value, reduce costs, and identify product defects earlier. Finally, a number of other techniques for long-term contracts, market-based buying practices, bench-marking processes, and elimination of non-value-added processes are being used (Kaufman 1994b).

DLA's cost avoidances from reengineering its business processes are impressive. During fiscal years 1993 to 1995, the agency achieved materiel savings and cost avoidances of over $2 billion by constraining materiel prices through operational efficiencies obtained in supply management and distribution areas. It expects over $8 billion more for fiscal years 1996 to 2001. In the area of contract administration, it gained over $9 billion in savings and cost avoidances during fiscal years 1993 to 1995. Furthermore, more than $18 billion in additional savings and cost avoidances are planned for fiscal years 1996 to 2001 (Defense Logistics Agency 1995b).

DLA Restructuring and Streamlining

As noted earlier, DLA's mission expanded greatly since 1962, and, in recent years, DMR decisions gave DLA more to do while DOD promised more budget cuts. While DLA was acquiring expanded contract administration functions and distribution depots, external factors such as budget cuts and the personnel drawdown were forcing DLA to reexamine the organization. Thus, the tumultuous environment necessitated that DLA restructure its field and headquarters organizations.

Field structure changes included mergers, closures, and consolidations as part of the BRAC process. Table 3.3 lists the field restructuring actions planned for completion in the 1990s. In the fall of 1992, the DLA Director, Vice Admiral Edward Straw, commissioned an independent study group to reassess the agency. In January 1993, the Director instructed some of DLA's executives, nicknamed the "Gang of Ten," to develop a plan for restructuring the headquarters. The goal was to achieve greater operating effectiveness within the headquarters. Soon thereafter, on 6 March 1993, DLA headquarters initiated its restructuring. Table 3.3 also indicates the major changes in the headquarters restructuring. Important changes included reductions in management spans of control and the implementation of employee teams to solve problems and improve processes. The changes are expected to streamline the flow of information, facilitate prompt decision making, provide greater flexibility in meeting new challenges quickly, empower employees to improve processes, leverage resources, and enhance responsiveness to customers (Defense Logistics Agency 1993a, 1993c).

Government Performance and Results Act (GPRA)

Congress passed the Government Performance and Results Act (GPRA) of 1993 (Public Law 103-62) to create standard planning and performance reporting processes in federal agencies. The intent of the act is to implement a results-oriented focus for government by shifting emphasis from program inputs to program execution and attainment of desired outcomes. The act requires all federal agencies, unless exempted by the Office of Management and Budget (OMB), to submit five-year strategic plans by 30 September 1997, annual performance plans for fiscal year 1999 in the fall of 1997, and performance reports for fiscal year 1999 by 31 March 2000 (Whittaker 1995; Laurent 1996; U.S. General Accounting Office 1996b). DLA volunteered to be DOD's pilot project for GPRA. Because of its already established orientation toward business practices and to further push itself to even better performance, DLA wanted to begin implementing GPRA provisions right away. On 31 January 1994, DLA, which was nominated by the Deputy Secretary of Defense, was designated by OMB to be a GPRA pilot project from 1994 to 1996.[6]

DLA's outstanding success at improving its business performance while downsizing has been recognized both within the DOD and nationally. On 8 March 1996, Secretary of Defense William Perry awarded the agency the Joint Meritorious Unit Award for extraordinary savings achieved from February 1994 to October 1995. The award cited the agency for supporting the national interest with actions that "directly improved the readiness of the

Table 3.3

Defense Logistics Agency Restructuring Actions

Field Organizations

1. Merge 2 of 6 Inventory Control Points to create a total of 5:

   Merge the Defense Electronics Supply Center (Dayton, Ohio) into the Defense Supply Center Columbus (Columbus, Ohio).

2. Close 8 of 33 Distribution Depots:
   a. Charleston, South Carolina
   b. Letterkenny, Pennsylvania
   c. McClellan, California
   d. Memphis, Tennessee
   e. Oakland (Alameda), California
   f. Ogden, Utah
   g. Pensacola, Florida
   h. San Antonio, Texas

3. Consolidate 5 Contract Management Districts into 2:
   a. Relocate Mid-Atlantic to East
   b. Relocate North Central to East and West
   c. Relocate South to East
   d. Relocate West to El Segundo, California

Headquarters

1. Organize for 2 principal business areas and a support element: Materiel Management, Acquisition, and Corporate Administration.
2. Reduce Director's span of control from 42 to 5 while eliminating "stovepipes," layering, and overlaps.
3. Establish an Executive Team of 5 for agency leadership.
4. Establish a Management Team of 13 for agency management.
5. Use policy, operations, and program teams and teaming principles to solve problems and improve processes.

Sources: "The Challenges Facing DLA" (Defense Logistics Agency, Public Affairs Office, 1993) and *The Roadmap to Transition: Headquarters Defense Logistics Agency* (Alexandria, VA: Defense Logistics Agency, January 1993).

Military Services while attaining $6.3 billion in savings for the Department of Defense." Additionally, one of DLA's supply centers, the Defense Personnel Support Center (DPSC), was one of only six federal government recipients of a 1995 Innovations in American Government Award given by the Ford Foundation and the John F. Kennedy School of Government at Harvard University. DPSC developed a "National Defense on the Offense" program that radically redesigned a century-old, bureaucratic approach to procuring and distributing about $3.5 billion in food, medical, and clothing supplies a year (Clark 1995; Corbin 1995b). The program incorporates

Table 3.4

Defense Logistics Agency Downsizing Evolution (Descriptors and Events)

Traditional Past	Recent Past 1988–1995	Reinventing Government 1993 and Beyond	Future 1997 and Beyond
Large	DMR	Executive Order 12839 to Downsize	QDR
Hierarchical	DOD Budget and Personnel Drawdowns	Presidential Memorandum on Downsizing	Possible BRAC 2001
Bureaucratic	BRAC 1988, 1991, 1993, and 1995	Government Performance and Results Act of 1993	More Downsizing
Budget Growth	Reengineering	Federal Workforce Restructuring Act of 1994	
	Restructuring and Streamlining	Downsizing	
	Downsizing		

sound business practices that allow the military to choose suppliers at the best prices and to respond effectively in times of national emergencies. For winning the award, DLA received a $100,000 Ford Foundation grant to provide leadership and assistance to other federal and state agencies wishing to replicate similar successful approaches. Established in 1985 to recognize state and local government initiatives, the Innovations Award program opened its competition to federal agencies for the first time in 1995.

Downsizing Activities

This section presents an overview of DLA's downsizing activities and is intended to provide the background necessary for understanding the results and analysis later in the chapter. It is clear that the six events described above preceded and combined to put DLA on a downsizing track well before the Clinton Administration's reinventing government initiative, presidential Executive Order 12839, and presidential memorandum of 11 September 1993 to downsize came along. The evolution of DLA downsizing is shown in Table 3.4. Traditionally, the agency was growth-oriented and operated in a hierarchical and bureaucratic manner. Between 1988 and 1995, key changes forced personnel reductions amid organizational trans-

Table 3.5

Defense Logistics Agency Downsizing Trends
Fiscal Years 1993 to 1996

End of Fiscal Year	Civilian Employees	Military Employees	Total Employees
1993	59,765	1,275	61,040
1994	55,537	1,178	56,715
1995	50,771	1,159	51,930
1996	47,543	1,120	48,663

Source: Defense Logistics Agency; Executive Directorate; Human Resources Staffing, Labor, and Employee Relations Group.

formation. By the time reinventing government dictated federal government downsizing, DLA was already doing so. At least until 2003, DLA will experience a continuation of the downsizing as a result of the QDR and possibly more BRAC exercises if Congress passes additional BRAC legislation.

From 1980 until 1992, DLA experienced continual growth from about 45,000 total employees in 1980 to 63,701 total employees in 1992. During this period, the growth was gradual, although the agency saw a little decline between 1987 and 1988 and between 1990 and 1991. The largest one-year gain occurred in fiscal year 1992, when 9,942 employees were added due to absorption of other DOD functions. However, since 1992, employee figures have dropped precipitously each year, as shown in Table 3.5. Reductions are expected to continue in future fiscal years and to reach approximately 47,312 employees at the end of 1997, 46,127 by the end of 1998, 44,547 by the end of 1999, and 41,718 by year-end 2000.

The downsizing since 1992 was targeted throughout the agency at all organizational levels: headquarters, primary-level field activities, management support activities, and field operating activities. Furthermore, downsizing was implemented through the reduction or elimination of individual positions, groups of positions, career fields, functions, management layers, and organizational units. Moreover, employees at all pay grade levels experienced a reduction in total numbers. For employees whose jobs were affected by the downsizing but who were not required or did not choose to leave DLA, the agency transferred or retrained them. Table 3.6 summarizes the tools used by DLA to achieve its personnel reductions.

The preferred strategy for personnel reductions, other than normal attrition, is the use of separation pay incentives from the VSIP or buyout legis-

Table 3.6

Defense Logistics Agency Tools for Downsizing

1. Normal attrition
2. Hiring freezes
3. Transfers within DLA
4. Retraining
5. Buyouts (voluntary separation incentive payments)
   a. Optional retirement
   b. Early retirement (early out)
   c. Resignation
6. Targeted reductions and eliminations
   a. Individual positions
   b. Groups of positions
   c. Career fields
   d. Functions
   e. Management layers
   f. Organizational units
7. Targeted levels
   a. All employee grade levels
   b. All organizational levels (headquarters, primary-level field activities, management support activities, and field operating activities)
8. Reengineering of business processes
9. Humanitarian approaches
10. Increased communications
11. Teaming of employees
12. Employee counseling centers
13. Outplacement services
14. Involuntary reductions-in-force (RIFs)

lation. Under the buyout provisions, eligible employees who resign voluntarily receive a payment equal to a severance allotment (based on a formula including salary and years of service) or $25,000, whichever is less. DOD has authorization to offer buyouts between December 1992 and 30 September 1999. However, DLA, like other DOD agencies, offers buyouts only in certain units of the agency and during specific windows of time when necessary to induce employees to leave voluntarily. The three possible categories for buyout eligibility (optional retirement, early retirement, and resignation) are explained in chapter 1. The details of the buyouts regarding buyout categories used, career fields eligible, windows, and "takers" varied throughout DLA. The total numbers of employees taking buyouts were 3,307 in fiscal year 1993, 3,433 in fiscal year 1994, 2,235 in fiscal year 1995, and 1,778 in fiscal year 1996. The least desirable downsizing strategy is the involuntary RIF. RIFs were used within the agency as a last resort. When a RIF did occur, it was because a location experienced a significant reduction in workload, BRAC closures, or skills imbalances.

Table 3.7 shows actual civilian downsizing statistics for fiscal years

Table 3.7

Defense Logistics Agency Civilian Downsizing Statistics by Strategy Categories

Activity	Optional Retirement with Buyout	Early Out with Buyout	Resign with Buyout	RIF	Other	Total Attrition
Fiscal Year 1993						
Inventory Control Points	32	0	4	2	462	500
Depot Regions	841	1,253	498	2	1,039	3,633
Service Centers	9	14	7	8	253	291
Contract Management Districts	541	4	100	18	794	1,457
HQ/MSA/FOA	4	0	0	0	265	269
Totals	1,427	1,271	609	30	2,813	6,150
Grade						
SES	0	0	0	0	0	0
GS/GM 15	2	0	0	0	23	25
GS/GM 14	15	3	1	2	53	74
GS/GM 13	62	13	2	0	123	200
GS 1–12	800	414	308	23	1,842	3,387
WG	548	841	298	5	772	2,464
Totals	1,427	1,271	609	30	2,813	6,150
Fiscal Year 1994						
Inventory Control Points	755	216	144	14	75	1,204
Depot Regions	164	365	334	58	448	1,369
Service Centers	120	64	19	3	231	437
Contract Management Districts	762	272	134	55	536	1,759
HQ/MSA/FOA	73	7	4	545	599	1,228
Totals	1,874	924	635	675	1,889	5,997
Grade						
SES	0	0	0	0	0	0
GS/GM 15	27	5	0	0	15	47
GS/GM 14	71	22	3	0	24	120
GS/GM 13	157	39	11	2	72	281
GS 1–12	1,318	472	378	84	1,276	3,528
WG	301	386	243	589	502	2,021
Totals	1,874	924	635	675	1,889	5,997

(Table 3.7 continued)

Activity	Optional Retirement with Buyout	Early Out with Buyout	Resign with Buyout	RIF	Other	Total Attrition
Fiscal Year 1995						
Inventory Control Points	158	114	69	14	445	800
Depot Regions	275	589	457	199	750	2,270
Service Centers	35	57	11	25	292	420
Contract Management Districts	177	102	42	1	476	798
HQ/MSA/FOA	78	65	6	1	86	236
Totals	723	927	585	240	2,049	4,524
Grade						
SES	2	0	0	0	0	2
GS/GM 15	14	10	0	0	8	32
GS/GM 14	18	19	1	0	19	57
GS/GM 13	68	53	6	0	71	198
GS 1–12	426	388	293	81	1,412	2,600
WG	195	457	285	159	539	1,635
Totals	723	927	585	240	2,049	4,524
Fiscal Year 1996						
Inventory Control Points	125	169	22	80	615	1,011
Depot Regions	149	220	171	54	860	1,454
Service Centers	23	31	5	14	279	352
Contract Management Districts	419	263	92	19	477	1,270
HQ/MSA/FOA	52	29	8	7	47	143
Totals	768	712	298	174	2,278	4,230
Grade						
SES	1	1	0	0	3	5
GS/GM 15	6	5	0	0	9	20
GS/GM 14	38	21	0	0	24	83
GS/GM 13	84	53	4	1	79	221
GS 1–12	531	475	193	128	1,590	2,917
WG	108	157	101	45	573	984
Totals	768	712	298	174	2,278	4,230

Source: Defense Logistics Agency; Executive Directorate; Human Resources Staffing, Labor, and Employee Relations Group.

1993, 1994, 1995, and 1996. Military downsizing figures are not shown because the number of military personnel in DLA is relatively small and military buyout programs are different from the civilian buyouts. The upper half of the table indicates losses of personnel according to downsizing strategy categories and by type of organization. Additionally, the lower half of the table breaks down personnel reductions by grade levels including executive (SES), general schedule/general management (GS/GM), and wage grade (WG), for the same downsizing categories. The category "other" includes regular retirements without buyouts, transfers, deaths, and other losses associated with normal attrition. Attrition for those years totaled 6,150, 5,997, 4,524, and 4,230, respectively. The figures differ from the attrition that can be calculated from Table 3.5 because the attrition in Table 3.7 includes transfers who remained within DLA. Regarding locations, note how the depot regions suffered a reduction of 8,726 workers out of the grand total of 20,901 personnel losses during 1993 to 1996. This loss equates to nearly 42 percent of all the downsizing. Also, the headquarters (HQ), management support activities (MSA), and field-operating activities (FOA) significantly increased their attrition from 269 in 1993 to 1,228 in 1994 before tapering off to 236 in 1995 and 143 in 1996. These figures indicate that personnel at the headquarters level and in management oversight positions were not immune from the downsizing.

In terms of attrition by grade levels, middle managers at the GS-14 and GS-15 levels and those at the GS-13 level, next in line to be managers, experienced consistent reductions throughout the four years, as indicated in Table 3.7. These losses reflect the inclusion of middle manager positions in the agency's downsizing program. Additional data in Table 3.8 show that the numbers of actual positions decreased at the GS-13 through GS-15 levels. For example, the numbers of positions for GS-13 grades declined from 2,838 at the end of fiscal year 1993 to 2,566 at the end of fiscal year 1996, a loss that equates to a 9.6 percent decrease. For GS-14 grades, there were 1,151 positions at the end of fiscal year 1993 and 995 at the end of fiscal year 1996, totaling a 13.5 percent drop. For GS-15 grades, the numbers were 339 and 284, for a 16.2 percent reduction. Obviously, on a percentage basis, positions for middle managers were drastically cut. On the other hand, the number of SES positions increased slightly, from 23 to 25.

Downsizing Interviews

An investigation of the downsizing processes within DLA was carried out by interviewing eight executives who were members of the SES. Refer to

Table 3.8

Defense Logistics Agency Civilian Positions
Fiscal Years 1993 to 1996
Number of Positions in Each Grade for Selected High Grades

End of Fiscal Year	GS-13	GS-14	GS-15	SES
1993	2,838	1,151	339	23
1994	2,688	1,060	309	29
1995	2,621	1,034	289	24
1996	2,566	995	284	25

Source: Defense Logistics Agency; Executive Directorate; Human Resources Staffing, Labor, and Employee Relations Group.

appendix C for the executive interview protocol. Following these interviews, additional interviews were conducted with three middle managers at the GS-14 and GS-15 grades. See appendix H for middle manager interview questions. Together, the interviews provided substantial description and explanation about downsizing conditions in the agency. To maintain confidentiality of the identities of respondents, their names are not revealed. For the SES officials, six of eight are from the headquarters and two are from the field, all eight have more than five years in the SES, and six of eight have three hundred or fewer employees. A total of 685 minutes was spent in interviews, with a mean interview time of one hour and 26 minutes. Table 2.9 contains demographic and employment data for the executives interviewed. Also, appendix E provides information about the nature of the positions held by the executives and some statistics on their interviews. For middle manager interviewees, all are assigned to headquarters positions, and they supervise from six to eighty employees. The mean interview time was 55 minutes.

An important part of executive interviews was the identification of critical incidents. Table 3.9 summarizes the critical incidents identified by the respondents. This part of the interviews obtained details about incidents or situations related to downsizing, in which the respondents were involved. See appendix D for an overview of the critical incident and behavior interview steps and techniques. Each interviewee was requested to discuss two "high point" incidents that resulted in significant accomplishments and one "low point" incident that prevented an accomplishment. The purpose of this part of the interviews was to obtain data on how the executives behaved in actual incidents involving downsizing. Some executives chose to focus on

Table 3.9

Defense Logistics Agency Critical Incidents

Interview		Critical Incident
DLA 1	1. High	Changed the organization to a business culture.
DLA 2	1. High	Successfully restructured and changed missions of units.
	2. Low	Managed the intraheadquarters transfer of employees.
	3. High	Eliminated two non-value-added work functions.
DLA 3	1. High	Reduced the workforce with minimal involuntary separations.
	2. Low	Did not convince the Director to manage and control individual departures in the downsizing.
	3. High	Managed the outplacement process with special care of employees during the consolidation of contract management organizations.
DLA 4	1. High	Quickly produced in writing a strategic plan for the organization's business.
	2. Low	Did not change pricing structure, causing the downsizing process to be imprecise.
	3. High	Reduced personnel faster than workload reduction and still achieved cost and performance improvements.
DLA 5	1. High	Membership in "Gang of Ten" directors who reengineered DLA from a bureaucratic to a change-oriented organization.
	2. Low	Experienced difficulty in creating a new culture from disparate cultures after downsizing actions.
DLA 6	1. High	Moved to a teaming concept for the organization, which positioned it for downsizing.
	2. High	Directed the process for disestablishing units in order to reapply resources to other units.
DLA 7	1. High	Made decisions on buyout policies.
	2. Low	Terminated 50 percent of a plant's positions.
	3. Low	Planned for a 10 percent reduction in positions.
DLA 8	1. High	Membership in "Gang of Ten" directors who reengineered DLA from a bureaucratic to a change-oriented organization.
	2. Low	Did not successfully create a joint DLA and General Services Administration enterprise.
	3. High	Changed from "inventory" to "buy response" business practices.
Total		High Point Incidents—13
		Low Point Incidents—7

fewer than the requested three critical incidents. Overall, DLA executives discussed thirteen high and seven low incidents that addressed downsizing conditions in rich detail.

Extensive within-case analysis was performed with interview data for the researcher to become intimately familiar with the DLA case. The analysis consisted of reviewing and summarizing the data, coding the data in a series of iterative steps, and then identifying themes and patterns. Appendix I explains the coding scheme, which was central to the analysis process. A thorough examination of the coded data results in the identification of specific, well-grounded themes and patterns. Table 3.10 is a thematic conceptual matrix for DLA downsizing conditions that contains ten downsizing aspects and corresponding characteristics representing the key themes and patterns that emerged for DLA. Furthermore, for each downsizing aspect, the characteristics are listed in decreasing order of support. In other words, characteristics are listed according to the strength of corroboration obtained from multiple and varying data sources and methods. Each set of downsizing aspects and characteristics is discussed in detail with supporting evidence in the next section. Quotes from executives and middle managers are included as support for each of the downsizing aspects.

Downsizing Conditions

Organizational Preparation for Downsizing

The data made it clearly evident that DLA had much experience in recent years in downsizing the agency. The changes brought about by the DMR, defense personnel drawdown, BRAC process, reengineering of business processes, and restructuring and streamlining actions combined to downsize the agency. As a result, DLA was ready for the downsizing initiated by the Clinton Administration's reinventing government effort. Unlike most agencies in the federal government, reinventing government did not alter the environment much for DLA, nor was the downsizing requirement perceived as a threat to the agency. All the executives interviewed agreed that DLA was experienced with downsizing. One executive strongly stated:

> I think that what has taken place in the shrinkage of the defense dollar puts us three or four steps out in front of that overall process initiated by the President to reduce the federal workforce. . . . Based on our last four, five years we can handle anything that comes along. We probably are as prepared as we could ever be to do anything that we ever needed to do related to downsizing. . . . We have been through it in about every way that we could have been.

Table 3.10

Defense Logistics Agency Downsizing Conditions

Downsizing Aspect	Characteristics
1. Organizational preparation for downsizing	a. Past experience from earlier Defense Department drawdowns b. Reengineer and reorganize first, then begin downsizing c. "You can never do enough" to prepare d. Downsizing would be more precise with performance management, information, and accounting systems
2. Organizational strategies for downsizing	a. Humanitarian approach b. Voluntary methods first: optional retirements, early out retirements, and resignations with buyouts c. Reductions-in-force at field level and none at headquarters d. Much consolidation and elimination of organizational units e. Doubts about the efficacy of employee teaming and empowerment f. Emphasis on reducing or eliminating administrative and no-value-added activities g. Increase in communication
3. Organizational downsizing in conjunction with other change	a. Downsizing is a later factor among other factors that are changing the organization b. Downsizing is the result of reengineering c. Downsizing is not used as an excuse or motive for other changes d. Downsizing helps change the organizational culture to business and team orientations
4. Middle manager reactions/concerns about downsizing	a. Some recognize opportunities b. Some feel disfranchised, threatened, frustrated, and insecure c. Concern for mission accomplishment d. Concern about workload, efficiency, performance, and productivity issues

(Table 3.10 continued)

Downsizing Aspect	Characteristics
5. Treatment of middle managers during downsizing	a. Assistance programs are available for personnel leaving b. Personnel remaining need better assistance programs and adjustment tools c. Personnel remaining experience workload increases and workload anxiety
6. Downsizing effects on middle manager behavior	a. Reengineering results in positive behavior b. Workload distribution issues are directly related to morale c. Managers remain committed, loyal, and motivated in response to the challenges faced d. Productivity and efficiency are up because the personnel loss rate exceeds the workload reduction rate
7. Conditions for resistance to change and downsizing by middle managers	a. Among the most senior managers at all manager levels b. When unable to cope with change c. When there is fear and a perception of threats d. When uncertain of new roles
8. Executive views of downsizing	a. Downsizing is subordinate to reengineering b. Downsizing is necessary and essential c. Downsizing results in positive by-product outcomes d. Downsizing is challenging, difficult, and painful e. Workforce capabilities are uncertain
9. Executive management practices during downsizing	a. More coaching, mentoring, encouraging, and lifting morale b. More delegation of authority and participatory style c. More attention to internal recruitment and placement of personnel d. More monitoring and evaluating work and performance e. No change from past in terms of specific types of actions f. More effort to accomplish more difficult work g. More communication h. Less formality and hierarchy i. More visibility

(Table 3.10 continued)

Downsizing Aspect	Characteristics
10. Executive competencies for downsizing	(See competencies and characteristics below)

a. Analytical
   Critically analyzes all processes.
   Understands dynamics and interdependencies.
   Establishes priorities.
   Examines how to balance mission requirements and lack of resources.
   Anticipates effects of decisions.
b. Vision
   Focuses on strategic issues and objectives.
   Identifies a future state or conditions for the organization to move toward.
   Seeks to use nontraditional solutions to change the organization.
c. Sensitivity and empathy for people
   Concerned about the total welfare of employees: professional, personal, health, family, and coping.
   Interested in and understands perspectives of others.
d. Commitment, energy, and inner strength
   Works tenaciously during downsizing.
   Makes personal sacrifices for the good of the organization and its employees.
   Is willing to make unpopular decisions.
   Tolerates the pain and difficulty of downsizing.
e. Leader and motivator through coaching, mentoring, and lifting morale
   For employees, encourages buy-in, persuades, instills confidence, and convinces.
   Facilitates employee work accomplishments.
f. Interpersonal skills
   Works closely with other decision makers.
   Works cooperatively with all interests.
g. Communication
   Shares information openly.
   Ensures employees operate with consistent data.
h. Team orientation
   Fosters conditions for all employees to work together toward common goals.
   Promotes participation and contributions in processes from all employees.
i. Flexibility
   Adapts well to multiple and changing circumstances.
   Works quickly with little notice and short planning.
j. Resourcefulness
   Accomplishes tasks and goals with innovation.
   Gets the job done not necessarily "by the book."

Six of the eight executives pointed out the central role reengineering and reorganizing had in preparing DLA for downsizing. These executives believed that reengineering should precede downsizing in order for an organization to operate effectively and efficiently in the future. That was exactly what DLA did: first it reengineered and reorganized to varying degrees throughout the agency at the headquarters and in the field. One executive located in the field felt this way:

First of all, we were doing it before there were such words as "reinventing government" and "reengineering" because our process really dates back to 1987 and 1988, begun long before it was vogue. . . . If you're downsizing and reorganizing and doing organizational changes without having first of all examined the business processes and changed them, it must be terribly frustrating. . . . I think we were damn lucky that we were in a position of having started our business process reengineering long before we needed to get into the numbers-driven objectives.

Despite being prepared for downsizing from past experience with it, some concern was expressed over not being prepared adequately for the human trauma dimension of downsizing. Most of the executives in the study showed a strong empathy for their employees because of the pressures and difficulties they faced. This theme is evident in other downsizing aspects also. One executive summed it up as follows:

I don't believe you can ever prepare a general workforce for downsizing. There is a bit of denial that goes on. I don't think you can prepare for that.

Another stated:

We took considerable pains to have what we call town hall meetings where we made the staff very much aware of actually what was happening and why. . . . Nevertheless, you can never do enough, and you certainly can't anticipate the unexpected.

Even though the agency was prepared for downsizing, downsizing remained difficult to implement. Although experience, reengineering, management empathy, and other factors discussed later prepared DLA and helped it achieve downsizing objectives, better management information systems could have given agency leaders greater confidence in their downsizing decisions. For example, one executive described how the decision to let anyone leave the organization through various incentives was not a wise decision because it created major skills imbalances and gaps in distribution functions. He recommended a process that would "come up with a scheme to orchestrate a flow of departures that was in concert with our work demands and our work measurement." Additionally, the following answer from a different interviewee was given in response to a follow-up question about preparation at the microlevel in DLA:

We haven't had a performance management system, an information system, and an accounting system with such extreme precision that I am able to determine with great precision precisely where the next move should be made. We've come a long way, but we're not there yet. Our operation research tools are better, and like any manager you wish they were better, but you have to go with what you've got.

Organizational Strategies for Downsizing

The organizational strategies aspect of downsizing revealed that the executives were united in how they favored and used a humanitarian approach whenever possible. This approach to downsizing was consistent with other characteristics appearing high on the lists for the "Executive Management Practices during Downsizing" and "Executive Competencies for Downsizing" aspects. Some executives were quite direct about their emphasis on a humanitarian orientation:

> We established what we called Transition Management Organizations and that was a very humanistic way of allowing that workforce to stay on to continue to do some work.

> I think we were interested in doing all of this downsizing management responsibly partly for humanitarian purposes and partly for how the agency appears purposes. . . . We tried to have certain public servants in important decision-making positions because those people were human kind of people who weighed the requirement to get the job done and . . . still had feelings.

Therefore, DLA relied first on voluntary methods for personnel reductions: normal attrition and buyouts for optional retirement, early retirement, and resignation. RIFs were avoided whenever possible and only used as a last resort because of the damage they do to personnel and organizations. Other major downsizing strategies included consolidations and elimination of organizational units (see Table 3.3). A lower-priority strategy was to reduce or eliminate administrative and no-value-added activities. A common element in any strategy was to increase communications to keep employees informed and reduce stress levels.

The use of employee teams was another strategy used by the agency. An interesting characteristic is that no consensus existed as to whether teaming increased or decreased management layers. One executive explained that the motive for teaming was to be more responsible to the customer and not to achieve personnel reductions. Another executive believed teaming was undertaken because it required fewer managers. As it turns out, DLA implemented teaming and management delayering as concurrent strategies during the past few years. One executive perceived that management layers had increased:

> I think, as an actual contradiction, the way we've implemented teaming around here, we've added management layers. And even though the restructuring was advertised as empowering people and decreasing the number of management layers by putting people on cross-functional teams, it's done the opposite. It's added layers.

Perhaps the explanation for the contradiction, or perceived contradiction at least, is that workload adjustments and eliminations were not sufficiently conducted. The issue of workload showed up again in the sections on "Middle Manager Reactions and Concerns about Downsizing," "Treatment of Middle Managers during Downsizing," "Downsizing Effects on Middle Manager Behavior," and "Executive Management Practices during Downsizing."

Moreover, middle managers identified a number of difficulties with the teaming approach. In some places, there was insufficient training for employee adaptation to teams, which resulted in problematic transitions to teams. Furthermore, in some offices, teams were not recognized as tools to make work processes more efficient but instead were considered additional work requirements. Two middle managers explained:

> The reductions in the numbers came first and then it led to an approach of "let's do teams." . . . Our teams are still developing. The jury on teams is still out. . . . The edict is "we will have teams." Training for teams came after the fact. . . . The team concept has some problems. In some places, the names were changed to teams. They're called teams, but they do things the same way as before. There are too few people in some places to do teams. There is not buy-in at all levels for teams. It is more of a directive for teams.

> We did not do a good job of explaining the team concept. Therefore, it was not embraced. . . . We started teaming two and a half years ago. Teaming was thought to be useful. On the day we were to become teams, the structure disintegrated. We did not follow through with training. We did have a four-hour session on team arrangements and four hours with teams. It was not sufficient to give team members what they needed. I think teams are good, but we did not give enough time to train the teams. And not all the teams at the headquarters are acting as teams. Workloads are interfering with team processes. My previous team was not a true team because it was not self-directed. But the leadership thinks they are serious about teams.

Regarding empowerment of employees, employees were not truly empowered because agency leaders did not give up power and remained controlling and directive. Additionally, empowerment principles were not fully understood. According to two middle managers:

> If the chain of command doesn't let go of authority, then there is no empowerment. . . . Executives are still more directive in style. They talk more and more of teams and empowerment, but they don't really give up authority and decision making. . . . Empowerment is working to some extent, but it will take a longer time. Employees should do it and see if they are told not to do it—don't wait.

> There is not a clear definition of "empowerment." I don't know if we can do
> it. It is an overworked word. It is ill-defined. . . . Empowerment is not fully
> explained as a concept. Employees think they can do what they want to do if
> they have empowerment.

Organizational Downsizing in Conjunction with Other Change

This category addresses the relationship between downsizing and other kinds
of change occurring for the agency. Earlier, this chapter discussed how other
external and internal changes preceded and drove downsizing actions. A critical juncture was the DLA decisions to undertake fundamental change in how it
conducts its work and to restructure from a functional to a business approach.
The agency "postured to operate in a businesslike manner as opposed to the
standard bureaucratic functional manner" in order to earn its revenues. Most of
the executives agreed that reengineering, reorganization, and streamlining resulted in the follow-on need to downsize. This view is succinctly stated by one
respondent: "Downsizing is not a driver. It's a result. It's never been used to do
anything else." However, once downsizing was under way, it did serve to
benefit the agency by helping move it toward its objectives. One executive
explained how "we're using the whole downsizing effort to change the culture"
to a business orientation. Another added that "the move to the multifunctional
teaming was really facilitated by the downsizing circumstances." Thus,
downsizing was a result of other changes; but downsizing, in turn, accelerated
desired changes.

Middle Manager Reactions and Concerns about Downsizing

Because middle managers are a specific target in downsizing efforts,
several questions in the interviews with executives focused on middle
manager reactions and concerns. Of course, the interviews with middle
managers provided their direct reactions and concerns. Overall, the majority of middle managers were very concerned about a variety of issues.
Although a minority of them recognized opportunities, the majority had
"negative" responses. A few GS-14s saw opportunity for potential open-
ings because GS-15s had left the organization, even though fewer GS-15
positions remained to aspire to.

Many middle managers felt disfranchised, threatened, frustrated, and in-
secure. One executive expressed that downsizing was a very threatening
process to middle managers because they viewed it personally:

> I don't know that they maintain an organizational perspective. It's all very
> personal. Anything that's a matter of the heart is hard to understand. So that

with this, it becomes a matter of the heart rather than a matter of doing business.

The result, according to another executive, was that it "diverts some of their energies ... and that impacts their job performance." Specifically, employees were apprehensive about reduced opportunities for career advancement, promotions, professional standing, and status. Middle managers complained:

> There will be no promotions for three to four years. We must create an environment of care and concern. This is a transitory time.

> Layers have been cut and middle managers down the chain have been hurt in status. It's hard on one's ego.

Several executives explained that many middle managers were especially concerned about the capability of the agency to accomplish its mission after downsizing. More specifically, middle managers had concerns about workloads, efficiency, performance, and productivity issues. The following were questions that the executives said typified middle manager concerns:

> Will we be actually able to do the mission?

> How do I get the job done while this downsizing is going on? How much will be demanded of me? Will all the output still be demanded but half the inputs gone? What is it we're going to stop doing? Or is management going to say "No, I still want everything done, so do it"?

> Who is going to be out there tomorrow to do the work? What work are we going to do tomorrow?

Treatment of Middle Managers during Downsizing

DLA organizations made a concerted effort to treat middle managers and other employees with dignity and respect during the downsizing process. Whether employees departed or remained with the agency, the intent was to "manage it responsibly" and to help employees "the best that we could." For those who left their jobs, a diversity of programs existed to assist them with retirement, transfer, or adjustment to new job requirements. Of course, there were buyout incentives and an effort to minimize RIFs. Also, field organizations had employee counseling centers that provided training, testing, interviews, and outplacement services. At the headquarters, personal consultations, information seminars, retirement day events, and outplacement services were available.

However, in the early downsizing stages, not as much attention was given to middle managers who remained with the agency. Because many resources were focused on departures, little time and resources were invested in assisting remaining personnel. Middle managers who remained needed programs to assist them with conditions such as skills imbalances, training lags, and demotivated employees within the workforce. The executives recognized these shortcomings, however, and voiced their intent to rectify it. One executive summed it very well: "Getting tools out there to do the job better. Accounting tools, financial tools, and automation tools. They need better tools to do the job."

The theme of excessive workload reappeared as an issue related to treatment of remaining middle managers. Remaining middle managers experienced workload increases, which led to increased anxiety about accomplishing their workloads. Although some workloads and functions were reduced or eliminated in some places, the norm was that decisions were not made about what work would no longer be performed. The consequence was that excessive work was expected to be performed by fewer remaining middle managers, who suffered enormous anxiety over those circumstances. According to an executive:

> Those who remain obviously carry even more responsibility for effecting the workload and I'm not sure that is recognized throughout the respective chains of command. It puts more pressure on the people remaining ... and while we all say "Well, we just have to prioritize and decide what we're not going to do," that ... isn't going to sell.... It'll be viewed as a cop-out rather than a reality of the workplace.

Another executive was more philosophical about the matter. Although his comment was lengthy, it is included in almost its entirety because the workload issue is a significant finding in this study.

> There is a part to downsizing that isn't being done by us, and I don't think by anybody, and that is the making of conscious decisions about what it is that we are not going to do.... We've got to come to grips with that at the senior management level, otherwise we are sending the wrong signals to the agency, workers, and mid-level management and that is we are saying take an already stretched workforce and stretch them a little bit more.... We have already been doing more with less for a long time, and now we want employees to do more than more with less and I don't think that is fair and I don't think that is right.... I think it is something that we will realize and we will wake up one day and say we just can't do this any longer at this level and we are not going to do it. And that is the statement we have to send to the administration and the statement we have to send to our leaders in the Pentagon.

Additionally, a middle manager stated the following about the employee-workload imbalance:

> Workloads don't decrease as much as personnel losses do. In fact, middle manager workloads have increased. At the headquarters, there is more workload on middle managers which should go to the action officers. It's hard because we're not supposed to "touch the ball" as a coach and because our bosses want so much. . . . We talk about reducing or eliminating workloads, but we're not good at it. . . . It makes sense that some workloads should go down, but it doesn't appear to be that way at headquarters because of initiatives and process improvements. We have not integrated initiatives, process improvements, and teams with functions thought of as normal duties. People see these things as an imposition, obstacles, and extra work.

Downsizing Effects on Middle Manager Behavior

Four characteristics were included in this aspect of downsizing. First, where reengineering was aggressively implemented before downsizing, middle managers were not threatened by downsizing. Because middle managers understood and accepted the new business orientation in reengineered organizations, they were much more likely to maintain high levels of morale, motivation, risk taking, and productivity despite downsizing actions.

Second, increased workload distributions had a direct negative effect on morale. Support for this characteristic came from comments such as "the number of early out acceptees is indicative . . . some people are tired of having a concomitant higher workload" and workloads must be "fairly administered because you run the real risk of just tearing morale to pieces."

Third, although middle managers were managing in a time of great change, most remained committed and loyal to the agency. Many middle managers maintained their motivation because they recognized that the challenges they faced required them to use their talents in innovative ways. More than half the executives commented about how downsizing brought out the best in most middle managers. A senior executive said:

> So middle managers have offered more to the agency than the executives. That's true. Executives continued to give leadership, tried to focus on some of the strategic issues. . . . But it's the middle managers who came up with all the innovations. . . . So it's the middle managers who carried this whole load. . . . They're the ones closest to the people who had to change, so they've been the change agents.

The fourth characteristic once again dealt with workloads. Some executives were proud of how productivity and efficiency rates were up because personnel loss rates exceeded workload reduction rates. One respondent stated that "people always come through when things get tough" and the employees "just keep pumping." However, another executive's analysis was more ominous. The following comment came from an executive not quoted on workloads in the previous section:

> I think that if you look at productivity, the productivity indices would have to be up because we're still carrying a tremendous workload. We haven't stopped, and I think it is an unfortunate circumstance. . . . We're still carrying one hell of a lot of workload that we brought from the old architecture and we need to start sifting through that and stop doing some things that don't have value.

A middle manager shares the pessimism:

> In some ways, quality of work and productivity have gone down because there are so many more things to balance and we have to deal with distractions from so much change. . . . Confidence in the world of work is reduced.

Conditions for Resistance to Change and Downsizing by Middle Managers

Other areas of interest are the conditions for resistance to change and resistance to downsizing by middle managers. There were middle managers who wanted to hold on to the "old" ways of doing business. As one would expect, many of the most senior managers who "simply could not see the need for change" fit this description. Also, middle managers who were unable to cope with change resisted. These types "either didn't want to or couldn't participate in the new work environment." A third kind of middle manager likely to resist included those who were fearful or felt threatened by the downsizing changes. Finally, those middle managers who were uncertain of their new roles tended to resist. As one executive noted, some "couldn't see their role in a changed organization" and if they had to "lead multifunctional teams or participate on a team" they "didn't exactly feel very secure." In fact, middle managers perceived their roles to be more difficult and expected them to remain difficult in the future:

> The job of the middle manager has become one of being a super action officer who manages a team, carries his or her own caseloads, and manages others with caseloads. You have to be more of a counselor and coach due to lower morale and more resistance. . . . Middle managers must try to talk with each other. They must hold each other up. They must be motivators to peers and team members.

Executive Views of Downsizing

The interview data revealed four patterns of executive views of downsizing: general view of downsizing, view of downsizing with other change, view of downsizing difficulty, and view of workforce capabilities and outcomes after downsizing. Under general view of downsizing, the executives believed downsizing is subordinate to reengineering. The earlier section on "Organizational Preparation for Downsizing" addresses this view further. Moreover, the executives strongly felt downsizing was "a necessary condition of doing business" and "an essential element of our strategy for the future."

Regarding view of downsizing with other change, an interesting contrast exists. Although three line executives made it clear that downsizing was not a driver, motive, or excuse for other change, four staff executives pointed out how downsizing, nevertheless, produced positive by-products. One flatly stated, "I think a by-product will be to get rid of dead weight people." Another said, "You can, generally speaking, through downsizing and streamlining get more bang for the buck and look better to your customer." As already noted in the aspect on "Organizational Downsizing in Conjunction with Other Change," downsizing was viewed as helping to change the culture and facilitating multifunctional teaming.

For view of downsizing difficulty, a consensus was that downsizing is extremely challenging, difficult, and painful. Direct quotes from different interviewees tell it best:

> And an awful lot of resistance. I'm telling you, painful. This is not comfortable. I'm pleased to say it worked. And I'm happy about what happened. But I can't tell you how painful the process is.

> I also see it as a difficult process. I see it as one that is causing a lot of pain out there both personally and professionally. I see it as one that may cause us some long-term effects.

> And that has been extremely difficult taking four disparate cultures, putting them together. It's been very difficult to declare victory when you turn on the switch in terms of a new organization. It's a continuous challenge.

Lastly, the pattern for view of workforce capabilities and outcomes after downsizing is that executives were greatly concerned about future capabilities. The agency had been implementing downsizing for quite some time. However, no one knew for sure how capable the workforce was throughout the agency. Nor did anyone know if mission accomplishment would be impaired if the agency was pushed to its limits in time of war. The executives expressed concerns about loss of experienced personnel, work skills imbalances, lack of resources and flexibility, experience and training gaps, and the need for reorientation training, education, tools, and techniques. Middle managers also recognized this serious problem:

> The biggest concern is that downsizing will continue and we won't be able to effectively guide people and still get the job done. The work has not gone down as much as the people have. That's absolutely true. . . . We have serious skills imbalances. Now it is somewhat serious. It will get very serious. And we're going to have trouble getting the mission done. And the executives agree with this. . . . NPR should not reduce middle managers significantly. We have a role to ensure the mission is carried out.

The good news, however, is that agency leaders did start to address those serious concerns. One agency executive asserted that the leadership was "beginning to now face the problem. . . . A lot of effort is now being geared up towards retraining."

Executive Management Practices during Downsizing

Several questions asked during the interviews with executives related directly to executive management practices during downsizing. To elicit varied responses, three questions were framed differently. They focused on "managing during downsizing," "new management challenges," and "new management styles, tactics, and strategies." Refer to appendix C for the wording of the interview questions. The research strategy was to combine the answers to achieve a more complete picture of executive management practices during downsizing.

Table 3.10 lists nine management characteristics identified from data analysis. The characteristics are those management practices by executives that were used or are recommended for use during downsizing. The order is based upon a combination of the frequency with which the practice was mentioned and the number of executives who mentioned the practice. Additionally, the critical incidents discussed by the executives were reviewed for behavior that reflected the practices. Therefore, the critical incidents provided additional support for the presence and order of the practices. Each listed item was identified at least three times and by at least two different executives.

Executive Competencies for Downsizing

The executive interviews were designed to include two opportunities for executives to identify executive competencies needed for downsizing. See appendix C for the interview protocol. First, the last section in Part I of the interviews asked executives, "What are the qualities, characteristics, and capabilities needed to perform those aspects of your position related to downsizing?" Second, one of the twenty questions in Part II asked, "What managerial competencies and skills do you believe are important for SES executives to exercise in managing during downsizing?"

Table 3.10 lists ten executive competencies identified from data analysis. The order is based upon a combination of the frequency with which the competency was mentioned and the number of executives who mentioned the competency. The table lists specific examples of behavior that illustrate the competencies. Additionally, the critical incidents discussed by the executives were reviewed for behavior that reflected the competencies. Therefore, the critical incidents provided additional support for the presence and order of the competencies. Each listed competency was identified at least three times and by at least two different executives. Therefore, although "background with functional or technical preparation," "sense of humor," "honesty and trustworthiness," and "empower others" were identified as competencies, none of them occurred frequently enough to be on the final list.

Summary of Major Findings

Table 3.11 shows the major findings of the DLA case study. The findings were reached after a systematic data analysis process of using multiple data sources, performing an iterative coding sequence, and identifying themes and patterns. The findings are written as results of the DLA case and can be considered lessons learned.

The discussion in the previous ten sections on downsizing aspects and characteristics support the findings in Table 3.11. However, two of the findings in the table receive more elaboration here. Half of the executives believed that the downsizing implemented, although difficult and painful, was less difficult than future downsizing will be. They believed that more difficult measures will have to be exercised that will cause continued resistance in subsequent stages of downsizing. The following quotes from executives provide evidence for the findings in the second, "Organizational Strategies for Downsizing," and seventh, "Conditions for Resistance," downsizing aspects:

> But now it's getting harder. We did this large reduction without a RIF. We did it through retirements, resignations, and reassignments. It's getting hard now, and I think there will be some negative reaction. . . . But when you make major geographic changes then you begin to get resistance. . . . The easy stuff is done. The hard stuff is coming.

Table 3.11

Major Defense Logistics Agency Findings

Downsizing Aspect	Finding
1. Organizational preparation for downsizing	Past experience and reengineering are not sufficient; management systems would improve preparation and implementation.
2. Organizational strategies for downsizing	More difficult personnel reduction strategies are expected to come later.
3. Organizational downsizing in conjunction with other change	Downsizing is not a primary change factor and should be preceded by reengineering.
4. Middle manager reactions/concerns about downsizing	Anxiety exists about roles and ability to accomplish mission.
5. Treatment of middle managers during downsizing	Remaining personnel need assistance programs and management tools to cope with organizational requirements.
6. Downsizing effects on middle manager behavior	Workload distribution is a key factor that needs adjustment.
7. Conditions for resistance to change and downsizing by middle managers	Resistance is expected to continue with subsequent downsizing.
8. Executive views of downsizing	Positive attitudes and concerns about workforce capabilities.
9. Executive management during downsizing	Management emphasis is turning to achieving personnel placement and workload synthesis.
10. Executive competencies for downsizing	Order of competencies is logical and consistent.

> But most of them [middle managers] are worried. And they're going to be more worried when they find out what else is going to happen around here.

The ten executive competencies identified in Table 3.10 are in a logical and consistent order for several reasons. The first two, which are "analytical" and "vision," were strongly emphasized in the data and are more strategic in nature. The next four, which are "sensitivity and empathy for people," "commitment, energy, and inner strength," "leader and motivator through coaching, mentoring, and lifting morale," and "interpersonal skills," are related to executives' individual behavior and interaction with other agency personnel. The last four, which are "communication," "team orientation," "flexibility," and "resourcefulness," are competencies executives exercise through organizational approaches, in general.

Four primary techniques were used to confirm the findings. First, triangulation was achieved by relying on different data sources and data collection methods. Second, weighting the evidence was practiced by exercising judgment about the quality of data and selecting the most valid data. Third, negative evidence was searched for to find any disconfirmations. And fourth, feedback from informants was used to validate the findings of the study.

Conclusions for Executive Management of DLA Downsizing

The last analytic exercise in the data analysis for the DLA case study was the generation of a causal network. The within-case displays in Tables 3.10 and 3.11 are steps in an inductive approach to building the causal network (Miles and Huberman 1994). For the DLA case, the causal network for downsizing appears in Figures 3.1 and 3.2. The causal network displays the most important variables and the relationships among them. The purpose of the causal network is to diagram an integrated understanding of the case. The causal network generated is the one that emerges from the data analysis. It subsequently will be synthesized in chapter 6 with the causal networks from the other two cases to generate a theoretical downsizing model and to produce hypotheses related to executive management during downsizing. In general, the causal network shows details of executive management of the DLA downsizing process. The figures include a two-dimensional section indicated by the dashed lines. The two dimensions are the downsizing process diagrammed in Figure 3.1 and executive management of downsizing depicted in Figure 3.2.

The far left side of Figure 3.1 identifies the following factors in the environment driving change for DLA: the end of the Cold War, the budget deficit, reduction of defense infrastructure, and the reinventing government initiative known as the National Performance Review. Each of these four major factors has the same effect on DLA. Each one drives DLA to downsize. Thus, consistent environmental forces precipitate the downsizing process. Therefore, although the downsizing process and management of it remain challenging and difficult, consistent factors minimize complexities that would be present in scenarios with contradictory environmental forces. Going from left to right, the two-dimensional, dashed line area represents the downsizing process and executive management of it. The downsizing process consists of three phases: process changes, personnel reduction strategies, and reorientations. Although there is some overlap among the phases, they generally follow the pattern shown. First, DLA implements reengineering, restructuring, and streamlining process changes throughout the agency. All of these process changes fundamentally modify agency activities to achieve organizational improvements. More particularly, reengineering makes radical change or significant alteration of work processes, restructuring realigns functional activities, and streamlining minimizes non-value-

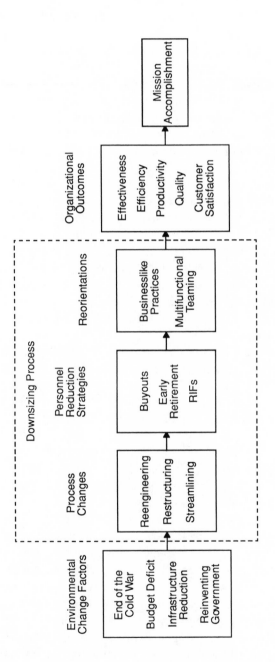

Figure 3.1 **Causal Network for Defense Logistics Agency Downsizing**

agency processes and
quire fewer personnel.
ts, early retirements,
chieve organizational
eorientations are to-
nctional teaming.
cutive management
illustrates this di-
LA's top leaders,
ry and concurrent
n analysis of the
promote change
leaders provide
ommunicate the
portion of the
cutive compe-
m part of the
iddle manag-
disfranchise-
efficiency,
nagers need
ment tools,
nanager re-
xpected to
d cooper-
e, coping

s/execu-
rganiza-
ciency,
ccom-

educ-
s far
, its
that
the

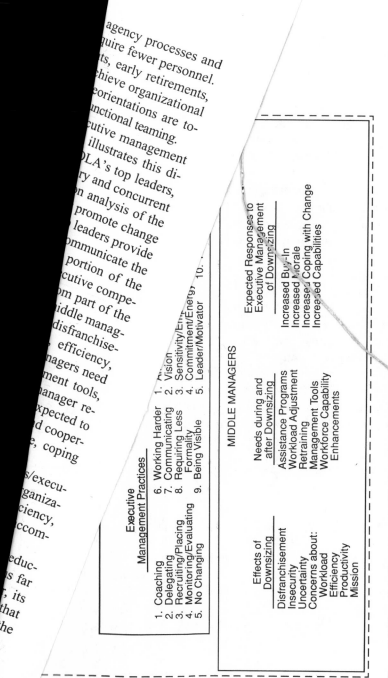

Figure 3.2 **Executive Management of Defense Logistics Agency Downsizing**

added steps while maximizing value-added steps in
systems. Next, the process changes enable DLA to re
Thus, personnel reduction strategies including buyou
and RIFs are employed. The first two phases help to a
reorientations in the third phase. For DLA, primary r
ward more businesslike practices and greater use of multif

The area within the dashed lines also represents exe
of the downsizing process explained above. Figure 3.2
mension with a pyramid. At the top of the pyramid are I
the military commanders who perform a critical prelimina
role for executive management of downsizing. Based upo
data, DLA top leaders exhibit four important strengths that
and enhance executive management of downsizing. The top
a clear vision, demonstrate leadership with firm direction, c
vision, and engender trust among employees. The middle
pyramid lists those executive management practices and exe
tencies needed by DLA for its downsizing process. The bott
pyramid indicates factors in three categories associated with m
ers. First, the effects of downsizing on middle managers are
ment, insecurity, uncertainty, and concerns about workload
productivity, and mission accomplishment. Second, middle ma
assistance programs, workload adjustment, retraining, manage
and other workforce capability enhancements. Third, middle m
sponses to improved executive management of downsizing are e
be increased buy-in, whereby middle managers trust in, accept, a
ate with the downsizing process, and increased levels of moral
with change, and capabilities.

Returning to Figure 3.1, the two-dimensional, downsizing proces
tive management dashed line area leads to desired and expected o
tional outcomes. Those outcomes are increased effectiveness, eff
productivity, quality, and customer satisfaction. Ultimately, mission
plishment is expected.

DLA's experience with downsizing reveals much about personnel r
tions being undertaken across the federal government. The agency th
has accomplished much success in managing its downsizing. Howeve
executives and middle managers know that DLA must build upon
success and make improvements for additional downsizing expected in
next few years.

Notes

1. Each military service managed certain categories of consumable items and ma

them available to all the services. In each case, they were called "single managers" and together within the three services there were eight single managers. See Nichols (1991) for a short history of the beginnings of DLA.

2. For an account of management improvements in DOD stemming from DMR, see Jones (1992).

3. The first DLA performance plan (Defense Logistics Agency 1994b) submitted in compliance with the Government Performance and Results Act explains DLA's budget relationship with DBOF.

4. The Quadrennial Defense Review is the fourth comprehensive review of the U.S. military since the end of the Cold War. It follows the 1991 Base Force Review, the 1993 Bottom-Up Review, and the 1995 Commission on Roles and Missions of the Armed Forces. The QDR is required by the Military Force Structure Review Act, part of the National Defense Authorization Act for Fiscal Year 1997. The QDR is a comprehensive examination of U.S. defense needs from 1997 to 2015 and includes perspectives on potential threats, strategy, force structure, readiness posture, military modernization programs, and defense infrastructure. Proposed QDR changes in defense manpower for 2003 further reduce the number of personnel already programmed to be lower in 2003. However, the QDR states that the "aim in taking these manpower reductions is to preserve the critical combat capabilities of our military forces—'the tooth'—while reducing infrastructure and support activities—'the tail'—wherever prudent and possible" (U.S. Department of Defense 1997, 31).

5. For an overview of how DOD and other federal agencies are using EDI to save money and boost efficiency, see Corbin (1992b).

6. See DLA annual performance plans and performance reports for details of its performance targets and achievements (Defense Logistics Agency 1994b, 1994c, 1995a, 1995c, 1996a, 1996b).

4

The Bureau of Reclamation: Downsizing with a New Mission

The Bureau of Reclamation is one of ten separate bureaus within the Department of the Interior (DOI).[1] The Interior Department was established in 1849, and its mission is to manage, preserve, and develop the nation's public lands and natural resources. In terms of budget and employment, only the National Park Service, Bureau of Land Management, and Bureau of Indian Affairs are larger within the Department of the Interior. For fiscal year 1997, BOR's budget authority was approximately $772 million, with an employment level of about 6,200 personnel.

A small headquarters for BOR is located with Interior Department offices in Washington, D.C. BOR projects and employees are organized into area offices in five separate regions throughout seventeen western states. The Reclamation Service Center in Denver, Colorado, provides technical, human resources, management, and administrative support services to the rest of BOR.

A revised BOR mission statement now guides the agency:

> To manage, develop, and protect water and related resources in an environmentally and economically sound manner in the interest of the American public. (Bureau of Reclamation 1992, iii)

Agency Background

The Reclamation Act of 1902 created the Reclamation Service that same year within Interior's U.S. Geological Survey. The original purpose of the agency was to administer the reclamation of arid and semiarid lands in western states. This management was to be achieved through construction of irrigation systems to store and distribute water, resettlement of people on the land, and development and improvement of economic stability (Warne

1973; Robinson 1979).[2] In 1907, the Reclamation Service was separated from the Geological Survey as an independent agency. Later, in 1923, the agency reorganized and was renamed the Bureau of Reclamation.

During its first decade, the Reclamation Service quickly established a respected reputation for constructing large dams and canals for agricultural irrigation. The "dam builders" repeatedly designed and built bigger and higher dams decade after decade (Warne 1973, 38). By the 1930s, though, BOR had expanded its programs beyond irrigation projects to include hydroelectric power generation, storage and delivery of safe municipal water supplies, and flood control. Throughout its history, BOR has prided itself on its record of engineering achievements and construction feats that have received worldwide acclaim. Consequently, early on, the agency developed a strong construction and engineering culture, which only recently began to change.

Over the years, BOR's mission grew to include other interrelated functions and projects: provision of industrial water supplies, improvement and protection of water quality, salinity control, river navigation, river regulation and control, fish and wildlife enhancement, recreation, conservation, environmental enhancement, and research on water-related activities. Today, Reclamation has federal oversight responsibility for 348 storage dams and reservoirs, 58 hydroelectric power plants, and 300 recreation sites (Bureau of Reclamation 1997).

In the past three decades, several trends pushed BOR away from water resources development and toward water resources management (Table 4.1). First, during the 1960s and 1970s, the environmental movement and new environmental laws presented BOR with difficult challenges (Lee 1980). The National Environmental Policy Act of 1969, the Federal Water Pollution Control Act of 1972, and the Endangered Species Act of 1973 combined to direct BOR toward greater awareness and incorporation of environmental factors into its decision making, project planning, and operations. Second, multiple constituent groups such as farmers, industrial water users, rural and urban water users, Native American tribes, recreationists, and environmentalists became active and made greater demands for water resources management. Third, changing public values and competing interests generated much controversy over water, its use, and its management.[3] Fourth, the number and scope of new construction projects diminished. All ongoing construction projects are expected to be completed by around 2000. Together, these trends led BOR to the conclusion that it must focus on water resources management to achieve multiple-purpose use of limited water supplies.

Since 1992 BOR has been dedicated to meeting the challenges associated

Table 4.1

Bureau of Reclamation Mission Transformation

Previous Mission	New Mission
1902 to 1991	1992 and beyond
Water resources development	Water resources management

with the management of finite water resources in the West. This part of the country is experiencing dramatic population growth and impacts to aquatic ecosystems. The agency is positioning itself to meet three principal challenges: securing and managing an adequate, sustainable water supply; addressing the decline of aquatic ecosystems; and managing social, economic, and political issues arising among water users.[4] However, it was not until the late 1980s that BOR finally took concrete steps to change its organization and focus in recognition of the trends and new realities described above. These recent actions are addressed in the next section.

Recent Organizational Changes

By the end of the 1980s, it was clear to BOR officials that the agency should be in the water resources management business. Although agency leaders recognized the need to change the agency's role, it still took a lengthy process between 1987 and 1993 to progress from initial recognition of the need to change to actual reorientation of the agency. The change evolution can best be described through a brief examination of four key BOR review, planning, and report efforts conducted during those years. During the period of 1993 to 1995, using the NPR as the change vehicle, BOR accelerated the transformation of its mission.

Assessment 1987

In March 1987, Secretary of the Interior Donald Hodel requested that BOR conduct an assessment of its role in managing water resources. The agency formed an Assessment Team to investigate opportunities to increase power operating efficiencies, water project efficiencies, and nonfederal partnerships. The outcome was a 10 September 1987 report titled *Assessment '87 . . . A New Direction for the Bureau of Reclamation* (Bureau of Reclamation 1987). The report claimed that the time had come for a "New Bureau of Reclamation":

This reality suggests strongly that the era of constructing large federally financed water projects is drawing to a close. . . . The key conclusion of the Assessment is that the Bureau's mission must change from one based on federally supported construction to one based on effective and environmentally sensitive resource management. . . . The Bureau should accelerate its transition . . . from a premier construction organization to a premier resource management organization. (Bureau of Reclamation 1987, i-ii, 2)

In October 1987, BOR followed with another document, *Implementation Plan: A New Direction for the Bureau of Reclamation.* In it were nine key recommendations and a broad-based strategic plan. The primary action taken was an organizational restructuring that included steps to relocate the headquarters to Denver and decentralize the agency. Also significant were redefined program priorities that helped initiate some cultural change. Although progress was made in the late 1980s, the momentum was lost in the early 1990s.

Strategic Plan

BOR next initiated development of a strategic plan in 1990. However, transformation of the agency slowed because emphasis was devoted to process while actual priority setting and implementation languished. Finally, two years later, it published in June 1992 *Reclamation's Strategic Plan: A Long-Term Framework for Water Resources, Management, Development and Protection* (Bureau of Reclamation 1992). The *Strategic Plan* consists of the following five sections, which have twenty-five program elements distributed among them: Managing and Developing Resources, Protecting the Environment, Safeguarding the Investment, Building Partnerships, and Fostering Quality Management.

Each program element has a guiding principle, a goal, several strategies for accomplishing the goal, and an implementation plan. The *Strategic Plan* thus provided the agency with specific concepts, objectives, and strategies to pursue in its annual programming and budgeting.

Commissioner's Program and Organization Review Team (CPORT)

The third major effort was initiated in May 1993 by Commissioner Dan Beard. He recognized that BOR's transition from a water resources development agency to a water resources management agency lacked sufficient progress, despite the good accomplishments of *Assessment '87* and the *Strategic Plan.* The Commissioner was committed to BOR's achieving the goal of becoming "the *premier water management agency in the world*" (Bureau of Reclamation 1993a,i), (italics in original). Therefore, he established a team of midlevel employees from across BOR to serve on the Commissioner's Program and Organization Review Team (CPORT). The purpose of the team was to recommend changes to assist BOR in completing its transition. The CPORT was advised to consider how the agency could operate more efficiently in the context of declining resources and how its programs must be carried out to be responsive to public values.

The *Report of the Commissioner's Program and Organization Review Team* was issued in August 1993 (Bureau of Reclamation 1993a). It presented an analysis of BOR's current programs and activities. Perhaps the greatest benefit of the *Report of the CPORT* was the internal debate it stimulated within the organization. The most important part of the report made recommendations for future activities and organizational changes to enable successful mission accomplishment. Many of the recommendations dealt with reducing bureaucracy, duplication, and inefficiencies and eliminating unnecessary internal reviews, excessive management oversight, and costly organizational layering. The recommendations formed the basis for specific decisions that followed in the next step. The next section on the agency's "blueprint" discusses the major changes that originated with the CPORT report.

Blueprint for Reform

Commissioner Beard quickly moved on to the fourth step in the sequence to reorient BOR. After considering the CPORT report, other forms of employee inputs, and deliberations among managers and executives, the Commissioner released his decisions on 1 November 1993 in *Blueprint for Reform: The Commissioner's Plan for Reinventing Reclamation* (Bureau of Reclamation 1993b). The *Blueprint* directs changes in functional processes and functional realignments.

In the category of functional processes, three areas of improvement are called for. First, policy guidance is broad and prior review and approval processes along with oversight processes are eliminated unless they add value. In addition, all regulations will be sunset at the end of fiscal year 1995 unless they are affirmed. Second, water resources management objectives drive the budget formulation and program execution processes. And third, authority and responsibility are delegated to lower levels, and excessive organizational layering is reduced. For functional realignments, several changes are mandated. First, the headquarters is designated only for Washington, D.C., offices. To correct diffusion of responsibility, responsibilities of offices in the Commissioner's Office are clarified. Moreover, both deputy commissioner and all five assistant commissioner positions are abol-

Table 4.2

Bureau of Reclamation Organization

Headquarters

Commissioner's Office located in Washington, D.C.:
  Operations Office
  Policy and External Affairs Office

Reclamation Service Center

Located in Denver, Colorado:
  Administrative Service Center
  Human Resources Office
  Management Services Office
  Program Analysis Office
  Technical Services Center

Regional Offices

Great Plains Regional Office (Billings, Montana)
Lower Colorado Regional Office (Boulder City, Nevada)
Upper Colorado Regional Office (Salt Lake City, Utah)
Pacific Northwest Regional Office (Boise, Idaho)
Mid-Pacific Regional Office (Sacramento, California)

Area Offices

25 located throughout 17 western states

Source: Bureau of Reclamation, Office of Public Affairs.

ished. Second, offices in Denver are redesignated as the Reclamation Service Center (RSC) with bureau-wide responsibility for technical services, human resources management, management services, and administrative services. The RSC's role is to provide customer-based support, not direction, review, and oversight. Third, field project offices are realigned into area offices, and more authority and responsibility are delegated to the area managers.

Implementation of the *Blueprint for Reform* occurred next. The Secretary of the Interior, Bruce Babbitt, officially authorized the BOR reorganization and restructuring by Secretarial Order on 13 April 1994. Since then, BOR has moved forward aggressively to implement the organizational changes outlined in the implementation plans they created. Table 4.2 lists the current offices within the BOR organization.

BOR and the NPR

It is significant to note how the BOR mission transformation is also a NPR reinvention effort at the same time. The new mission statement went into effect in 1992. However, the transition process to become a water resources management agency slowly began to occur between 1987 and 1993. In the spring of 1993, BOR kicked off its CPORT two months after the NPR began its six-month review of the federal government. Then, the *Blueprint for Reform* was announced in the fall of 1993 just two months after the NPR report was published. Many of the NPR principles were followed in BOR's realignment activities. In fact, NPR was used as the change mechanism to get BOR to finally and completely transform its mission, organization, and culture as it earlier stated it intended to do.

BOR is widely recognized as an exemplary reinvented agency (Kaufman 1994a; National Performance Review 1994, 13–14; Radin 1995, 114). It took advantage of the opportunity NPR gave it to make needed changes. One of the NPR report's 384 recommendations was DOI 12, "Create a New Mission for the Bureau of Reclamation" (National Performance Review 1993a, 144). The NPR status report highlighted BOR as one of five agencies "at the forefront of reinvention," which "represent the most comprehensive" government reinvention efforts (National Performance Review 1994, 24–25). BOR's accolades include being one of the first agencies to receive Vice President Al Gore's coveted Golden Hammer Award and winning a prestigious 1995 Innovations in American Government Award for reinvention successes. The "Reinvention of the Bureau of Reclamation" program was cited for its conversion into a leading water resource management bureau focused on conservation, water reuse, and environmental restoration, preservation, and enhancement. BOR, along with DLA, was among just six federal agencies and ten state and local government award winners in the Ford Foundation and Harvard Kennedy School of Government–sponsored competition (Clark 1995; Corbin 1995a). BOR used its $100,000 Ford Foundation grant to assist other federal and state agencies facing reform by establishing an Innovations Resource Center, a Reinvention Clearinghouse, and three regional one-day Reinvention Conferences.

Downsizing Activities

An overview of BOR's downsizing activities is included in this section to provide the background necessary for understanding the results and analysis that follow later in the chapter. Table 4.3 reflects how downsizing evolved in BOR by summarizing the changes experienced by the agency. Traditionally, the agency's water resources development mission locked it into an engineering and construction orientation. Organizationally, it operated as an autonomous, hierarchical, and bureaucratic empire. Then, the agency changed its mission to water resources management. The new mission,

Table 4.3

Bureau of Reclamation Downsizing Evolution (Descriptors and Events)

Traditional Past	Recent Past 1987–1995	Reinventing Government 1993 and Beyond	Future 1997 and Beyond
Water Resources Development Mission	Budget Decline	Executive Order 12839 to Downsize	*Strategic Plan: 1997–2002*
Engineering and Construction	Partnerships	*Report of the CPORT*	Culture Change
Autonomous	*Assessment '87*	Presidential Memorandum on Downsizing	
Hierarchical	*Strategic Plan*	*Blueprint for Reform*	
Bureaucratic	Water Resources Management Mission	Government Performance and Results Act of 1993	
	Transition to Decentralization	Federal Workforce Restructuring Act of 1994	
	Downsizing	Implementation Plans	
		Secretarial Order to Reorganize	
		Fewer Management Layers	
		Empowered Field Offices	
		Downsizing	

coupled with reinventing government initiatives, caused BOR to change itself to be more flexible through management delayering, field empowerment, and decentralization. The 1997 five-year *Strategic Plan* calls for continued culture change to meet new challenges of managing scarce water resources.

The effort to transform the agency's mission and culture amounts to an extraordinary level of change for the organization and its employees. Downsizing is an integral part of the many changes. The *Blueprint for Reform* acknowledged that "the reduction in Reclamation's program will be accompanied by a commensurate reduction in current staffing levels" (Bureau of Reclamation 1993b, 7). At the end of fiscal year 1993, the total number of BOR employees was 7,929. During fiscal year 1994, the number decreased by an extraordinary 1,274 or 16.1 percent for a year-end total of 6,655. Between fiscal years 1993 and 1996, the workforce was reduced by

Table 4.4

Bureau of Reclamation Downsizing Trends
Fiscal Years 1993 to 1996

End of Fiscal Year	Total Employees
1993	7,929
1994	6,655
1995	6,247
1996	6,200

Source: *Bureau of Reclamation Fiscal Year 1995 Annual Report* (Washington, D.C.: Bureau of Reclamation, n.d.), 40.

approximately 21.8 percent to a level of 6,200, where it has remained since then. Table 4.4 shows employee levels during the mid-1990s.

The downsizing occurred throughout the agency: Commissioner's Office, headquarters offices, the Denver Office (now the RSC), regional offices, and area offices within regions. The agency downsized by reducing or eliminating individual positions, groups of positions, career fields, functions, executive and management layers, and organizational units. Other actions included changing the nature of the work, establishing teams of employees to accomplish work, and empowering lower-level area offices. Table 4.5 lists the tools used by BOR to downsize its workforce.

Like DLA, the preferred strategy for personnel reductions, other than normal attrition, is the use of separation pay incentives from the VSIP or buyout legislation. However, agencies outside DOD had authorization to offer buyouts only from 30 March 1994 to 31 March 1995 under the first VSIP legislation. The buyout provisions permit eligible employees who resign voluntarily to receive a payment equal to a severance allotment (based on a formula including salary and years of service) or $25,000, whichever is less. The three possible categories for buyout eligibility (optional retirement, early retirement, and resignation) are explained in chapter 1. All three buyout categories were available in BOR. The least desirable downsizing strategy is the involuntary RIF. As in DLA, RIFs were used within the agency as a last resort.

BOR opened three buyout windows. The first window came in fiscal year 1994 from 4 April 1994 to 4 May 1994 and resulted in 801 "takers." None of them was extended on duty, and all left the agency right away to "clear the deck," according to an executive, prior to RIFs. Two windows in fiscal year 1995, from 2 October 1994 to 3 January 1995 and from 2 February 1995 to 31 March 1995, induced 466 employees to accept buyouts. Extensions to keep some of these personnel for limited periods were granted to make

Table 4.5

Bureau of Reclamation Tools for Downsizing

1. Normal attrition
2. Hiring freezes
3. Surplus Employee Placement Program for transfers within BOR
4. Retraining
5. Buyouts (voluntary separation incentive payments)
   a. Optional retirement
   b. Early retirement (early out)
   c. Resignation
6. Targeted reductions and eliminations
   a. Individual positions
   b. Groups of positions
   c. Career fields
   d. Functions
   e. Management layers
   f. Organizational units
7. Targeted levels
   a. All employee grade levels
   b. All organizational levels (Commissioner's Office, headquarters offices, service centers, regional offices, and area offices)
8. Planning and implementation documents
9. Increased communications
10. Teaming of employees
11. Empowering employees and lower-level organizations
12. Employee Assistance Program for counseling services
13. Employee Service Center for outplacement services
14. Involuntary reductions-in-force (RIFs)

future resource decisions on an orderly basis. Thus, 331 workers left with buyouts in fiscal year 1995, and 135 departed with buyouts in fiscal year 1996. The last window was scheduled to take advantage of the government-wide authority to the maximum extent possible before VSIP expired.

Table 4.6 shows actual downsizing statistics for fiscal years 1994, 1995, and 1996. The upper half of the table indicates losses of personnel according to downsizing strategy categories and by organization within BOR. The lower half of the table breaks down personnel reductions by grade levels for the same downsizing categories. The category "other" includes regular retirements without buyouts, transfers, deaths, and other losses associated with normal attrition. The bulk of BOR downsizing occurred in fiscal year 1994, when total attrition was 1,473. That figure differs from the attrition of 1,274, discussed above, which can be calculated from Table 4.4, because it includes transfers who remained within BOR. Regarding locations for fiscal year 1994, personnel reductions were relatively evenly distributed among

Table 4.6

Bureau of Reclamation Downsizing Statistics by Strategy Categories

Activity	Optional Retirement with Buyout	Early Out with Buyout	Resign with Buyout	RIF	Other	Total Attrition
Fiscal Year 1994						
HQ/Comm's Office	3	4	0	0	12	19
Reclamation Service Center	102	46	28	0	119	295
Administrative Service Center	9	6	6	0	41	62
Pacific NW Region	59	37	13	11	99	219
Mid-Pacific Region	51	55	7	0	78	191
Lower CO Region	71	57	33	1	115	277
Upper CO Region	64	49	13	20	97	243
Plains Region	38	37	13	13	66	167
Totals	397	291	113	45	627	1,473
Grade						
SES	1	0	0	0	2	3
GS/GM 15	11	3	0	0	4	18
GS/GM 14	28	18	0	1	6	53
GS/GM 13	56	23	6	0	16	101
GS 1–12	247	188	94	40	467	1,036
WG	54	59	13	4	132	262
Totals	397	291	113	45	627	1,473
Fiscal Year 1995						
HQ/Comm's Office	7	3	0	0	1	11
Reclamation Service Center	29	22	12	31	14	108
Administrative Service Center	0	3	9	0	9	21
Pacific NW Region	10	25	7	8	22	72
Mid-Pacific Region	10	5	3	0	19	37
Lower CO Region	31	25	31	29	21	137
Upper CO Region	13	13	12	12	20	70
Plains Region	19	24	18	19	9	89
Totals	119	120	92	99	115	545
Grade						
SES	3	0	0	0	1	4
GS/GM 15	3	0	0	0	0	3
GS/GM 14	8	11	1	0	0	20
GS/GM 13	24	16	1	2	5	48
GS 1–12	73	77	81	95	90	416
WG	8	16	9	2	19	54
Totals	119	120	92	99	115	545

(Table 4.6 continued)

Activity	Optional Retirement with Buyout	Early Out with Buyout	Resign with Buyout	RIF	Other	Total Attrition
Fiscal Year 1996						
HQ/Comm's Office	3	0	1	0	2	6
Reclamation Service Center	12	0	2	0	8	22
Administrative Service Center	7	2	0	0	12	21
Pacific NW Region	8	13	0	0	8	29
Mid-Pacific Region	5	9	1	1	19	35
Lower CO Region	10	19	6	13	13	61
Upper CO Region	8	11	1	4	10	34
Plains Region	10	6	1	1	10	28
Totals	63	60	12	19	82	236
Grade						
SES	0	0	0	0	0	0
GS/GM 15	1	0	0	0	0	1
GS/GM 14	11	2	0	0	1	14
GS/GM 13	9	13	0	0	6	28
GS 1–12	31	35	12	19	61	158
WG	11	10	0	0	14	35
Totals	63	60	12	19	82	236

Source: Bureau of Reclamation, Human Resources Office, Personnel Management Division.

the RSC and the five regions, with figures ranging from 167 to 295. Downsizing was not as dramatic in fiscal year 1995, when 545 employees exited, or in fiscal year 1996, when only 236 workers left.

In terms of attrition by grade levels, all levels of employees experienced a reduction in total numbers. Middle managers at the GS-15 and GS-14 levels and those at the GS-13 level, next in line to be managers, witnessed reductions of 22, 87, and 177, respectively, during fiscal years 1994 through 1996, as shown in Table 4.6. Also, seven executives left the agency during those three years. These losses reflect the inclusion of executive and middle manager positions in the agency's downsizing program. Additional data in Table 4.7 for the earliest downsizing show that the numbers of actual positions decreased at the GS-13 through GS-15 and SES levels. The numbers of positions for GS-13 grades were 689 at the end of fiscal year 1993 and 607 at the end of fiscal year 1994, a drop that equates to an 11.9 percent decrease. For GS-14 grades, there were 265 positions at the end of fiscal

Table 4.7

Bureau of Reclamation Positions
Fiscal Years 1993 and 1994
Number of Positions in Each Grade for Selected High Grades

End of Fiscal Year	GS-13	GS-14	GS-15	SES
1993	689	265	58	22
1994	607	210	35	19

Source: Bureau of Reclamation, Human Resources Office, Personnel Management Division.

year 1993 and 210 at the end of fiscal year 1994—a remarkable 20.8 percent drop. For GS-15 grades, the numbers were 58 and 35, for a staggering 39.7 percent reduction between fiscal years 1993 and 1994. Likewise, SES positions fell from 22 to 19, for a 13.6 percent decline in those same years.

The RSC experienced the most turbulence from the downsizing wave. To provide greater insight into downsizing actions within the RSC, Table 4.8 chronicles RSC downsizing steps during mid-1993 to early 1995.

Downsizing Interviews

An investigation of the downsizing processes within BOR was conducted by interviewing seven executives who were members of the SES. See appendix C for the executive interview protocol. After these interviews, additional interviews were carried out with four middle managers at the GS-14 and GS-15 grades. Middle manager interview questions are contained in appendix H. Combined, the interviews provided substantial description and explanation about downsizing conditions in the agency. To maintain confidentiality of the identities of the respondents, their names are not revealed. For the SES professionals, five of seven are from field organizations and two are from the headquarters, four of seven have less than five years in the SES, and four of seven have 330 or fewer employees. A total of 813 minutes was spent in interviews with a mean interview time of one hour and 56 minutes. Table 2.9 contains demographic and employment data for the executives interviewed. Also, appendix F provides information about the nature of the positions held by the executives and some statistics on their interviews. For middle manager interviewees, all are assigned to the RSC, and they supervise from six to twenty employees. The mean interview time was 65 minutes.

Table 4.8

Reclamation Service Center (RSC) Downsizing Actions

Date	Action
July 1993	Hiring freeze is enacted due to smaller projected workloads. Approximately 1,600 employees are in place in the Denver Office, excluding the Administrative Service Center.
August 1993	*Report of the CPORT* recommends shift in role for Denver Office from policy making, review, and oversight of regional and area offices to services and support.
November 1993	*Blueprint for Reform* sets forth *Report of the CPORT* changes, including reduction in management layers.
January 1994	Employee Service Center is established to help employees prepare for and look for new government jobs inside and outside BOR and in the private sector. Also, Employee Assistance Program is available with counseling services to assist employees through the change process.
March 1994	Staffing level projections for the restructured RSC estimate 300 to 400 positions are to be reduced by 1 October 1994.
April 1994	Secretarial Order officially approves BOR restructuring, implements *Blueprint for Reform* changes, removes line authority from the Denver Office, removes supervisory layers, changes the supervisor to staff ratio from 1 : 5 to 1 : 15, and changes the Denver Office to the RSC.
April 1994	In first VSIP buyout window, 177 employees (excluding the Administrative Service Center) accept buyouts between 4 April 1994 and 4 May 1994.
May 1994	Surplus Employee Placement Program is activated to help place employees in vacant positions in regional offices or the Administrative Service Center.
June 1994	1,417 employees are in the RSC, excluding the Administrative Service Center. Expected number of employees for the RSC in the future is 1,320.
June 1994	90-day RIF notices given to 88 employees who also receive outplacement services from a professional firm.
October 1994	Second VSIP buyout window is between 2 October 1994 and 3 January 1995.
February 1995	Third VSIP buyout window is between 2 February 1995 and 31 March 1995.

Sources: "Realignment Process for the Reclamation Service Center and Denver-Based Commissioner's Staff Fact Sheet," June 1994; and "Reclamation Service Center Announces Reduction-in-Force," press release, July 1994 (Bureau of Reclamation, Reclamation Service Center).

An important part of executive interviews was the identification of critical incidents. Table 4.9 summarizes the critical incidents identified by the respondents. This part of the interviews obtained details about incidents or situations related to downsizing, in which the respondents were involved.

Table 4.9

Bureau of Reclamation Critical Incidents

Interview		*Critical Incident*
BOR 1	1. High	Advocated delegation of authority and responsibility to field area offices.
	2. Low	Concurred with organizational units undergoing downsizing, performing workload estimates and analysis.
BOR 2	1. High	Involved in evaluating the need for changing the organization's mission, reorganizing, and downsizing.
	2. Low	Experienced rejection of a proposal to reduce the Reclamation Service Center by 50 percent.
BOR 3	1. High	Used and obtained positive results from employee-empowered teams that recommended downsizing actions.
	2. Low	Experienced difficulty and frustration of conducting the reduction-in-force process.
BOR 4	1. High	Used and obtained positive results from employee-empowered teams that recommended downsizing actions.
	2. Low	Experienced difficulty and frustration during implementation of the reduction in the number of SES executives in the organization.
BOR 5	1. High	Established a bureau-wide coordinated research program.
	2. Low	Observed insufficient consideration of longer-term human resource capabilities during the mission change and downsizing processes.
BOR 6	1. High	Gained experience with closing organizations that provided valuable insights about employee needs and emotions, which led to a proactive employee involvement process in the current downsizing.
	2. Low	Learned the lesson that an employee-empowered organization without structure and hierarchy may actually contribute to a threatening environment for employees who accept and find comfort in hierarchical structures.
BOR 7	1. High	Brought to closure a difficult process for reducing the number of SES executives in the organization.
	2. Low	Managed the process for downgrading and placing an SES executive.
Total		High Point Incidents—7
		Low Point Incidents—7

Refer to appendix D for a summary of the critical incident and behavior interview steps and techniques. Each interviewee was requested to discuss one "high point" incident that resulted in a significant accomplishment and one "low point" incident that prevented an accomplishment. The purpose of this part of the interviews was to obtain data on how the executives behaved in actual incidents involving downsizing. Overall, BOR executives discussed seven high and seven low incidents that addressed downsizing conditions in rich detail.

Extensive within-case analysis was performed with interview data for the researcher to become intimately familiar with the BOR case. The analysis consisted of reviewing and summarizing the data, coding the data in a series of iterative steps, and then identifying themes and patterns. Appendix I explains the coding scheme, which was central to the analysis process. A thorough examination of the coded data results in the identification of specific, well-grounded themes and patterns. Table 4.10 is a thematic conceptual matrix for BOR downsizing conditions that contains ten downsizing aspects and corresponding characteristics representing the key themes and patterns that emerged for BOR. Furthermore, for each downsizing aspect, the characteristics are listed in decreasing order of support. In other words, characteristics are listed according to the strength of corroboration obtained from multiple and varying data sources and methods. Each set of downsizing aspects and characteristics is discussed in detail with supporting evidence in the next section. Quotes from executives and middle managers are included as support for each of the downsizing aspects.

Downsizing Conditions

Organizational Preparation for Downsizing

BOR did not conduct any bureau-wide downsizing activities prior to the Commissioner's *Blueprint for Reform* and the NPR. Therefore, the agency's experience with downsizing was limited to parts that downsized intermittently in the 1980s. Overall, the interviews with executives revealed that BOR's preparation for downsizing was viewed with mixed opinion. On the one hand, executives believed BOR implemented downsizing with diverse organizational measures. On the other hand, they also expressed some doubts about the efficacy of those measures.

The agency "bent over backwards helping the people" by providing outplacement services during the downsizing. Additionally, BOR leaders increased communications with employees to provide timely information, help employees make decisions, and ease the transition. Despite the diverse

Table 4.10

Bureau of Reclamation Downsizing Conditions

Downsizing Aspect	Characteristics
1. Organizational preparation for downsizing	a. Establishment of outplacement activities and initiation of change management training b. With increased communications c. Some doubts about whether preparation was good enough d. Some employees do not trust management
2. Organizational strategies for downsizing	a. Participation of empowered employees in the planning of change b. Deliberate use of planning documents such as *Report of the CPORT, Blueprint for Reform,* and implementation plans c. Hiring freeze d. Buyouts e. Reductions-in-force f. Reduced management layers and hierarchy g. Elimination of overhead work, functions, supervisory positions, units, reviews and approvals, and regulatory oversight
3. Organizational downsizing in conjunction with other change	a. Reinventing government gives the agency an opportunity to make "changes we had to make anyway" b. Downsizing is part of the process for changing the agency's mission and culture from dam engineering and construction to water resources management
4. Middle manager reactions/concerns about downsizing	a. Strong feelings of not being valued and sense of reduced status and professional standing b. Less opportunity for advancement and promotion since there are significantly fewer middle manager positions c. Concern about the agency's new mission and general direction d. Feelings of vulnerability when hierarchy is removed

(Table 4.10 continued)

Downsizing Aspect	Characteristics
	e. Job as a middle manager is more demanding because of multiple changes, fewer resources, increased workloads, new skill mixes, increased span of control, and new role as a team leader
5. Treatment of middle managers during downsizing	a. Extensive effort to help find new jobs for those leaving through the availability of outplacement services b. Just beginning to strengthen the focus on those remaining by addressing new roles, management tools, retraining process, reengineering, continued participation in decision making, and team management
6. Downsizing effects on middle manager behavior	a. Morale and motivation are higher at the field area offices; morale and motivation are lower at the Reclamation Service Center and regional offices due to perception of being "losers" b. Commitment and loyalty remain high to the institution; trust and loyalty to top leaders among managers at the Reclamation Service Center is mixed c. Increase in risk taking due to emphasis on allowing managers to take risks d. Quality of work remains high e. Reduction in efficiency and productivity at times due to turmoil and workloads associated with change
7. Conditions for resistance to change and downsizing by middle managers	a. When holding on to desire to do "business as usual" b. When unable to recognize the reality of change and downsizing and cope with it c. At Reclamation Service Center, where many steps in the process were resisted, challenged, and questioned d. Among most senior managers
8. Executive views of downsizing	a. Downsizing is necessary and essential for the future b. "It should have been done sooner" c. Downsizing is challenging, difficult, and painful d. Uncertainty regarding whether sufficient attention was paid to human resource capabilities

(Table 4.10 continued)

Downsizing Aspect	Characteristics
9. Executive management practices during downsizing	a. More monitoring and evaluating work and performance b. More effort to accomplish more difficult work c. More coaching, mentoring, encouraging, and lifting morale d. More communication e. More delegation of authority and participatory style f. No change from past in terms of specific types of actions g. Less formality and hierarchy h. More attention to internal recruitment and placement of personnel i. More visibility
10. Executive competencies for downsizing	(See competencies and characteristics below)

a. Vision

Views situations from a broad perspective.

Considers what is best for the entire agency.

Knows what direction to lead to, provides employees an understanding of the direction, and maintains a consistency of purpose while leading toward goals.

b. Leader and motivator through coaching, mentoring, and lifting morale

Makes work conditions conducive to employees being as effective as possible.

Encourages employees to overcome difficulties, take risks, and succeed.

c. Sensitivity and empathy for people

Acts consistently when impacting employees' careers and lives.

Listens to employees.

Is sensitive to the needs of employees and understands their values.

Recognizes that employees hurt from downsizing and must heal.

Provides support systems to assist employees cope.

d. Analytical

Analyzes situations, determines factual bases, and makes difficult decisions.

Incorporates diverse ways of thinking about issues.

Thinks beyond the limits of own institution.

e. Commitment, energy, and inner strength

Committed to public service and institutional goals.

Is mentally and physically healthy for stressful work.

Perseveres through downsizing difficulties.

f. Honesty and trustworthiness

Places public service and public interests above individual interests.

Gains credibility by being honest, candid, and forthright.

Earns trust from others in own integrity and vision.

g. Communication

Clearly communicates goals and information.

Creates environment where subordinates give candid feedback.

Tells others what they do not want to hear but need to hear.

h. Empower others

Sets clear boundaries and expectations and then allows employees freedom to accomplish goals.

(Table 4.10 continued)

Downsizing Aspect	Characteristics
	Does not control; instead, delegates authority and trusts others with it.
i. Interpersonal skills	Interacts constructively with peers and superiors.
	Helps "build bridges" of positive relations with others.
j. Patience	Understands it takes time for employees to accept, make, adapt to, and have ownership of change.
	Resists urges to make things happen too fast.
	Is willing to see things through over long periods.

assistance programs, the executives were not entirely confident that they were sufficient. One detects an ambivalence in an interview response:

> We did the best that we could. We put in a lot of effort early in terms of communicating with our employees. We implemented things such as an Employee Service Center. . . . And what we did was conduct training for people in change management and personal transitions. We've actually had a paid contractor on board who actually specializes in outplacement activities. So we did. We prepared them as well as we could prepare them. Or, we tried to. Again, some folks dealt with them very professionally. Others had a very hard time with that.

Lack of employee trust was another theme that emerged regarding preparation for downsizing. Some employees had a distrust of the agency's downsizing process. That distrust originated from a lack of trust some employees had for some agency leaders. More specifically, employees believed there was not "a clear sense of where we ought to be" and were "thinking there's a hidden agenda" associated with the downsizing. The lack of trust by employees over downsizing actions translated into an executive view that any organization's preparation for downsizing might be limited. The following quote from an executive makes the point:

> [Preparation is] probably as good as you can get, which is never good enough. I mean, we did far more than I've ever been familiar with doing. We did a lot of communication. We had a lot of all-employee meetings. We put out a lot of local area network messages. We got the outplacement contractors on board. We used change management training, and yet the comment you hear most frequently is "nobody's telling us anything and they're keeping secrets." I mean, I don't think you can ever be totally prepared for something like this.

Every executive interviewed expressed some degree of concern about the level of preparation BOR had before and during the downsizing. Although one executive felt the agency was well prepared, even he admitted that "it didn't make it easier" and "this is still something that we need to deliberately pursue."

Organizational Strategies for Downsizing

A noteworthy aspect of the downsizing approach taken by BOR was the empowerment of employees and their inclusion in the planning process. As already discussed, a team of employees from throughout the agency served on the CPORT. Interestingly, the unit most affected by downsizing, the Denver Office (before it became the Reclamation Service Center), was not represented on the CPORT. The team's recommendations in the CPORT report became the core elements in the *Blueprint for Reform* plan to restructure the agency. Employee participation in change efforts also continued during the actual implementation of the restructuring. For example, six employee teams with some middle managers devised the plan for the formation and implementation of the Technical Services Center (TSC) within the RSC. The teams proposed the workload, workflow process, organizational structure, and staffing plan for the TSC.

Central to the agency's downsizing approach was a disciplined use of planning documents and implementation plans. The strategy of developing and implementing detailed plans was largely responsible for the quick progression from CPORT formation in May 1993 to reorganization implementation in the summer of 1994. One executive praised the strategy as follows:

> We followed a very deliberate and predetermined process: . . . a definition of our new mission, organizational changes to support the new mission, executive analysis of that, the Commissioner's direction, implementation plans for achieving that, implementation teams to carry out the implementation plans, and the change implemented in just fifteen months. Maybe fifteen months sounds like a long time, but it's an incredible achievement when we look back from where we were to where we are today.

BOR used a variety of personnel reduction strategies prior to evoking RIFs. Voluntary methods were relied on first. The RSC in Denver used a "three-pronged approach": (1) a hiring freeze, (2) optional and early out retirements with buyouts, and (3) RIFs. Of course, a limited amount of attrition occurred during the hiring freeze. Additionally, internal transfers or placements were made to minimize the number of personnel subjected to RIFs.

The prime objective of downsizing was to make the RSC a more efficient, effective, and customer-responsive organization. One way to do this was to reduce costs through reducing unnecessary management layers and excessive hierarchy. Specific changes included cutting the number of SES positions from twenty-two to nineteen between 1993 and 1994, reducing management layers in all chains of command, lowering the supervisor-employee ratio from about 1 : 5 to closer to 1 : 15, decreasing reviews to a single level, and delegating responsibility to employees at lower levels. An executive described the delayering process with fervor:

> We had an organization that was six or seven layers deep: assistant commis-
> sioner, deputy commissioner, division chief, branch chief, section head, unit
> head, individual supervisor, and individual worker. So you had this 800 or 1,100
> person organization with all this hierarchy, grossly inefficient, and with horrid
> approval processes. We said we can't tolerate this in the future. . . . So what
> we're going to do is eliminate five of the seven hierarchical layers. . . . And we
> actually cut out, just eliminated, did away with, abolished, four or five layers.

Another executive commented:

> We've gone from the old hierarchical division-branch-section organizations
> to work groups, leadership groups, and organizations that will be using self-
> directed teams.

Other organizational strategies for downsizing included reduction or elimination of overhead work, functions, supervisory positions, units, reviews and approvals, and regulatory oversight. According to one interviewee, BOR was guided by certain "downsizing philosophies" like empowered workers, empowered field organizations, efficient and effective operations, and less control and more service. But, the implementation of empowerment principles had its growing pains. Two different middle managers commented:

> Empowerment has occurred, but we have not taken full advantage of it.
> That's because there is a learning curve. It will be slow.

> Empowerment is occurring, yes and no. It depends on how you define *em-
> powerment*. A lot of middle managers have trouble defining it. They ask,
> "What's my role and my accountability?" It is occurring in some places.
> Some people do well; some don't. Some fight it. It's happening differently in
> different places.

Organizational Downsizing in Conjunction with Other Change

Behind the rhetoric about BOR reinventing itself, one finds a more accurate account of the agency's transformation. Put simply, the reinventing govern-

ment initiative and its timing presented an opportunity for BOR leaders to use
it as the mechanism to make changes the agency already needed and planned to
make. BOR's traditional project work was being curtailed and, therefore, so
was annual funding. Reinventing government includes principles, such as cutting red tape, reducing operating costs, and empowering employees, that BOR
knew for years it should follow. When the federal government launched a
program to transform outdated bureaucratic systems, the agency could not
permit itself *not* to change its orientation completely.

Every executive interviewed admitted that reinventing government was
an opportunity the agency took advantage of. This characteristic of BOR
reinvention is rarely made known in media reports about BOR's transformation. Three executives were direct on this issue:

> We had to do something. And seizing the opportunity . . . to make it part of
> the fundamental changes was the reason for our success.

> Yes, we were fortuitous, and we made changes we had to make anyway.

> It just so happens that it's exactly what the National Performance Review put
> out by Vice President Gore calls for and it's why we were so lined up with
> the Clinton Administration's objectives. . . . I mean we were institutionally
> lined up to achieve what the White House wanted us to achieve because of
> our problematic change.

Furthermore, the executives acknowledged that downsizing helped bring
about specific changes such as mission change, culture change, and a business orientation. In other words, downsizing was used as a tool to achieve
other change objectives. In this way, downsizing was a means to an end.
The following remarks came from yet another three executives. Again, they
were very clear:

> We're definitely using the downsizing to change the focus of where Recla-
> mation is going from being a construction organization to a water manage-
> ment organization.

> I think the agenda of the Commissioner was the change of cultural aspect,
> and this was an ideal mechanism to use.

> I think what downsizing will do is it will force us to do business differently.

Middle Manager Reactions and Concerns about Downsizing

Middle managers are a specific target in downsizing efforts. Therefore,
several questions in the interviews with executives focused on middle manager reactions and concerns. Moreover, middle managers gave direct feed-

back during their interviews. Overall, the majority of middle managers had deep concerns about a diversity of issues. A minority of them recognized opportunities for themselves in the future. However, the majority of them had "negative" responses to the downsizing. This section addresses middle manager concerns about loss of status, fewer advancement opportunities, and the agency's new mission. Additionally, two other interesting themes emerged and are discussed: a sense of vulnerability among middle managers following dismantling of hierarchical structures, and the demanding nature of middle manager jobs.

First, middle managers, in general, had a mixture of emotions, including anger, frustration, and resentment. The many changes resulted in loss of positions, titles, and work responsibilities. Therefore, they had strong feelings of not being valued by the organization. One middle manager stated:

> Some employees love the change and think, "It's about time." But some can't handle it. They fear for their jobs and their ability to do them. They don't trust management. They are concerned for their livelihood. If they changed jobs and supervisors, it resulted in difficulties.

Remarks from two different executives added support:

> Because these people were used to being treated with a great deal of respect. Respect that goes with winners and they had a sense of pride in what they did because they realized that they were the best. . . . And then to be told that they weren't good, that what they did was bad . . . was very, very painful.

> Our people have very high standings, nationally and internationally. They're highly regarded worldwide. And when they lost their organizational titles and their grades and their standings in their organization, they lost their standings in their community worldwide. . . . They lost a lot of their personal self-worth, and it was very difficult for them.

Second, younger managers saw far less opportunity for advancement and promotion as there were fewer middle manager positions to aspire to. The delayering, position downgradings, and position eliminations decreased opportunities. That the new environment for middle managers is more difficult is reflected in the comments of two middle managers:

> Many employees are concerned about whether they will still have a job later. Different functions were put together with little preparation or experience.

> Some employees don't see promotion opportunities with fewer positions available. The twenty-five-year people were at all levels, and some felt as if they were demoted.

An executive was empathetic:

We've had people who were in management and supervisory positions who are not now. And we've had people who now have to become group leaders when they don't know how to be group leaders. We've had increased span of control where somebody might have had four or five people reporting to him, he now has fifteen or twenty, and we don't quite know how to handle that just yet. Those are the basic things that surface most often.

Third, middle managers were concerned about the definition of the new mission and the direction of the agency. This issue was sensitive since it challenged the vision of BOR's leadership. The evidence strongly suggests that some middle managers did not "buy in" to the whole change process. Moreover, some middle managers did not understand what it is they should "buy in" to. Three quotes from three different executives support this point:

They're concerned about the general direction we're going as an agency. Many of them believe that the decision to get out of construction was politically motivated and not in the public interest.

I think we need to understand clearly what we are trying to accomplish. One of the difficulties we had in this organization is that our mission hasn't been fairly clearly articulated to the employees and they are having some difficulty understanding what is our new mission.

What is the shared vision by the employees of this organization? I challenge you to get on the elevator, punch any button, get off, and ask the first ten people you run into, "What is the vision of this organization? Where are we going?" And if you ask the Commissioner, "Where are we going?" I'd bet you a month's salary you don't get anything close to the same answer by the majority of those people.

Further analysis points to how the Commissioner's goal of becoming "the premier water management agency in the world" was considered by many middle managers to be too vague to be meaningful. A middle manager points out:

There is erosion of technical skills. People are not sure what they are supposed to be doing. There is confusion about responsibilities. But it is evolutionary. Initially, there were concerns and worries. Now, the take-the- initiative types like it. However, the spoon-fed ones are concerned and scared and lack a sense of security.

Fourth, an interesting observation is that some middle managers actually had a difficult time adjusting to the new decentralized organization with less hierarchy. It is commonly believed that employees do not like overly structured and hierarchical organizations because they stifle creativity and initiative while being very controlling. However, in BOR, some workers preferred the structure and felt uncomfortable without it. One executive described the phenomenon in a low point critical incident. According to this executive:

> The majority of people who are scientists and engineers like order and structure and the predictability of it.... And they find comfort in hierarchy.... But when you removed it, they felt vulnerable.

The executive described the event as an incident requiring strategy adjustment to avoid undesirable outcomes. The lesson in this downsizing incident is that organizational behavior can be unpredictable. As the executive stated, empowerment can be positive or negative for an individual and "there's no such thing as one size fits all when you're addressing organizations because they're very dynamic."

Finally, the job of the middle manager and first-line supervisor became more demanding. The middle manager now must contend with fewer budget and personnel resources, increased workloads, new workforce skill mixes, an increased span of control, and a new role as a team leader. On top of all this, the middle manager must be an agent for change. Two middle managers were anxious to address the issue of a more demanding job:

> Middle managers are working our butts off. We're working harder. I work thirteen to fourteen hours a day and six days a week. It's the same with others. It's a hard time for middle managers who are trying to loosen control, trust people, and empower people. We have less rope from the executives who are still holding us accountable for not making mistakes. The pressure and stress are tremendous. Some of it is the fault of middle managers for not changing. Some are fighting it tooth and nail and are experiencing lots of stress and feel like they are losing control. There is still a lot more work.... The middle managers are being forced to become coaches, resource providers, part of leadership, and not be controllers, watchers, and supervisors. Some are having difficulty with this. They are now mostly team facilitators getting teams resources and dealing with problems that prevent teams from doing their jobs. You're not the all-knowing manager any more. We're just trying to survive.

> There has been a change in the role of the manager. That person is now free of technical responsibilities. Managers have more responsibility to assist team leaders. The manager's role now is to coach, mentor, allocate resources, and do peer review.... The biggest change for middle managers is that their jobs used to be 80 percent technical and 20 percent management. Now it is 95 percent management and 5 percent technical. They now serve as coaches and mentors to work with the team leaders to get them resources.

Executives were aware of what middle managers were going through.

One executive reflected on how well middle managers were doing despite the tough times:

> I think in the cases of a lot of my middle managers, they struggle more. They have less of the big picture and more of what's happening directly in their own organizations. And they're acting very, very professionally. They're trying as best as they can try, but it's harder for them. They have to make the specific tasks happen.

Treatment of Middle Managers during Downsizing

The aspect pertaining to the treatment of middle managers during downsizing has two characteristics. The first is that the agency initially focused the majority of its attention during downsizing on middle managers and other employees who left the organization. The second is that eventually the agency turned its attention to the needs of middle managers and other personnel who remained with the organization.

In January 1994, the RSC established the Employee Service Center to assist employees through the reorganization process. The center provided multiple services such as answers to questions about the BOR restructuring, an automated government job application form, a list of government and private sector job opportunities, and job-hunting videos. Additionally, employees were authorized to use agency computers and official duty time to prepare job applications and were allowed time off to attend job interviews and job fairs. Another help service was the Employee Assistance Program, which provided professional counseling assistance to employees. And in May 1994, the Surplus Employee Placement Program was activated to help place employees in regional offices and the Administrative Service Center. All these programs operated to assist middle managers and rank-and-file workers in getting new jobs prior to a RIF. In fact, these extensive efforts in conjunction with the buyout incentives were successful in minimizing the number of RSC employees who suffered a RIF. Although eighty-eight people received RIF notices on 29 June 1994, only twenty-one actually were forced to leave without jobs.

After BOR implemented the many organizational changes that resulted in large numbers of personnel leaving, agency leaders began to focus on remaining employees. The executives recognized the need to prepare middle managers for their new roles. They know they must ensure that middle managers receive necessary management tools and retraining. Moreover, they know they must see to it that process reengineering, middle manager participation in decision making, and team management practices persist into the future. Evidence that the agency at first did not do as much as it needed to do is found in the following executive remarks:

> We probably have put more emphasis on the people who are leaving than on people who are staying. One of the things we're trying to do now is focus on those people who are remaining . . . and we're trying to deal with that by putting our emphasis right now on getting people to function most effectively in their new roles that they're going to have in the restructured, realigned organizations . . . to try to equip people to be successful.

Downsizing Effects on Middle Manager Behavior

Five characteristics were identified in this aspect of downsizing. First, morale and motivation were higher at the field area offices and lower at the RSC and regional offices. Generally, morale and motivation levels in BOR correlated with levels of authority and responsibility held by organizational echelons. Consequently, because area offices gained authority and responsibility due to decentralization and empowerment, their middle managers had higher morale and motivation. Conversely, the RSC and regional offices lost power and, thus, their middle managers had lower morale and motivation. Two executives used the term *losers* to explain how employees perceived themselves at the RSC and regional offices. According to an executive:

> Morale in the field has never been higher. . . . They're excited about it. They feel empowered. They feel important. . . . From a year ago and up until recently, morale in Denver had never been lower. Because we were the losers in this. That's how it was viewed. . . . Right now the regional offices are feeling awfully bad because they're giving up their authority to the field. And they're downsizing. And the morale in the regional offices is very low.

Second, commitment and loyalty among middle managers remained high to the institution. As already noted, the BOR workforce had a long record of accomplishments, traditionally had a strong sense of pride and self-respect, and had a high worldwide reputation. Through the changes, middle managers retained their support for the welfare of the agency and their desire for the agency to succeed in its new mission. Middle managers asserted, "Commitment and loyalty are still there," and "I have not detected any changes in commitment and loyalty." However, some middle managers at the RSC developed a lack of trust in and loyalty to the agency's top leaders, which took a while to wane. The issue of trust surfaced earlier in the discussion for the downsizing aspect of "Organizational Preparation for Downsizing." The primary source of the distrust appears to have been the way the Commissioner communicated to employees the need to change the agency. The following quote reflects this assertion:

> I think that there's a real disappointment on their part that they don't feel that they were treated with respect by the top leadership, the Commissioner. They feel that, you know, that what they did was bad. They don't feel their accomplishments were recognized for what they were, within the context of when they were done. . . . And then to be told that they're no good, that they're losers. . . . There was a real resentment for that.

Another executive lends support to the contention that the cause for much of the lack of faith in top management was the Commissioner:

> There is incredible loyalty to the institution, kind of a mixed bag on loyalty to management. The Commissioner has a very high following in the field, a lesser following in this office. There's a lot of folks in this office that don't feel very supportive or committed to him. People are feeling better about that all the time in here by the way. . . . Some people are unhappy with our leadership that we've provided.

However, it is difficult to separate all the possible reasons for middle managers' dissatisfaction and to ascertain conclusively the cause of the lack of trust and loyalty to management. With so much change occurring in the organization at the same time, it is plausible that any of a number of events could have contributed to lack of trust and loyalty by some middle managers. Still another executive provides support for this view:

> During this process, I don't think that employees had any trust of management. And yet when you asked them who management was, they couldn't tell you. We said, "Who's management? Do you trust me?" "Well, yeah, I trust you." "Do you trust your supervisor?" "Well, yeah." "Well, do you trust that person's supervisor?" "Well, yeah, I think so." And then you go, "Who's management?" "Well, somebody knows something they aren't telling us and they're keeping it a big secret." So trust was a real issue. It didn't seem to be focused at all. . . . I mean, their trust issues weren't in what was happening in total. It was what was happening that day to them.

Third, risk taking increased due to an emphasis on allowing and expecting middle managers to take risks in the new environment. Most of the increased risk taking occurred in the field among area managers. It coincided with greater levels of empowerment. The Commissioner encouraged risk taking and innovation and issued "forgiveness coupons," an innovation to stimulate risk taking, to be redeemed if managers made mistakes. However, there were a few individuals who reacted by withdrawing from taking risks. One executive described it this way:

> Some of our middle management has sort of locked in and tried to become invisible. . . . The other thing is that they sometimes take the approach of disappearing when their employees are empowered because I sense it's a defense mechanism. . . . Some of them distance themselves even in meetings. . . . Those are people who feel particularly vulnerable and threatened.

Fourth, the quality of work remained as high as in the past. It is too early to measure any improvements in quality of work that might come from the restructuring. There was a link between the high level of commitment middle managers had to the agency and the high quality of work produced on behalf of the agency. However, one detects a concern among middle managers about the possibility of diminished quality and productivity if a high operations tempo continues:

> Ninety-five percent of the employees have a job ethic to keep working. But it can only go so far and then it is directly related to falling quality of work and productivity.

> The biggest problem is that there are no reductions in program requirements, but they expect the same quality, timeliness, and support with less staff or no staff. We are at the break point and only getting out the crisis issues. Some things are not being dealt with. We can't continue at the same quality levels. People are doing their best just to get the job done. More is being spent on overtime. We are using flexible work schedules. Job pride carries them on.

Fifth, efficiency and productivity among middle managers decreased at certain times in the past year. During those times that employees experienced more change, they also felt more anxiety, which was manifested in less efficiency and productivity. For example, during the few days before RIF notices were delivered at the end of June 1994, "people probably did nothing." One executive commented that at times, BOR was "in a state of uncertainty and confusion" where "the destruction that comes from organizational change and mission change is very significant and it most showed itself in the area of morale and productivity, not quality of product."

Conditions for Resistance to Change and Downsizing by Middle Managers

Conditions for resistance to change and resistance to downsizing by middle managers are other areas of interest. There were middle managers who were reluctant to change from the "old" ways of doing business. Several executives explained that the organization used the phrase "business as usual" to describe functions and processes that were most comfortable to middle managers. The first type of resisters were those who wanted to do business as usual and who thought that the changes would be superficial. These resisters were told by executives, "You need to work on our priorities, not what you're comfortable with." A second group of resisters were those who did not recognize the reality of change and were unable to cope with it. These resisters were described with the following words: "unable, don't know how, or in some cases, don't have the capability to change." Also, some middle managers understood the need for change but resisted because they were "very uncomfortable with the process." The third instance of resistance came from middle managers at the RSC in Denver, which experienced the most change and downsizing. An executive relayed the frustration of middle managers when he said:

> People resisted to what we wanted to do at every turn. . . . And they believed in the rightness of their position, therefore they resisted. They questioned, they questioned, they questioned. They challenged, they challenged, they challenged.

A fourth source of resistance came from some of the most senior managers, who were referred to as the "old guard."

Executive Views of Downsizing

The interview data revealed four patterns of executive views of downsizing: general view of downsizing, view of downsizing with other change, view of downsizing difficulty, and view of workforce capabilities and outcomes after downsizing. For general view of downsizing, almost all the executives thought downsizing was "necessary" or "essential" and would be to the long-term benefit of the agency. A typical response to the question of how they viewed downsizing was: "We needed to do it because it's essential for our future survival." Furthermore, there existed a belief that "it should have been done sooner" and "at least several years ago."

Earlier, in the section on "Organizational Downsizing in Conjunction with Other Change," it was noted how downsizing helped change the mission, culture, and business orientation. Additionally, downsizing aided the agency in matching people with certain skills, position responsibilities, and position levels. An example of how this matching was accomplished was described by an executive who stated:

> I think that what we have done with the group managers and the technical specialists is we have placed people who have more human resources skills

into positions where that is needed. . . . So, I think that was one of the very positive things of the restructure that we were able to realign some people and to get them in better spots in the organization.

Regarding view of downsizing difficulty, a consensus was that downsizing is extremely challenging, difficult, and painful. Direct quotes from different respondents emphasized this characteristic:

> The hard part is making it work. And that's the thing that is very difficult. Implementation is hard.

> If we would have done it sooner, we wouldn't have to have done it so painfully. . . . It's painful, and if you're close to retirement, you probably don't want to take that kind of pain.

A critically important fourth pattern emerged regarding executive views of workforce capabilities and outcomes after downsizing. Most line and staff executives were concerned about whether human resource capabilities will be sufficient to accomplish the BOR mission. It is clearly evident that BOR implemented a comprehensive set of planned changes through a diversified set of strategies. Yet some uncertainty existed about the following seven areas: (1) fewer resources, (2) workload estimates, (3) imbalances between employees and workloads, (4) skill capabilities, (5) skill mixes, (6) workplace tools and retraining, and (7) maintaining the delegation of responsibility. Three different middle managers expressed opinions with a great amount of trepidation:

> Administratively, we made cuts before the work was known. The cuts were not workload related. The whole process is backward. We have the same work, volume, and quality with fewer people. It is difficult coping with the current workload. Decisions were not thought out due to outside constraints. We need to adjust the workload instead of adding work.

> We've had some significant shifts of people into newer jobs they are not skilled to handle. The middle managers worry. Absolutely. We hear about lack of capability from everybody. It is a major concern. Some people don't train very well. Even the good ones take time. We've had some of the wrong workers leave the agency, too, to some extent. On the information resource management side, we lost seven really top young people hired in the last five to seven years. They were innovative, creative, had skills and inquisitiveness. Two were RIFed and five left to the private sector or other agencies. It was also true on the engineering side.

> For workforce capability, we lost people. Top management has not adjusted demands, and we are told we must do the same work with fewer people. The director is reducing the number of employees and not programs. It will lead

to suffering of quality and it will push good people out the door. We have a lot of professional, dedicated, and technically oriented people who are being lost. If this nonsensible approach continues, we will damage the field and make this a second-rate agency.

Executives were well aware of the issues expressed by the middle managers. One executive shared their concerns:

I don't think that we're going to be able to deliver as good a quality of product and as efficiently as we did in the past because we don't have the personnel to do it. . . . I don't think there's been a great deal of sensitivity with respect to where people fit in. . . . The question you're asking me is how are we implementing ourselves and I'm telling you my view is we're not implementing ourselves very effectively.

That opinion was buttressed by another executive. Furthermore, he pointed out that executives are determined to ensure employees have what they need to get their jobs accomplished:

Now the jury is out on whether or not in the long run we are able to gain the level of efficiency that we need to gain. . . . We have people that were displaced from jobs that they sought out to jobs that they've been involuntarily placed into, jobs that they may feel not well-equipped to perform. . . . We're focusing our energies into reequipping our employees to do a different function.

Executive Management Practices during Downsizing

Several questions asked during the interviews with executives related directly to executive management practices during downsizing. To elicit varied responses, three questions were framed differently. They focused on "managing during downsizing," "new management challenges," and "new management styles, tactics, and strategies." See appendix C for the wording of the interview questions. The research strategy was to combine the answers to achieve a more complete picture of executive management practices during downsizing.

Table 4.10 lists nine management characteristics identified from data analysis. The characteristics are those management practices by executives that were used or are recommended for use during downsizing. The order is based upon a combination of the frequency with which the practice was mentioned and the number of executives who mentioned the practice. Additionally, the critical incidents discussed by the executives were reviewed for behavior that reflected the practices. Therefore, the critical incidents provided additional support for the presence and order of the practices. Each listed item was identified at least three times and by at least two different executives.

Executive Competencies for Downsizing

The executive interviews were designed to include two opportunities for executives to identify executive competencies needed for downsizing. Refer to appendix C for the interview protocol. First, the last section in Part I of the interviews asked executives, "What are the qualities, characteristics, and capabilities needed to perform those aspects of your position related to downsizing?" Second, one of the twenty questions in Part II asked, "What managerial competencies and skills do you believe are important for SES executives to exercise in managing during downsizing?"

Table 4.10 lists ten executive competencies identified from data analysis. The order is based upon a combination of the frequency with which the competency was mentioned and the number of executives who mentioned the competency. The table contains specific examples of behavior that illustrate the competencies. Additionally, the critical incidents discussed by the executives were reviewed for behavior that reflected the competencies. Therefore, the critical incidents provided additional support for the presence and order of the competencies. Each listed competency was identified at least three times and by at least two different executives. Therefore, although "resourcefulness," "background with functional or technical preparation," "team orientation," and "flexibility" were identified as competencies, none of them occurred frequently enough to be on the final list.

Summary of Major Findings

Table 4.11 shows the major findings of the BOR case study. The findings were reached after a systematic data analysis process of using multiple data sources, performing an iterative coding sequence, and identifying themes and patterns. The findings are written as results of the BOR case and can be considered lessons learned.

The discussion in the previous ten sections on downsizing aspects and characteristics support the findings in Table 4.11. However, one of the findings in the table receives more elaboration here: executive views of downsizing reveal that downsizing was difficult and the resultant human resource capabilities uncertain. Despite these generally pessimistic characteristics, the study identified an approach used to contend with these issues. The executives observed and had faith in the value of a team orientation

Table 4.11

Major Bureau of Reclamation Findings

Downsizing Aspect	Finding
1. Organizational preparation for downsizing	Mixed views of preparation.
2. Organizational strategies for downsizing	Extensively planned, diversified, and comprehensive strategies.
3. Organizational downsizing in conjunction with other change	Changing the mission and downsizing were necessary and overdue.
4. Middle manager reactions/concerns about downsizing	Insecure about personal and institutional futures and some concern about mission and vision.
5. Treatment of middle managers during downsizing	Remaining personnel need more assistance to move forward.
6. Downsizing effects on middle manager behavior	Positive at area offices, more negative elsewhere, and some lack of trust at the Reclamation Service Center.
7. Conditions for resistance to change and downsizing by middle managers	Personnel are struggling with the transition.
8. Executive views of downsizing	Belief that a team orientation, coupled with employee and lower organizational-level empowerment, leads to greater buy-in.
9. Executive management during downsizing	Management is uncertain of, but very interested in, determining success of changes.
10. Executive competencies for downsizing	Order of competencies is consistent.

coupled with employee empowerment and lower-organizational-level empowerment. They believe that this combination of strategies resulted in greater employee buy-in to the change and downsizing processes and raised performance levels. In fact, two executives were so enthusiastic about the approach that they identified it as high point critical incidents. One executive commented:

> What happened with that particular team, and I think this is probably pretty true whenever you have employee empowerment, is they came together. . . . It's been very, very important to us getting through this process because . . . they're committed to each other.

However, implementing teaming in the agency's organizations still had some growing pains. According to a middle manager:

> We have a lot of resistance for going to teaming from the specialist concept. . . . A team leader is a horrible job because you must do teams on top of regular

work. We rushed into teaming without adequate team training, a sensible approach, and organized planning. We have made a commitment to the team process, but without adequate support and less work, it is stifling to work as a team and decide as a team.

The ten executive competencies identified are listed in Table 4.10 in a consistent order. A trend is that those competencies most related to the areas where BOR had the most difficulties during downsizing are the ones appearing toward the top of the list. Although the executives may not have been consciously aware of it, they seemed to identify most frequently those competencies associated with areas of BOR downsizing difficulties. Perhaps an explanation can be found in the tendency for executives to focus on issues paramount to them; hence, they speak of areas of difficulty. This chapter reports these areas of difficulty. For instance, the section on "Middle Manager Reactions and Concerns about Downsizing" discusses a perceived lack of vision. "Vision" is the first competency listed for the executives. Second, uncertainties regarding workforce capabilities after downsizing were addressed in the section on "Executive Views of Downsizing." Correspondingly, the need to exercise "analytical" skills was identified by executives as the fourth competency on the list. A third example is trust, which was discussed in the "Organizational Preparation for Downsizing" section and in the "Downsizing Effects on Middle Manager Behavior" section. The executives, then, identified "honesty and trustworthiness" as a competency, ranked sixth.

Four primary techniques were used to confirm the findings. First, triangulation was achieved by relying on different data sources and data collection methods. Second, weighting the evidence was practiced by exercising judgment about the quality of data and selecting the most valid data. Third, negative evidence was searched for to find any disconfirmations. And fourth, feedback from informants was used to validate the findings of the study.

Conclusions for Executive Management of BOR Downsizing

The last analytic exercise in the data analysis for the BOR case study was the generation of a causal network. The within-case displays in Tables 4.10 and 4.11 are steps in an inductive approach to building the causal network (Miles and Huberman 1994). For the BOR case, the causal network for downsizing appears in Figures 4.1 and 4.2. The causal network displays the most important variables and the relationships among them. The purpose of the causal network is to diagram an integrated understanding of the case.

132

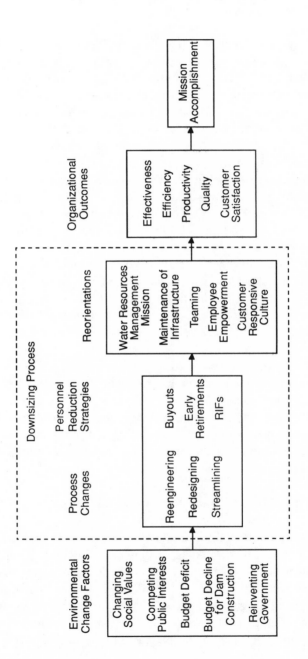

Figure 4.1 **Causal Network for Bureau of Reclamation Downsizing**

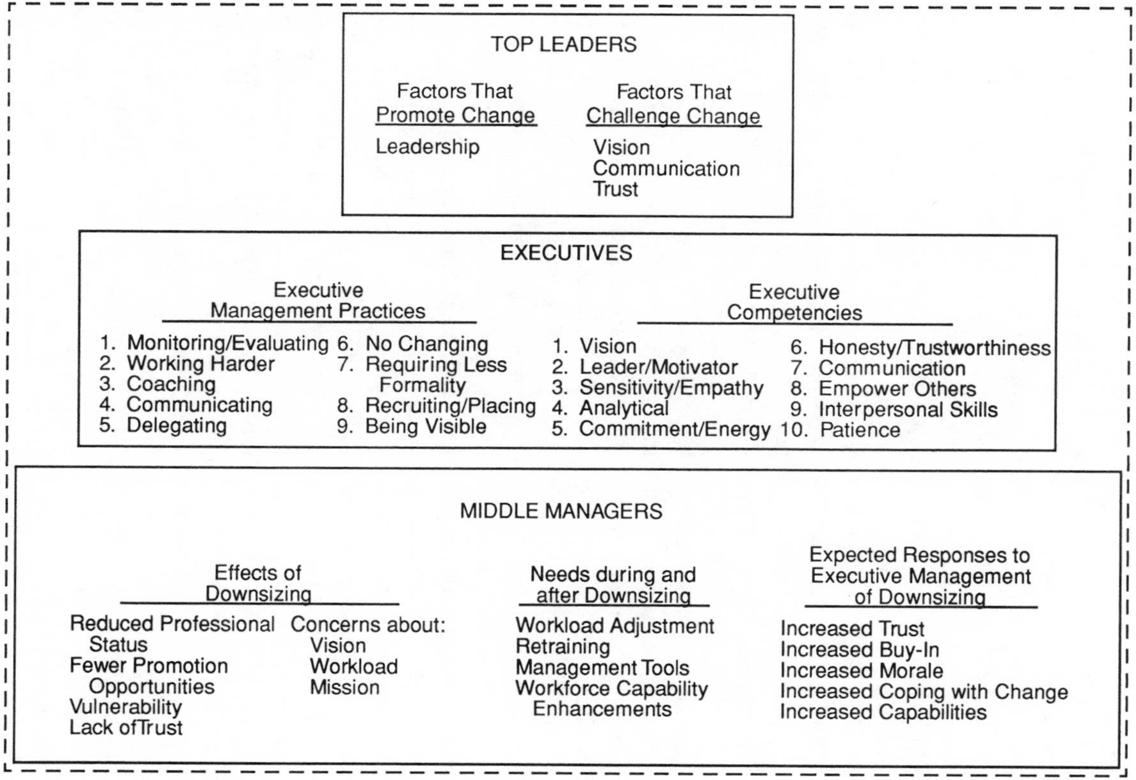

TOP LEADERS

Factors That Promote Change	Factors That Challenge Change
Leadership	Vision
	Communication
	Trust

EXECUTIVES

Executive Management Practices

1. Monitoring/Evaluating
2. Working Harder
3. Coaching
4. Communicating
5. Delegating
6. No Changing
7. Requiring Less Formality
8. Recruiting/Placing
9. Being Visible

Executive Competencies

1. Vision
2. Leader/Motivator
3. Sensitivity/Empathy
4. Analytical
5. Commitment/Energy
6. Honesty/Trustworthiness
7. Communication
8. Empower Others
9. Interpersonal Skills
10. Patience

MIDDLE MANAGERS

Effects of Downsizing

Reduced Professional Status
Fewer Promotion Opportunities
Vulnerability
Lack of Trust

Concerns about:
Vision
Workload
Mission

Needs during and after Downsizing

Workload Adjustment
Retraining
Management Tools
Workforce Capability Enhancements

Expected Responses to Executive Management of Downsizing

Increased Trust
Increased Buy-In
Increased Morale
Increased Coping with Change
Increased Capabilities

Figure 4.2 **Executive Management of Bureau of Reclamation Downsizing**

The causal network generated is the one that emerges from the data analysis. It subsequently will be synthesized in chapter 6 with the causal networks from the other two cases to generate a theoretical downsizing model and to suggest hypotheses related to executive management during downsizing. In general, the causal network shows details of executive management of the BOR downsizing process. The figures include a two- dimensional section indicated by the dashed lines. The two dimensions are the downsizing process diagrammed in Figure 4.1 and executive management of downsizing shown in Figure 4.2.

The far left side of Figure 4.1 identifies the following factors in the environment driving change for BOR: changing social values, competing public interests, the budget deficit, budget decline for dam construction, and the reinventing government initiative known as the National Performance Review. Changing social values refer to the general trend away from a priority on economic development and toward greater emphasis on environmental considerations. Competing public interests refer to the multiple constituencies making demands on scarce water resources. These two factors forced BOR to change its mission. The other three factors, budget deficit, budget decline, and the reinventing government initiative, drive BOR to downsize. Therefore, BOR is experiencing complexities associated with changing its mission at the same time that it downsizes. This combination of events creates an especially challenging and difficult scenario for the executives attempting to manage the downsizing process. Going from left to right, the two-dimensional, dashed line area represents the downsizing process and executive management of it. The downsizing consists of three phases: process changes, personnel reduction strategies, and reorientations. Although there is some overlap among the phases, they generally follow the pattern shown. The process changes are reengineering, redesigning, and streamlining, and each fundamentally modifies agency activities to achieve organizational improvements. More particularly, reengineering makes radical change or significant alteration of work processes; redesigning reduces or eliminates some functions, hierarchical levels, and organizational units considered to be duplicative or unnecessary; and streamlining minimizes non-value-added steps while maximizing value-added steps in agency processes and systems. However, BOR is jointly employing personnel reduction strategies and implementing process changes throughout the agency. The personnel reduction strategies include reliance on buyouts, early retirements, and RIFs. The first two phases help to achieve organizational reorientations in the third phase. For BOR, primary reorientations are toward the new water resources management mission, maintenance of infrastructure, greater use of teams, greater employee empowerment, and a stronger customer-responsive culture.

The area within the dashed lines also represents executive management of the downsizing process explained above. Figure 4.2 illustrates this dimension with a pyramid. At the top of the pyramid are BOR's top leaders, the Commissioner and a few other political appointees who perform a critical preliminary and concurrent role for executive management of downsizing. Based upon analysis of the data, BOR top leaders contend with three factors that challenge change and make executive management of downsizing difficult. Early in the downsizing process, BOR top leaders did not provide a clear vision, communicate the vision so that it was understood and accepted by all employees, and engender sufficient trust by employees in actions taken by top leaders.[5] However, the top leaders did provide firm leadership direction for downsizing by making it clear that the agency would definitely reorient itself and do so with staff reductions. This leadership strength helped to promote necessary change. The middle portion of the pyramid lists those executive management practices and executive competencies that are needed by BOR for its downsizing process. The bottom part of the pyramid indicates factors in three categories associated with middle managers. First, the effects of downsizing on middle managers are reduced professional status, fewer promotion opportunities, vulnerability, lack of trust, and concerns about vision clarification, workload, and mission accomplishment. Second, middle managers need workload adjustment, retraining, management tools, and other workforce capability enhancements. Third, middle manager responses to better executive management of downsizing are expected to be increased trust; increased buy-in whereby middle managers trust in, accept, and cooperate with the downsizing process; increased morale; increased coping with change; and increased capabilities.

Returning to Figure 4.1, the two-dimensional, downsizing process/executive management dashed line area leads to desired and expected organizational outcomes. Those outcomes are increased effectiveness, efficiency, productivity, quality, and customer satisfaction. Ultimately, mission accomplishment is expected.

BOR is experiencing difficulty with downsizing primarily because it is downsizing while simultaneously adjusting to a new mission. The BOR case highlights that downsizing is indeed a challenging experience, and the resultant human resource capabilities are uncertain. Nevertheless, the agency has made noteworthy progress and its Innovations in American Government Award reflects its success. The men and women of BOR at the executive and middle manager levels have managed to steer the agency through the personnel reduction stage of downsizing. Now, these dedicated public managers are focusing on the agency's important water resources management mission.

Notes

1. The name "Reclamation" is often used to refer to the Bureau of Reclamation. "BOR" is used in this book for convenience to be consistent with "DLA" for the Defense Logistics Agency and "FDA" for the Food and Drug Administration.

2. For a historiography and guide to literature on BOR, see Lee (1980).

3. In recent years, several books have been published about reclamation events and controversies. These books have a range of views about BOR's role. See Worster (1985), Reisner (1986), and Wilkinson (1992).

4. The *Bureau of Reclamation Strategic Plan: 1997–2002* (Bureau of Reclamation 1997) explains the challenges and opportunities facing the agency and its plans to address them. The *Strategic Plan* was submitted prior to the end of fiscal year 1997 in compliance with the Government Performance and Results Act. The five-year plan includes the agency's mission statement, long-term strategic goals, and strategies for achieving the goals.

5. According to Radin (1995, 114) in her study of NPR "success stories," Department of Interior staff emphasized that better communication and training were required to minimize the effects of the tremendous cynicism within the department.

5

The Food and Drug Administration: Downsizing and Upsizing

The Food and Drug Administration is a regulatory agency within the Department of Health and Human Services (HHS). The Department of Health, Education, and Welfare (HEW) was established in 1953 to unify administration of federal health, education, and Social Security programs. In 1979, the education function was transferred to a new Department of Education and HEW was redesignated HHS. FDA is organizationally located within the Public Health Service, which is one of the six primary operating organizations of HHS. Seven other agencies, including the Centers for Disease Control and Prevention and the National Institutes of Health, along with FDA, constitute the Public Health Service. FDA is operating in fiscal year 1997 with a budget of approximately $996 million and 9,358 employees.

FDA is a consumer protection agency that regulates a wide variety of products. The committee report that accompanied the passage of the Federal Food, Drug, and Cosmetic Act of 1938 states that FDA's responsibility is "to protect public health and promote honesty and fair dealing in the market place."[1] The mission of FDA is to enforce laws to ensure public health is protected against impure and unsafe foods, drugs, and cosmetics; unsafe medical devices; and unsafe radiation-emitting products, as well as to ensure that these products are truthfully and informatively labeled.[2] The headquarters for FDA is scattered throughout the metropolitan Washington, D.C., area at forty locations with most of its offices located in Rockville, Maryland. About half the agency's personnel are located in FDA's six centers. Approximately one-third of FDA personnel are employed in the field, which consists of 21 district offices and 130 inspection posts throughout six regions of the United States. Table 5.1 identifies the current structure and offices within FDA.

Table 5.1

Food and Drug Administration Organization

Headquarters
Located in Washington, D.C., metropolitan area:
    Office of the Commissioner (OC)
    Office of External Affairs
    Office of Management and Systems
    Office of Policy
Centers (Headquarters Components)
Located in Washington, D.C., metropolitan area except for one center:
    Office of Operations
    Office of Regulatory Affairs (ORA)
    Center for Biologics Evaluation and Research (CBER)
    Center for Drug Evaluation and Research (CDER)
    Center for Devices and Radiological Health (CDRH)
    Center for Food Safety and Applied Nutrition (CFSAN)
    Center for Veterinary Medicine (CVM)
    National Center for Toxicological Research (NCTR), Jefferson, Arkansas
Regions and District Offices
Northeast Region
    District Office, Boston, Massachusetts
    District Office, Brooklyn, New York
    District Office, Buffalo, New York
Mid-Atlantic Region
    District Office, Baltimore, Maryland
    District Office, Cincinnati, Ohio
    District Office, Newark, New Jersey
    District Office, Philadelphia, Pennsylvania
Southeast Region
    District Office, Atlanta, Georgia
    District Office, Nashville, Tennessee
    District Office, New Orleans, Louisiana
    District Office, Orlando, Florida
    District Office, San Juan, Puerto Rico
Midwest Region
    District Office, Chicago, Illinois
    District Office, Detroit, Michigan
    District Office, Minneapolis, Minnesota
Southwest Region
    District Office, Dallas, Texas
    District Office, Denver, Colorado
    District Office, Kansas City, Kansas
Pacific Region
    District Office, Los Angeles, California
    District Office, San Francisco, California
    District Office, Seattle, Washington
Inspection Posts
130 located throughout the United States

Source: FDA Almanac: Fiscal Year 1996, DHHS Publication (FDA) 96–1254 (Rockville, MD: Food and Drug Administration, Office of Public Affairs, July 1996).

Agency Background

In 1906, the Food and Drugs Act was passed to prohibit interstate commerce in misbranded and adulterated foods, drinks, and drugs. From 1906 until 1927, the Bureau of Chemistry of the U.S. Department of Agriculture (USDA) enforced the law. Then in 1927, the Food, Drug, and Insecticide Administration of USDA was created and acquired enforcement authority. A few years later in 1931, it was renamed the Food and Drug Administration. Finally, in 1940, FDA was transferred from USDA to the Federal Security Agency, which became HEW in 1953.[3] In 1968, FDA became a part of the Public Health Service in HEW when a reorganization of federal health programs took place.

Congress established the Public Health Service in 1798. Since that time, Congress passed much legislation to broaden its activities for accomplishing its mission of protecting and advancing the physical and mental health of U.S. citizens. The Public Health Service Act of 1944 revised existing legislation related to the Public Health Service. During the five decades since then, expanded responsibilities and organizational changes occurred. Certainly, integration of FDA into the Public Health Service was one of the most important changes.

FDA has the responsibility and authority to enforce numerous laws related to protecting the public's health. However, most of FDA's duties involve enforcing three major statutes (Food and Drug Administration 1987, 9–11; Food and Drug Administration 1989). First, the Federal Food, Drug, and Cosmetic Act of 1938 is enforced by FDA. Congress has amended the law many times since 1938. About 90 percent of FDA's workload is directed at enforcing this act. The statute and its amendments are aimed at regulating foods, human and animal drugs, medicated animal feeds, medical devices, and cosmetics. Additionally, the act permits FDA to inspect imported products, grant premarket approvals, establish quality standards, and conduct factory inspections. Moreover, the law allows warning letters, recalls, seizures, injunctions, and criminal prosecutions for violations. The second statute is the Public Health Service Act of 1944. FDA is responsible for enforcing sections of this act that relate to biological products such as vaccines, serums, and blood and control of communicable diseases. The third statute, the Fair Packaging and Labeling Act of 1966, requires FDA to enforce honest and informative labeling of foods, drugs, medical devices, and cosmetic products.

Today FDA is considered by many to be the principal consumer protection agency. In fiscal year 1996, FDA provided consumer protection from over $1 trillion worth of products at a cost of less than $4 per person (Food and Drug Administration 1996, 14). Looked at another way, FDA is responsible for products that account for 25 cents out of every dollar spent by the nation's consumers. FDA's 1,100 investigators and inspectors oversee almost 95,000 regulated businesses, visit more than 15,000 facilities a year, and collect about 80,000 domestic and imported product samples for examination (Food and Drug Administration 1995a).

Recent Organizational Changes

The government increased the scope of FDA's regulatory function in recent years in concert with expansion of the number of products and the growth and complexity of scientific means of analyzing those products. During a period when many federal agencies are experiencing budget reductions, the FDA budget is growing. The agency requires more funds to keep up with the pace of regulation and oversight of foods, drugs, cosmetics, and medical devices. The FDA budget increased every year during the 1990s. For example, FDA budgets for fiscal years 1993, 1994, 1995, and 1996 were $809 million, $921 million, $948 million, and $981 million, respectively (Food and Drug Administration 1994a, 11; Food and Drug Administration 1995b, 17; Food and Drug Administration 1996, 15). Concomitantly, during each year since 1993, the agency has received increasingly higher levels of user fees from industry. The trend has been to supplement federal funding with user fees to provide a greater budget to perform the regulatory mission. Two of the agency's largest user fee programs are described next.

Prescription Drug User Fee Act Program

Congress passed the Prescription Drug User Fee Act of 1992 (PDUFA) (Public Law 102-571) in October 1992. The law permits FDA to collect fees from industry during fiscal years 1993 to 1997 to augment FDA resources devoted to reviewing new human drug and biological product license applications. The purpose of the act is to expedite the drug review and approval process within specified time periods (U.S. General Accounting Office 1994a). The addition of more than six hundred personnel in the Center for Drug Evaluation and Research (CDER) and in the Center for Biologics Evaluation and Research (CBER) for the program has resulted in an expedited process to make safe new drugs available more quickly. The program is so successful that decisions on breakthrough drugs are made in six months or less and on all other drugs in twelve months or less (Friedman 1997). FDA has consistently exceeded its annual performance goals in almost every category. According to the legislation, for fiscal years 1993

Table 5.2

Food and Drug Administration Downsizing Trends
Fiscal Years 1993 to 1996

End of Fiscal Year	Total Employees
1993	9,378
1994	9,691
1995	9,570
1996	9,397

Source: Food and Drug Administration, Office of Human Resource Management Services, Classification Services Staff.

through 1997, FDA's PDUFA program was expected to receive $36 million, $54 million, $75 million, $78 million, and $84 million, respectively. The original PDUFA program expired 30 September 1997, and FDA received reauthorization from Congress to extend the program for another five years through fiscal year 2002.

Mammography Quality Standards Act Program

The Mammography Quality Standards Act of 1992 (MQSA) (Public Law 102-539) established new mammography standards and mandated inspections of mammography facilities. The Center for Devices and Radiological Health (CDRH) inspects 10,000 facilities annually. User fees help implement the requirements and pay for additional personnel. For fiscal year 1997, the MQSA program received approximately $13 million in user fees, which funded approximately thirty-five employees.

Downsizing Activities

This section presents an overview of FDA's downsizing activities and provides the background necessary for understanding the results and analysis later in the chapter. The previous section discusses how FDA relies on user fees to accomplish its mission. These user fee programs coupled with downsizing requirements force the agency to face the dilemma of increasing and decreasing personnel at the same time. For FDA, downsizing requirements are contradictory and confusing to user fee program requirements. On the one hand, FDA must comply with NPR's mandate to reduce its employment levels like all other federal agencies. On the other hand, user fee legislation requires additional employees to expedite work processes. Be-

---

Table 5.3

Food and Drug Administration Tools for Downsizing

1. Normal attrition
2. Hiring freezes
3. Voluntary early retirements (early outs) without buyouts (separation incentive payments)
4. Targeted reductions and eliminations
   a. Managerial positions
   b. Deputy positions
5. Reinventing Administrative Management Program

---

cause of these opposing actions, FDA's total employment has remained relatively stable during the past five years. Table 5.2 shows the employment trends for FDA in recent years. Total employment was 9,378 employees at the end of fiscal year 1993, increased to 9,691 at the end of fiscal year 1994, dropped slightly to 9,570 at the end of fiscal year 1995, reached 9,397 at the end of fiscal year 1996, and stands at 9,358 midway through fiscal year 1997. Total employment is expected to level off to 9,338 at the end of fiscal year 1997 and remain at that level through the year 2000.

Because FDA needed to add employees while it was downsizing, it did not have a robust downsizing program. The agency relied on normal attrition, targeted reductions at some management positions, and did not offer buyouts. Table 5.3 summarizes the tools used by FDA in its modest downsizing effort.

User fee programs allow the number of FTE employees to increase. Most of the growth occurred in CDER, CBER, and CDRH. OMB authorized FDA to grow by more than six hundred positions in fiscal year 1994 for programs in these centers. Approximately one-third of the additional positions are at the senior level (GS-14, GS-15, and SES) due to the need for physicians and expert scientists.[4] Table 5.4 shows employment statistics for fiscal years 1993 through 1996. The table includes figures for the number of GS-13, GS-14, GS-15, and SES employees as well as numbers for employees in special categories. The data are broken out according to the major organizations within FDA. Personnel located in field regional offices, district offices, and inspection posts are employees of the Office of Regulatory Affairs (ORA).

With the exception of the SES category, every category of high-grade employees shown in Table 5.4 increased from fiscal year 1993 to fiscal year 1996. The number of SES officials declined by one. Overall, the number of high-grade employees increased from 4,125 in 1993, which was 43.9 percent of the FDA total, to 4,706 in 1996, which was 50.1 percent of the FDA total. The total number of GS-14, GS-15, and SES personnel climbed from 1,425 in 1993

(15.2 percent) to 1,587 in 1996 (16.9 percent) of the agency's total employees. Obviously, the number of employees in the top grades is extremely high.

Although FDA was authorized to increase personnel, presidential Executive Order 12839 and the presidential memorandum to downsize the federal government applied to FDA also. Of course, downsizing is a difficult task for all agencies to implement. In the case of FDA, though, downsizing is extremely troublesome because of the agency's unique circumstances. FDA and other organizations of the Public Health Service have a higher than normal senior-level grade structure compared to other federal agencies. FDA employs large numbers of professional staff including physicians, scientists, researchers, chemists, epidemiologists, and others who command salaries at senior-level grades because of their expertise. Furthermore, special pay and compensation authorities are in operation to attract and retain these specialized personnel. Because NPR principles focus on cost reduction and downsizing emphasizes cutting management positions, senior-level grades are primary targets for reinventing government. Clearly, across-the-board federal government downsizing has the potential to result in adverse consequences for FDA since the agency requires so many senior positions. Therefore, it was wise for OMB to grant the Public Health Service an exemption from reductions for some senior-level categories.

FDA attempted to achieve NPR goals in all of its organizations. For downsizing, the agency used normal attrition as the primary method. Additionally, it did not offer any VSIP buyouts in any fiscal year. Furthermore, the agency received VERA from OPM to offer early retirements without buyouts during a short window period near the end of fiscal year 1994. Where losses did occur, FDA tried to reduce organizational layering and duplication, administrative support staff, and the ratio of managers and supervisors to employees. No involuntary RIFs were used at any time. For streamlining, FDA initiated more than thirty regulatory reinvention projects since March 1995 to reduce regulatory burdens and streamline the regulatory process.

In summary, FDA was required to downsize and began downsizing implementation actions in its organizations. However, downsizing was conducted on a restrained basis. Even though three centers added personnel and FDA grew overall, the agency still went through downsizing experiences. Therefore, FDA was a suitable agency to be included in this study of downsizing. Its unique circumstances make it an interesting case study.

Downsizing Interviews

The investigation of the downsizing processes within FDA was conducted by interviewing eight executives who were members of the SES. Refer to

Table 5.4

Food and Drug Administration Employment Statistics
Employees by Grade for Selected High Grades

Center	GS-13	GS-14	GS-15	Corps	ST/ SBRS	AD	SES	Total Employ- ees All Grades	% of FDA Total
End of Fiscal Year 1993									
OC	216	133	59	33	0	0	17	1,119	11.9
ORA	597	159	52	82	0	0	11	3,514	37.5
CDER	368	222	113	116	0	80	21	1,467	15.6
CBER	125	62	37	61	0	101	7	779	8.3
CDRH	284	136	68	127	1	5	6	1,008	10.7
CFSAN	239	128	69	45	1	39	8	923	9.8
CVM	91	52	18	11	0	13	6	282	3.0
NCTR	47	28	10	4	1	13	3	286	3.0
Totals	1,967	920	426	479	3	251	79	9,378	100.0
End of Fiscal Year 1994									
OC	243	126	58	29	0	1	17	1,101	11.4
ORA	632	147	52	82	0	0	9	3,606	37.2
CDER	418	220	121	131	0	102	23	1,563	16.1
CBER	150	67	42	63	0	105	6	821	8.5
CDRH	339	135	68	134	1	7	6	1,120	11.5
CFSAN	265	127	72	45	1	30	7	936	9.7
CVM	100	50	19	11	0	14	5	284	2.9
NCTR	49	26	11	4	1	15	4	260	2.7
Totals	2,196	898	443	499	3	274	77	9,691	100.0
End of Fiscal Year 1995									
OC	278	139	76	27	0	3	19	1,177	12.3
ORA	637	134	47	87	0	0	12	3,360	35.1
CDER	468	237	128	132	0	106	21	1,645	17.2
CBER	163	81	38	74	0	106	6	868	9.1
CDRH	374	137	75	130	2	10	6	1,137	11.9
CFSAN	277	121	65	41	1	20	10	871	9.1
CVM	106	45	19	12	0	2	5	263	2.7
NCTR	46	27	12	3	1	12	4	249	2.6
Totals	2,349	921	460	508	4	259	83	9,570	100.0
End of Fiscal Year 1996									
OC	233	146	85	31	0	4	25	1,072	11.4
ORA	673	132	45	90	0	0	10	3,306	35.2
CDER	470	266	147	140	2	96	16	1,664	17.7
CBER	178	97	45	78	4	105	4	886	9.4

(Table 5.4 continued)

Center	GS-13	GS-14	GS-15	Corps	ST/ SBRS	AD	SES	Total Employ- ees All Grades	% of FDA Total
CDRH	365	166	72	132	5	11	6	1,126	12.0
CFSAN	253	138	62	40	3	31	9	846	9.0
CVM	103	46	19	12	0	1	5	256	2.7
NCTR	37	31	12	3	6	13	3	241	2.6
Totals	2,312	1,022	487	526	20	261	78	9,397	100.0

Source: Food and Drug Administration, Office of Human Resource Management Services, Classification Services Staff.

Note: Corps: Commissioned Corps
ST/SBRS: Scientific and Technical/Senior Biomedical Research Service
AD: Administratively Determined (Staff Fellows and Visiting Scientists)
OC: Office of the Commissioner
ORA: Office of Regulatory Affairs
CDER: Center for Drug Evaluation and Research
CBER: Center for Biologics Evaluation and Research
CDRH: Center for Devices and Radiological Health
CFSAN: Center for Food Safety and Applied Nutrition
CVM: Center for Veterinary Medicine
NCTR: National Center for Toxicological Research

appendix C for the executive interview protocol. Detailed accounts of downsizing conditions were provided through extensive description and explanation. To maintain confidentiality of the respondents, their names are not identified. Two of the eight interviewees were assigned to higher head-quarters organizations and six worked in centers. Executives were selected for interviews from two centers that were simultaneously downsizing and growing (CDER and CBER) and from the Center for Food Safety and Applied Nutrition (CFSAN), which was downsizing only. In addition, exec-utives from the Office of the Commissioner and ORA were interviewed. Five have more than five years in the SES, and six have 160 or fewer employees. A total of 653 minutes was spent in interviews with a mean interview time of one hour and 22 minutes. Table 2.9 contains demographic and employment data for the executives interviewed. Also, appendix G contains information about the nature of the positions held by the execu-tives and some statistics on their interviews.

An important part of the interviews was the identification of critical incidents. Table 5.5 summarizes the critical incidents identified by the re-spondents. This part of the interviews obtained details about incidents or situations related to downsizing in which the respondents were involved. See appendix D for an overview of the critical incident and behavior inter-

Table 5.5

Food and Drug Administration Critical Incidents

Interview			Critical Incident
FDA 1	1.	High	Positioned the organization for downsizing by proactively merging FDA and state training groups.
	2.	Low	Made mistakes in the process of designing and procuring an automated nationwide management information system.
	3.	High	Positioned the organization for downsizing by increasing automation.
FDA 2	1.	High	Guided the effort to combine the on-site management review program and internal controls program that later became a Reinventing Administrative Management Program model.
	2.	Low	Experienced difficulty in getting superiors to accept that certain activities should be eliminated in the downsizing environment.
	3.	High	Helped shift attitudes toward positive thinking about streamlining, resource savings, and downsizing by promoting Reinventing Administrative Management Program.
FDA 3	1.	High	Initiated an innovative program aimed at preventing food problems versus inspecting for problems.
	2.	High	Initiated innovative programs to leverage fewer resources by forming partnerships with organizations, states, and industry.
	3.	Low	Did not successfully persuade another federal agency to form a partnership.
FDA 4	1.	High	Maintained equity among center divisions while balancing user fee growth and downsizing personnel actions.
	2.	Low	Managed and coped with the dual requirements to hire and reduce senior-level positions.
FDA 5	1.	High	Implemented the new food labeling program and now enforcing it without additional resources.
FDA 6	1.	High	Completed pesticide monitoring databases and a pesticide analytical manual for outsiders in order to reduce work of limited personnel.
	2.	Low	Faced with reductions in research, reviews, monitoring, and regulation activities due to hiring freeze and limitations on promotions to GS-14.
	3.	High	Successfully delivered internally produced materials for toxicology test despite reduced resources.
FDA 7	1.	High	Proposed a comprehensive plan for FDA centralization and decentralization of administrative activities.
	2.	Low	Faced increased workloads with reduced positions.
FDA 8	1.	High	Suggested creative approaches to solve dilemma of hiring and reducing senior-level positions.
	2.	Low	Reduced administrative staff through random attrition without reducing administrative responsibilities.
Total			High Point Incidents—12
			Low Point Incidents—7

view steps and techniques. Each interviewee was requested to discuss two "high point" incidents that resulted in significant accomplishments and one "low point" incident that prevented an accomplishment. The purpose of this part of the interviews was to obtain data on how the executives behaved in actual incidents involving downsizing. Some executives chose to address fewer than the requested three critical incidents. Overall, FDA executives discussed twelve high and seven low incidents that revealed downsizing conditions.

Extensive within-case analysis was performed with interview data for the researcher to become intimately familiar with the FDA case. The analysis consisted of reviewing and summarizing the data, coding the data in a series of iterative steps, and then identifying themes and patterns. Appendix I explains the coding scheme, which was central to the analysis process. A thorough examination of the coded data results in the identification of specific, well-grounded themes and patterns. Table 5.6 is a thematic conceptual matrix for FDA downsizing conditions that contains ten downsizing aspects and corresponding characteristics representing the key themes and patterns that emerged for FDA. Furthermore, for each downsizing aspect, the characteristics are listed in decreasing order of support. In other words, characteristics are listed according to the strength of corroboration obtained from multiple and varying data sources and methods. Each set of downsizing aspects and characteristics is discussed in detail with supporting evidence in the next section. Quotes from executives are included as support for each of the downsizing aspects.

Downsizing Conditions

Organizational Preparation for Downsizing

FDA was not very well prepared for downsizing. In general, FDA did not believe that downsizing on a large scale would be required of the agency. The widespread belief in FDA was that even if the agency must downsize, it would not have to downsize as much as other federal agencies. The primary reason for this thinking was the inconsistency between the simultaneous requirements to add more personnel for user fee programs and reduce personnel in compliance with NPR initiatives. This contradictory condition caused confusion and disincentives to prepare seriously for downsizing. More will be discussed in later sections about how these circumstances affected other downsizing aspects.

Seven of eight executives interviewed held the view that the agency was not prepared for downsizing or was in a state of denial regarding downsiz-

Table 5.6

Food and Drug Administration Downsizing Conditions

Downsizing Aspect	Characteristics
1. Organizational preparation for downsizing	a. In a state of denial that the agency will actually downsize b. Very little planning for downsizing
2. Organizational strategies for downsizing	a. Absence of a genuine agency-wide downsizing program due to simultaneous requirements to grow and downsize b. Reinventing Administrative Management Program (RAMP) c. Normal attrition d. Hiring freeze e. No buyouts f. No reductions-in-force g. Early retirements h. Some downsizing measures at lower levels
3. Organizational downsizing in conjunction with other change	a. Downsizing precedes reinvention and streamlining b. Downsizing forces innovative ways to become more efficient c. Downsizing is not used as an excuse for other changes
4. Middle manager reactions/concerns about downsizing	a. Disbelief that downsizing is serious or credible for FDA b. Apprehension about accomplishing the mission of protecting the public health c. Feelings of anxiety about job functions and workloads d. Concern about reduced opportunities for career advancement, promotions, and professional standing
5. Treatment of middle managers during downsizing	a. No formal programs to assist departing or remaining employees in transition b. Some decentralized efforts to help remaining employees cope with changes c. Actions to minimize perception of organizations as "haves" and "have nots"

(Table 5.6 continued)

Downsizing Aspect	Characteristics
6. Downsizing effects on middle manager behavior	a. Commitment, loyalty, and quality of work remain high b. Generally, morale and motivation are negative c. Risk taking and productivity vary within the agency d. Managers have limits at which behavior becomes negative
7. Conditions for resistance to change and downsizing by middle managers	a. When implementation processes are viewed as flawed b. When unable to recognize the reality of change and downsizing c. When reorganizing to achieve greater efficiency
8. Executive views of downsizing	a. "What does the nation want FDA to do?" should be answered first b. Reduction in mission activities and workloads should precede any downsizing c. Current process for implementing downsizing in FDA is disturbing and difficult d. Downsizing without workload changes will result in negative outcomes
9. Executive management practices during downsizing	a. More coaching, mentoring, encouraging, and lifting morale b. More communication c. More effort to accomplish more difficult work d. More monitoring and evaluating work and performance e. More attention to internal recruitment and placement of personnel f. More delegation of authority and participatory style g. Less formality and hierarchy h. No change from past in terms of specific types of actions
10. Executive competencies for downsizing	(See competencies and characteristics below)

a. Analytical
Determines and adapts to resource shortfalls.
Analyzes requirements versus resources mix and creatively determines new ways to operate more efficiently.
Makes difficult choices among competing priorities.

(Table 5.6 continued)

Downsizing Aspect	Characteristics

b. Commitment, energy, and inner strength
Maintains composure in difficult times.
Faces adversity, finds ways to overcome it, and moves toward goal accomplishment.
Utilizes coping mechanisms to deal with frustrations.
c. Leader and motivator through coaching, mentoring, and lifting morale
Encourages more and directs less.
Keeps employees focused on objectives and goals.
Finds ways to reward and express satisfaction with employee performance.
Gains the confidence of the total organization.
d. Background with functional or technical preparation
Has quality knowledge and expertise in functional area.
Understands the agency's operations at both the higher headquarters and center levels.
Is "bottom line" oriented with experience in realignments and personnel allocations and a proclivity for data management.
e. Interpersonal skills
Builds and mends relationships.
Interacts effectively with dissatisfied employees during difficult times.
Creates networks to enhance relationships.
f. Communication
Increases communication quality up and down the management chain.
Articulates information to demonstrate win-win situations.
Conducts ongoing communications to dissipate unnecessary concerns and suspicions.
g. Sensitivity and empathy for people
Puts self in position of employees and realizes how downsizing is affecting them daily.
Acts creatively to satisfy employees' needs.
Helps remaining employees adjust to changes.
h. Team orientation
Focuses on group efforts, not on individual accomplishments.
Builds teams by convincing managers to cooperate.
i. Flexibility
Operates effectively in diverse situations.
Responds well to diverse needs and opinions.
j. Resourcefulness
Recognizes opportunities and seizes them.
Gets the job done in spite of rules and regulations.

---

ing. One representative statement came from an executive who said, "I don't think we're well prepared at all . . . and unfortunately, we usually wind up in the reactive instead of the proactive mode." In addition, a strong sense of denial exists regarding whether the agency really is subject to downsizing or whether it actually is downsizing. One executive was very succinct on this point:

> I think all of those who are espousing the "I'll wait it out and this too shall pass" attitude are basically exercising a denial.

Another made it clear that the downsizing effort is minimal:

> I still believe it's because we haven't come to grips with the fact there is really downsizing taking place. . . . To me, downsizing means that you approach it in some sort of organized fashion. . . . We're kind of just nibbling at the edges all the way around. You know, losing a few here, losing a few there, not being able to replace, but there's no orchestrated downsizing that's going on.

Additionally, very little planning occurred in case the agency was forced to increase the scope of its downsizing. Where the planning did occur, it tended to be in the centers that were not affected by user fee growth. At that level and below, managers were beginning to search and plan for ways to adapt to having fewer people.

Organizational Strategies for Downsizing

There was no genuine agency-wide strategic program that provided an aggressive agency approach to downsizing. However, the Reinventing Administrative Management Program (RAMP) did exist to implement the NPR program. The purpose of RAMP was to improve efficiency of administrative and management systems through process improvements, management initiatives, and automation throughout FDA. The primary elements of RAMP were for FDA organizations to reach the goals of reducing its number of administrative staff personnel and decreasing their supervisory ratios over the next five years. However, whereas the NPR calls for a federal workforce downsizing of 12 percent, RAMP streamlining plans estimated an FDA staff reduction of only 5.5 percent. A 26 May 1994 Streamlining Plan summary narrative stated, "We believe this is the most severe reduction in staffing that we can realistically achieve over the next four years, without doing serious damage to our ability to protect the public health."

The main strategies for achieving personnel reductions were normal attrition coupled with a hiring freeze. The problem with normal attrition was that it occurred relatively slowly and randomly throughout the agency and "penalized offices unfairly." Therefore, the hiring freeze operated with flexibility, such as allowing one employee to be hired for every three that left, in order to ensure proper skills balancing. However, CDER, CBER, and CDRH were exempt from the hiring freeze in order to increase their personnel.

Furthermore, the agency did not offer any buyouts because "it doesn't make any sense in an agency that's still hiring to be paying people to leave." Also, FDA did not conduct any RIFs. But, near the end of fiscal year 1994, it announced a voluntary early retirement option. To qualify, employees had to be 50 years old with at least twenty years of service or be any age with at least twenty-five years of service. The application window started on 4 August 1994 and required takers to separate by 30 September 1994. A total of seventy-eight employees, thirty-eight from headquarters and forty from the field, accepted the early out opportunity (Food and Drug Administration 1994b, 1, 5).

Within the centers and in field district offices, some progress was made in achieving other elements of the NPR. For example, whenever possible, organizations hired below the senior-level grades and delayed any promotions to GS-14. If a branch or division chief retired, then branches or divisions were realigned to reduce managerial positions, layers, and supervisory ratios. In some offices, all deputy positions were eliminated. One executive described these approaches as "not a planned and orderly way of doing business."

The strategies used by FDA reflect a relatively modest approach to cutting personnel. There are several reasons why the agency's downsizing was limited. First, the agency strongly believed that it could not afford to reduce its employee levels in light of a regulatory mission that was growing in scope and complexity. Second, three centers had a statutory requirement to add personnel. Third, OMB granted the Public Health Service and FDA exemptions from downsizing. A statement from one of the agency's executives captures the sentiment:

> I mean, we believe that we'll be told there's some numbers that we have to get to. And we'll be working to get to those numbers ... but, when it gets down to the actual bottom line, there isn't a single soul in this agency who believes that we will ever be forced to let people go.

Organizational Downsizing in Conjunction with Other Change

FDA downsizing was driving other changes within the agency. The downsizing, although kept to minimum levels, was precipitating other reinvention objectives and streamlining actions. The significance was that FDA chose to let downsizing drive any form of reengineering rather than to reengineer first and then determine necessary downsizing levels. A respondent explains this situation as follows:

> We have a top-down pressure situation wherein you're given specific marching orders and targets as opposed to reinvention efforts, which require fewer people. Now, necessity being the mother of invention ... you're going to have to figure out how to do the same job with fewer people. So, that's going to cause you to reinvent. But, it's not like "We've now redone this process,

so it only takes half as many people to do it." It's "You're only going to have half as many people so you better reinvent the process in order to be able to deal with this."

Therefore, downsizing forced innovative ways to become more efficient. In several of the high point critical incidents, executives identified cases where management actions resulted in work process improvements that require fewer resources. For example, the Hazard Analysis Critical Control Point (HACCP) system is a preventive approach to ensuring the safe processing and importing of seafood. Instead of the classical inspection-sampling-regulatory action approach, the HACCP approach prevents problems. The use of HACCP leverages funding and employee resources. According to the executive in charge of the effort, "It's not a downsizing event per se, but it's the kind of thing you have to do to allow that to occur and not shirk your responsibilities in terms of seafood safety."

On the other hand, FDA did not use downsizing as an excuse for other change. As a center executive stated, "I don't know of any instances when we use the excuse of downsizing as a means of accomplishing something that we wanted to do anyhow." For instance, the plan by ORA to restructure its nineteen laboratories would be carried out even if NPR and downsizing principles did not exist. Consolidation of the laboratory system into five multidisciplinary laboratories and four special-focus laboratories will take place between 1997 and 2014. One executive stated:

> Well, that's one of our proactive ways to face this. However, if we didn't have an NPR driving us, we still think that would be the proper thing to do. . . . I can't say it was driven by NPR, but I will in all candor tell you we'll take credit for it under NPR.

Middle Manager Reactions and Concerns about Downsizing

Because middle managers are a specific target in downsizing efforts, several questions in the interviews with executives focused on middle manager reactions and concerns. Unlike in the DLA and BOR cases, no middle managers were interviewed in FDA. According to executives, many middle managers found it difficult to believe that anyone would seriously want to downsize FDA. To these middle managers, it simply was not credible to try to downsize FDA, which they perceived had a crucial mission and was already "stretched very thin." Closely associated with that reaction was an apprehension that downsizing threatened the ability of the agency to accomplish its valuable mission. They believed their responsibility for protecting the public health should not be interfered with. For some of the middle managers, then, the NPR and downsizing efforts evoked reactions of defensiveness. The following are some descriptions of middle manager responses to downsizing according to their executive superiors:

"So what are we downsizing to? Doesn't anybody care about the babies of America that are going to have glass in their baby food?" We get a lot of "wrapped in the flag" arguments when we do these kinds of things.

We have some very dedicated people trying to carry out a mission, and you hear lots of analogies like, "Well, a B-1 bomber costs X zillion dollars, and why not eliminate one of those and then it will pay the entire agency budget for twenty years." So, there is always a feeling, I think, of "Why us versus someone else?"

We're paid to be skeptical. That's part of our job in looking at things. We're supposed to be unbiased and a little bit on the skeptical side and say, "We want to see the hard data before we make our decision." I mean they're saying, "Fine, we understand the theory; let's see the hard data of how this thing really works out."

Many middle managers also had feelings of anxiety about the functions and workloads of their jobs after downsizing was implemented. There was little concern about losing their jobs because there were no RIFs and the agency was primarily relying on normal attrition and voluntary early retirements to downsize. However, middle managers were concerned about how streamlining, reorganizations, increased spans of control, and workloads from departed employees would affect their jobs. There was a general concern expressed as, "What does this mean for me?" These middle managers perceived that they would be expected to perform more work to compensate for employees who had left. In fact, the evidence from the case indicates that very little work was being eliminated.

Finally, there was a strong sense of discouragement about reduced opportunities for career advancement, promotions, and professional standing. An account from one respondent who felt the impact on his organization tells it best:

The GS-13s have not been promoted now for almost a year. Many of those people ... fully deserved to be promoted to a GS-14 level, and we were working our way through that when the freeze came in. Some of those people are seriously adversely affected from a career point of view. On the other hand, there are many young scientists who deserved to be promoted because they are becoming internationally known and are considered experts in their fields. ... To be quite honest with you, some of those are looking outside the government for other employment and some of them are being hired, which is a loss to us. . . . There is some concern about their personal standing, loss of professional standing because their ability to keep current and to continue certain research programs is reduced. . . . They're not able to remain competitive with the outside world because of lack of resources.

Treatment of Middle Managers during Downsizing

Because there was an absence of sizable downsizing beyond normal attrition and a narrow early retirement option, FDA did not have any formal assistance programs for departing or remaining employees. Whereas buyouts, RIFs, and major reorganizations result in large employee transitions, the more limited downsizing measures by FDA were not as disruptive. Consequently, there were no employee service centers or job transition programs for the agency's employees affected by the downsizing.

To assist their remaining employees adjust to changes resulting from NPR and downsizing, some centers did establish initiatives. For example, one center gave awards in lieu of promotions and planned to create an emeritus status for some former employees. Also, a change management course was offered in some places within the agency. A frustrated interviewee revealed that the further "you go down in the organization you'll see people like me reacting to NPR and downsizing by actually doing things like reorganizing and putting systems into place to help us out."

Another characteristic of the treatment of middle managers during downsizing aspect deals with organizations perceived to be "haves" and those perceived to be "have nots." Centers or units of centers that are authorized to grow due to user fees were considered "haves" because they gained more resources and organizational advantages. Others were called "have nots." To minimize any actual or perceived unfair differences among organizations, some actions were taken. For example, in one center, managers were directed to pay close attention to workload and performance expectations. From this goal, consideration was given to information management systems or contracting out as alternatives to helping achieve efficiencies. The aim was to "try to keep the center from becoming a group of 'haves' and 'have nots' and the morale problems that come from that."

Downsizing Effects on Middle Manager Behavior

The effects of downsizing on middle manager behavior varied by type of behavior and organization within FDA. First, there was almost complete consensus that commitment, loyalty, and quality of work remained high throughout the agency. Regarding commitment and loyalty, a hierarchy seemed to exist, with the greatest commitment and loyalty being to the public's health and then to other entities like the Clinton Administration, the agency, or the Commissioner. Second, generally, morale and motivation were negative to varying degrees across the agency. Of course, morale and motivation varied by individual and one could find middle managers with both high and low levels of morale and motivation in any FDA organization. However, every executive interviewed gave some indication that morale and motivation were problems that stemmed from the downsizing, its uncertainty, and the changes associated with it. According to an executive, "The mere mention of it brings morale down." Third, risk taking and productivity varied within the agency. Some middle managers took risks because "they saw the potential to be very effective" or because they had to respond where others did not. Conversely, some middle managers did not take risks because their motivation was lacking.

An interesting theme emerged regarding middle managers who maintained positive behavioral responses. There was a limit to how long middle managers could maintain positive behavior unless improvements were made in their work environments. For example, two respondents in different centers asserted the following about commitment:

> Middle managers are still committed. I don't know at what point that will change, but it will start to deteriorate.

> I think commitment is beginning to wane. You can only step on folks so long and for so many things and they really get tired.

Another felt this way about motivation:

> So, while you can be motivated up to a point, if you feel that you're being abused then that's going to affect your motivation to do any more. It's like, I mean, what difference does it make, no matter what I do, they just want more and more and more. And that's a problem.

Conditions for Resistance to Change and Downsizing by Middle Managers

Resistance to change and downsizing was another area investigated regarding middle managers. Resistance naturally existed because the agency's personnel were skeptical about whether downsizing should or would occur. The resistance aspect was tied to the denial attitude and disbelief by agency employees that were addressed in previous sections. Therefore, the first condition associated with the resistance was when implementation processes were viewed as flawed. Some middle managers considered downsizing for FDA to be flawed because they believed the agency needed more employees, not fewer employees. Also, they thought concurrent hiring and downsizing activities were contradictory. A second condition was when middle managers were unable to recognize the reality of change and downsizing. Because some middle managers strongly believed that NPR and downsizing were political, short-term events, they failed to see the reality that downsizing was extensive across the government. They resisted because they did not want "to be the first in line" to downsize and thought that "if you can hold this off for a little while, it will all go away." Finally, a third condition for resistance was when reorganizations took place to achieve downsizing objectives such as greater efficiency. This condition held true for centers growing from user fees like CBER and for those not affected by user fees such as CFSAN. An executive stated:

> I went through a reorganization in my own group and I heard from every single director who had some problem with the results of downsizing. And they lobbied and they cried and they stomped their feet and they did all kinds of things, but I had to make the ultimate decision, which I did. So, they were very resistant to change.

Executive Views of Downsizing

The executives expressed their views of downsizing in rational and philosophical terms. They completely understood the underlying principles of the NPR and downsizing and, for the most part, accepted them. When it came to the application of downsizing to FDA, though, the executives were much more willing to challenge the wisdom of it. The trouble with downsizing FDA, according to them, was that it was inconsistent with expectations of the American people, activities required by law to be accomplished, and the magnitude of the workload distributed throughout the agency. Four major themes that emerged highlight the views of the executives interviewed.

First, most of the executives asserted that fundamental questions related to what the agency should do needed to be answered prior to making any downsizing decisions. The most important question was, What activities do American citizens, private industry, health professionals, consumer groups, Congress, and the Clinton Administration expect FDA to perform? The reason clarification and prioritization of mission activities needed to occur first was that the agency performed a myriad of important functions and services to protect the public's health. The executives believed there was no way to sustain the current level of activities with fewer resources. Therefore, according to the executives, the agency must either receive external guidance or make internal decisions regarding its priorities. Neither occurred to any significant degree. The following comments were extracted from a more lengthy philosophical opinion given by one bewildered executive:

> I guess I am concerned that the right questions are not always asked about what is it that we really want our government to do and in particular FDA.... My observation is that the expectations all the way around are very high.... I wish there was some mechanism for looking at these broader questions up front.

Another frustrated executive was more outspoken:

> If someone would come and tell me what I shouldn't be doing or Congress would tell us we are doing drug reviews incorrectly ... I consider downsizing a rational approach. I am a taxpayer also, and I don't think I need to be paying taxes for people doing work that is not needed. But, I haven't heard anybody tell me that there is anything that we are doing that doesn't need to be done and the idea of just downsizing for the sake of downsizing without some logic ... doesn't make any sense.... So, it is a dumb, futile exercise.... Instead, they are going to rely on us to tell them what we are not going to do and that is silly.... No commissioner in my twenty-eight years in this agency has ever been willing to say, "I am not going to do X anymore because I don't have resources."

Second, and closely associated with the first, executives thought decisions should consciously be made to reduce particular mission activities and workloads prior to downsizing implementation. Otherwise, they believed remaining employees in a downsized FDA would be left with "undiminished responsibilities" because "this agency has never figured out how to stop doing anything." A typical attitude is reflected by the following quote:

> The downsizing effort is predicated on the fact that there are lots of people performing useless functions.... I don't believe that I have any of those kinds of people. I have just barely enough people to take care of the responsibilities that are laid upon me.

However, in those few cases where work was terminated, there was a feeling that "we're cutting out things that we don't want to cut out and that's hurting." Translated, it means that because so much work was important, reducing the work caused dismay. This dilemma was related to the next view held by the executives.

The third general view was that the downsizing process was very disturbing to executives and difficult for them to implement. In the interviews, executives described the FDA downsizing circumstances with phrases like "it presents some really special problems," "we have this real bizarre situation," "I have a great deal of trepidation," and "we are not sure how to respond." Each of these short quotes came from different executives. In summary, the executives felt that it was "a complicated exercise because of the schizophrenic nature of it that is unique in many respects to FDA."

Finally, there was a common belief that if the agency downsized and workloads were simply transferred to remaining employees, then negative outcomes would result. The fear was that the agency would not be able to ensure safety of the nation's food, drugs, cosmetics, and medical devices. The argument was that "there will be public consequences to any dramatic downsizing" and "one possibility if they cut too much is that you could then have some public health disasters." Take for example, the area of food oversight. According to an executive:

> I'm concerned about how thin we can get and still provide protection of the nation's food supply.... There are a whole series of new and important changes to our food supply and at the same time we're reducing the number of people in the foods area to deal with this.... I think that we're going to see more mistakes and more problems unless we can be extraordinarily efficient and the regulated industry gives us complete cooperation.

Executive Management Practices during Downsizing

Several questions asked during the interviews with executives related directly to executive management practices during downsizing. To elicit varied responses, three questions were framed differently. They focused on "managing during downsizing," "new management challenges," and "new management styles, tactics, and strategies." See appendix C for the wording of the interview questions. The research strategy was to combine the answers to achieve a more complete picture of executive management practices during downsizing.

Table 5.6 lists eight management characteristics identified from data analysis. The characteristics are those management practices by executives that were used or are recommended for use during downsizing. The order is based upon a combination of the frequency with which the practice was mentioned and the number of executives who mentioned the practice. Additionally, the critical incidents discussed by the executives were reviewed for behavior that reflected the practices. Therefore, the critical incidents provided additional support for the presence and order of the practices. Each listed item was identified at least three times and by at least two different executives.

Executive Competencies for Downsizing

The interviews were designed to include two opportunities for executives to identify executive competencies needed for downsizing. Refer to appendix C for the interview protocol. First, the last section in Part I of the interviews asked executives, "What are the qualities, characteristics, and capabilities needed to perform those aspects of your position related to downsizing?" Second, one of the twenty questions in Part II asked, "What managerial competencies and skills do you believe are important for SES executives to exercise in managing during downsizing?"

Table 5.6 lists ten executive competencies identified from data analysis. The order is based upon a combination of the frequency the competency was mentioned and the number of executives who mentioned the competency. The table contains specific examples of behavior that illustrate the competencies. Additionally, the critical incidents discussed by the executives were reviewed for behavior that reflected the competencies. Therefore, the critical incidents provided additional support for the presence and order of the competencies. Each listed competency was identified at least three times and by at least two different executives. Therefore, although "vision," "patience," "empower others," and "sense of humor" were identified as competencies, none of them occurred frequently enough to be on the final list.

Summary of Major Findings

Table 5.7 shows the major findings of the FDA case study. The findings were reached after a systematic data analysis process of using multiple data sources, performing an iterative coding sequence, and identifying themes and patterns. The findings are written as results of the FDA case and can be considered lessons learned.

The discussion in the previous ten sections on downsizing aspects and characteristics support the findings in Table 5.7. The ten executive competencies identified are listed in Table 5.6 in a coherent order for the FDA case. FDA is experiencing "a world where you're getting mixed messages" that necessitates "coping mechanisms . . . to cope with the frustrations of the duality of our situation." Therefore, the primary competencies required for the circumstances described in this chapter relate to executives' being

Table 5.7

Major Food and Drug Administration Findings

Downsizing Aspect	Finding
1. Organizational preparation for downsizing	Employees are in denial that downsizing will occur on a large scale.
2. Organizational strategies for downsizing	The approach is piecemeal.
3. Organizational downsizing in conjunction with other change	Personnel reductions are preceding redesigning and streamlining activities.
4. Middle manager reactions/concerns about downsizing	Defensive of agency welfare and mission and distressed over reduced promotion opportunities.
5. Treatment of middle managers during downsizing	Some positive actions implemented in lieu of an unnecessary formal program for remaining employees.
6. Downsizing effects on middle manager behavior	Despite low morale and motivation, commitment and loyalty remain high but have limits.
7. Conditions for resistance to change and downsizing by middle managers	Downsizing implementation is viewed as flawed and leads to resistance.
8. Executive views of downsizing	Belief that mission priorities should be clarified and workloads should be reduced.
9. Executive management during downsizing	Management emphasis is on getting agency to be more efficient.
10. Executive competencies for downsizing	Order of competencies is coherent.

prepared for an incongruent environment. Consequently, "analytical," "commitment, energy, and inner strength," and "background with functional or technical preparation" are three of the top four competencies ranked by the executives.

Four primary techniques were used to confirm the findings. First, triangulation was achieved by relying on different data sources and data collection methods. Second, weighting the evidence was practiced by exercising judgment about the quality of data and selecting the most valid data. Third, negative evidence was searched for to find any disconfirmations. And fourth, feedback from informants was used to validate the findings of the study.

Conclusions for Executive Management of FDA Downsizing

The last analytic exercise in the data analysis for the FDA case study was the generation of a causal network. The within-case displays in Tables 5.6

and 5.7 are steps in an inductive approach to building the causal network (Miles and Huberman 1994). For the FDA case, the causal network for downsizing appears in Figures 5.1 and 5.2. The causal network displays the most important variables and the relationships among them. The purpose of the causal network is to diagram an integrated understanding of the case. The causal network generated is the one that emerges from the data analysis. It subsequently will be synthesized in chapter 6 with the causal networks from the other two cases to generate a theoretical downsizing model and to produce hypotheses related to executive management during downsizing. In general, the causal network shows details of executive management of the FDA downsizing process. The figures include a two-dimensional section indicated by the dashed lines. The two dimensions are the downsizing process diagrammed in Figure 5.1 and executive management of downsizing depicted in Figure 5.2.

The far left side of Figure 5.1 identifies the following factors in the environment driving change for FDA: the growth and complexity of food, drug, medical device, and cosmetic products; the growth and complexity of the scientific process to review those products; user fee legislation authorizing personnel growth; the budget deficit; and the reinventing government initiative known as the National Performance Review. The growth and complexity of products and scientific review and the increase in personnel due to user fee legislation operate to pressure FDA to grow in size. Conversely, the budget deficit and reinventing government drive FDA to downsize. Obviously, these two forces are in contradiction. As a result, FDA is experiencing a frustrating quandary for executive management of the downsizing process. Going from left to right, the two-dimensional, dashed line area represents the downsizing process and executive management of it. The downsizing consists of three phases: personnel reduction strategies, process changes, and reorientations. Although there is some overlap among the phases, they generally follow the pattern shown. First, FDA is exercising limited personnel reduction strategies that consist of normal attrition, hiring freezes, and early retirements without buyouts. Next, FDA is implementing redesigning and streamlining process changes on a limited scale in places. The process changes fundamentally modify agency activities to achieve organizational improvements. More particularly, redesigning reduces or eliminates some functions, hierarchical levels, and organizational units considered to be duplicative or unnecessary and streamlining minimizes non-value-added steps while maximizing value-added steps in agency processes and systems. The first two phases help to achieve organizational reorientations in the third phase. For FDA, the primary reorientation is toward expediting the review and approval processes for products.

163

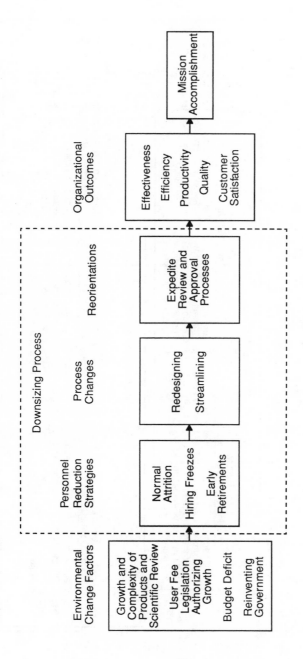

Figure 5.1 **Causal Network for Food and Drug Administration Downsizing**

164

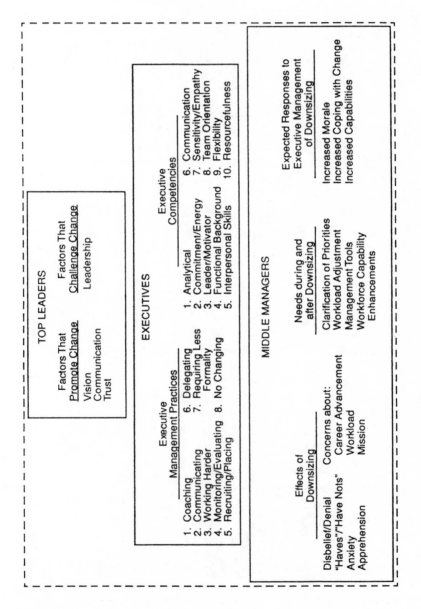

Figure 5.2 **Executive Management of Food and Drug Administration Downsizing**

The agency's Reinventing Administrative Management Program exists to support the downsizing process.

The area within the dashed lines also represents executive management of the downsizing process explained above. Figure 5.2 illustrates this dimension with a pyramid. At the top of the pyramid are FDA's top leaders, the Commissioner and a few other political appointees who perform a critical preliminary and concurrent role for executive management of downsizing. Based upon analysis of the data, FDA top leaders exhibit three important strengths that promote change and enhance executive management of downsizing. The top leaders provide a clear vision, communicate the vision, and engender trust among employees. However, there is one area in which top leaders challenge change and inhibit executive management of downsizing. FDA top leaders, early in the downsizing process, did not provide needed direction through their leadership. In other words, they offered insufficient guidance to help executives deal with the problems associated with the contradictory requirements to upsize (grow) and downsize. The middle portion of the pyramid lists those executive management practices and executive competencies that are needed by FDA for its downsizing process. The bottom part of the pyramid indicates factors in three categories associated with middle managers. First, the effects of downsizing on middle managers are disbelief and denial that downsizing are expected of FDA; a sense of "haves" and "have nots" among organizations within FDA; and anxiety, apprehension, and concerns about career advancement, workload, and mission accomplishment. Second, middle managers need clarification of priorities, workload adjustment, management tools, and workforce capability enhancements. Third, middle manager responses to better executive management of downsizing are expected to be increased morale, increased coping with change, and increased capabilities.

Returning to Figure 5.1, the two-dimensional, downsizing process/executive management dashed line area leads to desired and expected organizational outcomes. Those outcomes are increased effectiveness, efficiency, productivity, quality, and customer satisfaction. Ultimately, mission accomplishment is expected.

FDA is a federal agency that found itself in complicated circumstances as a result of a web of NPR requirements to downsize and legislation to grow. FDA's employment of many high-grade employees makes downsizing particularly troublesome. Over time, the agency successfully managed to reduce personnel in some offices to balance the addition of employees in some of its centers. The FDA case points out the need to consider differences among agencies before levying across-the-board requirements.

Notes

1. This quote was taken from the script accompanying a set of briefing charts describing FDA and the Office of Regulatory Affairs (ORA). It came from the text used to describe a chart titled "Our Mission." The script and briefing charts were obtained from an ORA executive during an interview on 12 September 1994.

2. For a review with facts and figures of how FDA fulfilled its regulatory mandates during fiscal year 1996, see the 1996 *FDA Almanac* (Food and Drug Administration 1996).

3. A more detailed, but still brief, summary of FDA's history is provided by Young (1983) and Janssen (1992). Young (1983) also presents a short bibliography for additional information on FDA's history.

4. Obtained from a memorandum titled "FDA Senior-level Staffing Reduction Plan (Civilian Staff), FY 1994" from FDA Deputy Commissioner for Management and Systems to Deputy Assistant Secretary for Health Management Operations, 20 October 1993. For further detailed information on FDA staffing, see other internal memoranda on senior-level staffing reductions, hiring freeze, preliminary fiscal year 1995 ceilings, average salaries, and early out retirement and buyouts between May 1994 and July 1994.

6

Managing Downsizing:
Lessons Learned

The Defense Logistics Agency, Bureau of Reclamation, and Food and Drug Administration case studies appear in the three previous chapters. Downsizing phenomena in each case were explained by addressing the agency's recent organizational changes and downsizing activities and discussing investigation results, analysis, and major findings. Data analysis in each case study resulted in explanation-building and a network stipulating a set of causal links. The purpose of chapter 6 is to move from within-case analyses to a comparative, or cross-case, analysis to generate lessons learned. The comparative analysis identifies underlying similarities and differences, synthesizes interpretations across cases, deepens understanding and explanation, and enhances generalizability. Appendix J describes the analytical process for conducting the comparative analysis.

The chapter includes four focuses. First, comparisons are made of (1) environmental factors influencing the downsizing process and (2) characteristics of the downsizing process. Second, lessons learned are identified for organizations and downsizing, middle managers and downsizing, and executives and downsizing. Furthermore, a comparative analysis of the study's executive competencies and the OPM executive competencies is presented. These comparisons and lessons learned represent the findings of the study. Third, a theoretical model for executive management of downsizing is developed. And fourth, seven hypotheses for executive management of downsizing are advanced. Together, the comparisons, lessons learned, model, and hypotheses form the final downsizing theory building product from the case studies.

Comparisons of Agency Downsizing Processes

This section presents two tables that contain information about the downsizing processes of DLA, BOR, and FDA. The tables summarize similarities and differences among the three agencies.

First, Table 6.1 shows the results of a comparison of environmental change factors influencing the downsizing processes of the agencies. There are four categories of change factors: political, economic, social, and technical. For DLA, political and economic factors galvanize the downsizing process. The overriding political factor is the end of the Cold War. The major economic factor is the budget deficit. These two factors combine to result in another economic factor: reduction in the defense infrastructure. Additionally, the reinventing government initiative, known as the National Performance Review, is a political and economic factor. For BOR, political, economic, and social factors are the most influential in spurring agency downsizing. Economically, the budget deficit, budget decline for dam construction, and reinventing government initiative act on the downsizing process. Socially, changing social values regarding protecting the environment and competing public interests for water usage impinge on the downsizing process. Reinventing government is also a political factor and served as a catalyst for BOR's downsizing process. Finally, for FDA, technical factors join the political and economic factors as important influences. The political factor of the reinventing government initiative combines with the economic factors of the budget deficit and reinventing government to drive FDA toward downsizing. However, the technical factors of (1) growth and complexity of food, drug, medical device, and cosmetic products and (2) growth and complexity of the agency scientific review process combine with the political factor of user fee legislation, requiring the hiring of additional personnel, to drive FDA to grow. In summary, political, economic, social, and technical factors in the external environment of the agencies affect how they downsize. Each agency has a different combination of environmental factors that create the context for downsizing and influence the downsizing process. Two factors, the budget deficit and the reinventing government initiative, operate to affect all three agencies.

Table 6.2 provides greater insight into how the factors in Table 6.1 affect the downsizing processes of the agencies in the study. Table 6.2 displays the results of a comparison of characteristics of the downsizing processes of the agencies. The table is a six-by-three matrix containing descriptors that reveal similarities and differences in six categories among the three agencies. First, regarding the direction of change that external environmental factors cause, DLA and BOR are driven consistently toward downsizing. But FDA experiences factors that result in the contradictory impetuses to grow and to downsize. Second, downsizing is difficult for each agency, but each agency has a different type of difficulty. The type of difficulty for DLA is "direct" in that it derives from factors pointing the agency toward

Table 6.1

Comparison of Environmental Change Factors Influencing the Downsizing Process

	Defense Logistics Agency	Bureau of Reclamation	Food and Drug Administration
Political	End of the Cold War Reinventing Government	Reinventing Government	User Fee Legislation Reinventing Government
Economic	Budget Deficit Infrastructure Reduction Reinventing Government	Budget Deficit Budget Decline for Dam Construction Reinventing Government	Budget Deficit Reinventing Government
Social		Changing Social Values Competing Public Interests	
Technical			Growth and Complexity of Products Growth and Complexity of Scientific Review

Table 6.2

Comparison of Characteristics of the Downsizing Process

	Defense Logistics Agency	Bureau of Reclamation	Food and Drug Administration
Direction of Change	Consistent: Downsizing	Consistent: Downsizing	Contradictory: Growth and Downsizing
Type of Difficulty	Direct: Downsizing	Complex: New Mission and Downsizing	Complex: Growth and Downsizing
Extent of Downsizing Process	Extensive	Extensive	Minimal
Type of Downsizing	Antecedent	Archetypic	Discrepant
Predominant Feature of Downsizing	Continuation of Earlier Changes	Central to Transforming Agency	Contradictory to Concurrent Growth
Downsizing Experience	Challenging Difficult Painful	Challenging Difficult Painful	Challenging Difficult Painful

downsizing. BOR has "complex" difficulty because it is changing its mission at the same time that it is downsizing. FDA also has "complex" difficulty because it is simultaneously growing and downsizing. The third descriptor is the extent of the downsizing process. In DLA and BOR, it is "extensive." These agencies experienced aggressive process changes and high attrition rates during their downsizings. Meanwhile, FDA's downsizing is classified as "minimal" since it adds personnel as well as loses them and its process changes are not widespread. Fourth, for type of downsizing, each agency is characterized differently. DLA's downsizing is labeled "antecedent" because that agency started downsizing a few years before other agencies in the federal government. As a result, DLA and other DOD organizations share valuable guidance and lessons learned with civilian agencies. BOR is classified as "archetypic" since it serves as a prototype for how agencies can reinvent and downsize comprehensively. FDA is called "discrepant" because the agency has unusual circumstances requiring it to simultaneously grow and downsize. Fifth, the predominant feature of downsizing for each agency is consistent with the other characterizations. What stands out is that DLA's downsizing is a continuation of past organizational changes, BOR's downsizing is a central part of its mission transformation, and FDA's downsizing is contradictory to its concurrent growth mandate. Finally, the downsizing experience for each agency is challenging, difficult, and painful regardless of the unique circumstances of each agency.

Organizations and Downsizing

The next step in the comparative analysis identifies cross-case patterns, which constitute lessons learned, pertaining to organizational dimensions of downsizing. The dimensions of interest are (1) preparation for downsizing, (2) personnel reduction strategies for downsizing, and (3) downsizing process changes and reorientations. Table 6.3 shows eleven lessons learned for organizations and downsizing. The lessons for the three dimensions are buttressed by affirmative evidence and/or absence of disconfirming evidence. Except for one lesson learned, all the lessons have supporting evidence from each of the three cases. The one exception is number 9, "Downsizing is an opportunity to help agencies change missions and cultures." For this lesson, the DLA and BOR cases provide evidence. The FDA case does not have affirmative evidence for the lesson because the agency was not trying to change its mission or alter its culture in a significant way. However, there is no disconfirming evidence that if FDA sought to change its mission or culture that downsizing would not be an "opportunity to help" it do so.

Table 6.3

Lessons Learned for Organizations and Downsizing

Preparation for Downsizing

1. Agencies are not completely prepared for downsizing.
2. Agencies conduct downsizing in an imprecise manner.
3. Agency downsizing is difficult no matter how much planning and preparation are conducted.
4. Agencies prefer greater time periods to plan, prepare for, and implement downsizing.

Personnel Reduction Strategies for Downsizing

5. Agencies rely on voluntary methods first.
6. Agencies use RIFs as a last resort.

Downsizing Process Changes and Reorientations

7. Overall, despite some reduction and elimination of activities, functions, and programs, agencies do not reduce or eliminate workloads for remaining employees as much as they should.
8. Agencies do not use downsizing as an excuse for other changes.
9. Downsizing is an opportunity to help agencies change missions and cultures.
10. Agencies pursue activities during and after downsizing that increase efficiencies and other businesslike practices.
11. Agencies prefer to implement personnel reductions after reengineering, redesigning, restructuring, and streamlining take place.

Middle Managers and Downsizing

Another important part of the study examined the effects of downsizing on middle managers. This section describes the comparative analysis that uncovers lessons learned related to middle managers and downsizing. Table 6.4 lists eleven lessons for middle managers and downsizing. The lessons are authenticated by affirmative evidence and/or absence of disconfirming evidence. All the lessons have supporting evidence from each of the three cases. Two of the lessons receive weak support from one of the three cases. First, for lesson number 5 dealing with middle manager concerns about careers, the DLA case only weakly supports this finding. Second, for lesson number 9 related to transition assistance for departing middle managers in FDA, there are no formal agency-wide assistance programs but some decentralized help. Therefore, sufficient evidence exists to give some support for this finding.

Table 6.4

Lessons Learned for Middle Managers and Downsizing

1. Middle managers remain committed and loyal to their agencies.
2. Middle managers are concerned about the continued capability of their agencies to accomplish their missions.
3. Some middle managers recognize opportunities and are somewhat optimistic.
4. Many middle managers have feelings of disfranchisement, insecurity, and vulnerability.
5. Many middle managers have apprehension about reduced opportunities for career advancement, promotions, professional standing, and status.
6. Many middle managers have anxiety about job functions, workload distribution, and performance, efficiency, and productivity issues.
7. Morale and motivation among many middle managers are generally negative.
8. Risk taking, quality of work, efficiency, and productivity among middle managers vary depending on location and workplace factors within agencies.
9. Agencies adequately provide transition assistance to middle managers who leave agencies.
10. The following are becoming priorities as agencies focus attention on remaining middle managers: change management, new roles, retraining, management systems, team management skills, and other assistance programs.
11. Middle managers believe their jobs in the future will be much more challenging than in the past.

Executives and Downsizing

The research focused centrally on executives and downsizing. Executives perform a critical role in managing downsizing processes in agencies. The comparative analysis search reveals lessons learned regarding executive views of downsizing, executive management practices during downsizing, and executive competencies for downsizing.

Executive Views of Downsizing

Six lessons from executive views of downsizing emerged and appear in Table 6.5. Again, the lessons are substantiated by affirmative evidence and/ or absence of disconfirming evidence. Each lesson has supporting evidence from all three cases. The following remarks further explain the lessons. The numbers correspond with the listed lessons in the table.

1. Every executive interviewed in each agency displayed a recognition that reinventing government and downsizing were realities facing the federal government. Although some executives disagreed with some aspects of implementation, they accept the fundamental premises for reinventing government and downsizing. Even in FDA, where the executives are disturbed

Table 6.5

Lessons Learned from Executive Views of Downsizing

1. Executives have an outlook that reinventing government and downsizing are realities of the environment for their agencies.
2. Executives believe downsizing is necessary and essential for their agencies when the following conditions exist:
   a. The mission is changed or curtailed.
   b. Downsizing and growth are not simultaneous requirements.
3. Executives think organizational reengineering, redesigning, restructuring, and streamlining should precede personnel reductions.
4. Executives maintain that workload distribution after downsizing is a critical factor related to employee behavior and performance.
5. Executives consider downsizing to be challenging, difficult, and painful.
6. Executives are uncertain of and concerned about the future workforce capabilities of their agencies after downsizing.

by the difficulties associated with downsizing and growth, they still accept that some downsizing in some parts of the agency will occur.

2. This lesson stipulates the conditions for when executives believe downsizing to be necessary and essential. Of course, these conditions were met in the cases of DLA and BOR. Consequently, their executives expressed how downsizing was "necessary" and "essential." Because FDA has simultaneous requirements to downsize and grow, its executives did not describe downsizing as being necessary and essential for their agency.

3. If personnel reductions occur, executives think some kind of organizational process changes, like reengineering, redesigning, restructuring, or streamlining, should happen first. The philosophy is that the agency should first establish its mission, functions, structure, processes, and priorities and then reduce personnel as necessary. The downsizing experience at DLA closely approximated this sequence. BOR conducted the two tasks somewhat simultaneously. At FDA, the order was reversed.

4. The issue of workload distribution for employees after downsizing is one of the most significant lessons to emerge from the research. The data were analyzed in many different ways, and the need to adjust workload was constantly identified. Consequently, there are ample references to this issue in the DLA, BOR, and FDA chapters.

5. Another consistent lesson is the view by executives that downsizing is *challenging, difficult,* and *painful.* These three words were commonly used by executives in each agency in their descriptions of critical incidents and answers to a wide range of questions. Although the downsizing contexts vary for DLA, BOR, and FDA, each agency shares the agony of downsizing.

6. Concern by executives about future workforce capabilities after

downsizing is another vital lesson. Not only do executives have some doubts about workforce capabilities, but they also reflect the apprehension by middle managers about workforces accomplishing their missions to acceptable standards. In DLA, some uncertainty surrounds workforce skill mixes. In BOR, some ambivalence exists as to whether human resource capabilities were paid sufficient attention. And in FDA, the perception of "haves" and "have nots" surfaced regarding personnel resource capabilities in various organizations. For DLA and BOR, buyouts introduced a degree of randomness to workforce skill losses. For FDA, the hiring freeze constrained the replacement of personnel lost through normal attrition.

Close examination of the lessons learned for organizations and downsizing, middle managers and downsizing, and executives and downsizing reveal four highly incontrovertible findings: (1) downsizing is difficult, (2) reengineering, redesigning, restructuring, and streamlining should precede personnel reductions, (3) workload distributions need adjustment, and (4) workforce capabilities are uncertain.

Executive Management Practices during Downsizing

Executives manage downsizing with a number of practices. The term *management practice* means any management style, tactic, or strategy used to contend with challenges associated with downsizing. Nine general management practices were identified during the within-case analyses. The practices, referred to previously as characteristics in DLA Table 3.10, BOR Table 4.10, and FDA Table 5.6, appear again in Table 6.6 as a set of lessons learned for executive management practices during downsizing. In chapters 3–5, the management practices were listed in the earlier tables based upon a combination of the frequency with which the practice was mentioned and the number of executives who mentioned the practice. This time, the order of the practices in Table 6.6 is arrived at by averaging the placement of practices in the previous tables. Thus the practices near the top of Table 6.6 were also near the top of the tables for the case studies.

Not too much emphasis should be placed on the order. What is conveyed is a general sense of which management practices were most prevalent across the cases. With one exception, every practice in Table 6.6 was found in each case study. The only anomaly is that number 9, "more visibility," did not appear in the FDA case study. *More visibility* means the executive increases her level of availability and contact with employees. However, there is no counterevidence in the FDA case, such as lack of visibility helping downsizing, to invalidate the finding that visibility is a viable management practice. In addition, number 7, "no change from past," means that

Table 6.6

Lessons Learned for Executive Management Practices during Downsizing

1. More coaching, mentoring, encouraging, and lifting morale
2. More monitoring and evaluating work and performance
3. More effort to accomplish more difficult work
4. More communication
5. More delegation of authority and participatory style
6. More attention to internal recruitment and placement of personnel
7. No change from past in terms of specific types of actions
8. Less formality and hierarchy
9. More visibility

some executives do not change from any past management actions to suit downsizing. The study considers this posture to be, in itself, a practice.

Executive Competencies for Downsizing

Executives who achieve effective and superior organizational performance have specific characteristics or competencies that affect their behaviors. For this research, *executive competencies for downsizing* are defined as underlying characteristics of executives such as motives, traits, self-concepts, bodies of knowledge, and skills that relate to effective and superior management of downsizing.[1] Fifteen SES competencies were identified during the within-case analyses. The competencies, referred to previously as characteristics in DLA Table 3.10, BOR Table 4.10, and FDA Table 5.6, appear again in Table 6.7 as a set of executive competencies for downsizing. Note that the executive competencies were listed in the earlier tables based upon a combination of the frequency with which the competency was mentioned and the number of executives who mentioned the competency. This time, the order of the competencies in Table 6.7 is arrived at by averaging the placement of competencies in the previous tables. Thus the competencies near the top of Table 6.7 were also near the top of the tables for the case studies.

Just as for the management practices in Table 6.6, not too much emphasis should be placed on the order of the executive competencies in Table 6.7. Three factors are important, though, about the list of executive competencies. First, the competencies appearing higher on the list are those most common in the case studies and found to be necessary for downsizing. Second, the competencies lower on the list are less prevalent but still necessary for downsizing. Third, regardless of its position on the list, each competency appeared in at least two of the three case studies. In fact, twelve of the fifteen competencies emerged from all three case studies. Number 12,

Table 6.7

Executive Competencies for Downsizing Compared with U.S. Office of Personnel Management Competencies

1. Analytical
    (2.) Creative Thinking
    (4.) Decisiveness
    (5.) External Awareness
    (15.) Planning and Evaluating
    (16.) Problem Solving
    (20.) Technology Management
2. Leader and motivator through coaching, mentoring, and lifting morale
    (9.) Influencing/Negotiating
    (11.) Leadership
3. Commitment, energy, and inner strength
    (17.) Self-Direction
4. Sensitivity and empathy for people
    (8.) Human Resources Management
    (10.) Interpersonal Skills
    (13.) Managing Diverse Workforce
5. Vision
    (3.) Customer Orientation
    (21.) Vision
6. Communication
    (14.) Oral Communication
    (22.) Written Communication
7. Interpersonal skills
    (1.) Conflict Management
    (9.) Influencing/Negotiating
    (10.) Interpersonal Skills
8. Background with functional or technical preparation
    (6.) Financial Management
    (19.) Technical Competence
9. Team orientation
    (18.) Team Building
10. Flexibility
    (7.) Flexibility
11. Resourcefulness
    (7.) Flexibility
12. Honesty and trustworthiness
    (12.) Management Controls/Integrity
13. Empower others
    (11.) Leadership
14. Patience
15. Sense of humor

Note: Items 1.–15. identify the executive competencies for downsizing found in this study. Items (1.)–(22.) shown in parentheses refer to Office of Personnel Management (OPM) executive competencies. See appendix A for definitions of OPM competencies.

"honesty and trustworthiness," was not found in the FDA case study. Additionally, number 14, "patience," was not identified in the DLA case study. And number 15, "sense of humor," was not uncovered in the BOR case study. Nevertheless, these executive competencies remain listed because sufficient evidence exists in at least two case studies and no disconfirming evidence warrants elimination of any of the competencies.

Because data about SES competencies were gathered during the research, an opportunity exists to compare the study's findings with OPM's current competencies. OPM plans to release changes in 1998 to its competencies and Executive Core Qualifications. Recall that the section on "Managerial Competence Models" in chapter 2 described OPM's Leadership Effectiveness Framework and its twenty-two competencies. Table 2.1 lists the twenty-two competencies. According to OPM's *Guide to SES Qualifications* (U.S. Office of Personnel Management 1994), LEF competencies are attributes of executives who successfully demonstrate key characteristics that are behavioral activities. A matching analysis was conducted to pair this study's competencies with OPM's competencies. Specific examples of behavior that illustrate and help define the study's competencies are found in DLA Table 3.10, BOR Table 4.10, and FDA Table 5.6. Also, definitions of OPM's competencies are in appendix A. Table 6.7 groups OPM competencies under corresponding competencies found in this study. OPM competencies are identified with numbers within parentheses and with upper and lower case letters to avoid confusion. Four OPM competencies— number (7), "Flexibility"; number (9), "Influencing/Negotiating"; number (10), "Interpersonal Skills"; and number (11), "Leadership"—appear under more than one of this study's competencies.

This study's executive competencies for downsizing include two competencies that have no counterparts among the OPM competencies. Number 14, "patience," and number 15, "sense of humor," are traits that emerged as executive competencies. A *trait* is a dispositional way in which a person responds to an equivalent set of stimuli (McClelland 1951). None of the twenty-two OPM competency definitions in appendix A includes any mention of the word *patience*. Furthermore, none of the five Executive Core Qualifications in appendix B references *patience*. The meaning of "patience," as defined by the data in the study, is to recognize and willingly accept that events and adaptations take extended periods of time to be completed. The only OPM competency that comes close to having the same meaning is number (7), "Flexibility," defined as "Adapts to change in the work environment; effectively copes with stress." However, other data in this study led to "flexibility" as a separate competency with a meaning similar to the OPM definition. Therefore, there is justification for OPM to add "patience" as a twenty-third competency in the LEF. Alternatively, OPM could extend the definition of "Flexibility" so that "patience" becomes another dimension of "Flexibility." Of the study's fifteen executive competencies in Table 6.7, "sense of humor" had the weakest amount of evidence from the case studies supporting it. There was a significant gap between "sense of humor" and the next competency above it, "patience," in terms of the amount and quality of evidence. Moreover, none of the OPM competency definitions includes any reference to "sense of humor." This study does not find sufficient evidence for OPM to add a new competency for "sense of humor" or to expand any of the twenty-two competency definitions to include "sense of humor" as a new dimension.

Two of the study's other competencies on the list of executive competencies for downsizing in Table 6.7 are closely aligned with OPM competencies and strongly established in the case studies. Competency number 2, "leader and motivator through coaching, mentoring, and lifting morale," has similarities to OPM competencies number (9), "Influencing/ Negotiating," and number (11), "Leadership." However, neither of the OPM competencies as defined has quite the same meaning as the study's competency. Therefore, this study suggests that OPM should consider modifying its "Leadership" competency definition to include a dimension that includes "coaching, mentoring, and lifting morale." Additionally, competency number 3, "commitment, energy, and inner strength," is similar to OPM competency number (17), "Self-Direction." The OPM LEF would be more complete if it added the phrase "possesses commitment, energy, and inner strength" to the definition of "Self-Direction."

A Theoretical Model for Executive Management of Downsizing

Figure 2.1 diagrammed an initial theoretical model of the downsizing change process. The theoretical model was part of a theoretical framework that functioned to guide the conduct of the research. The model represents a macroview of downsizing phenomena. The completion of in-depth case studies of downsizing in DLA, BOR, and FDA and a comparative analysis results in a revised theoretical model. Figures 6.1 and 6.2 illustrate the revised model for executive management of downsizing in federal agencies. The variables and the relationships among them in the new model evolved from the findings in the case studies. A process of synthesizing the causal networks of downsizing for the three agencies and integrating the most salient cross-case patterns generated Figures 6.1 and 6.2. The revised theoretical model is a cross-case causal network that uses variables estimated to be the most influential in explaining downsizing phenomena. The theoretical model possesses several attributes. First, the model is ordered temporally. It includes variables associated with timing before, during, and after downsizing. Second, the model links the variables according to causes and effects in a linear chain. Third, downsizing phenomena are now explained with greater specificity. Fourth, the model is representative of the individual case accounts. And fifth, the model makes conceptual, empirical, and theoretical sense.

The following describes the relationships portrayed in Figures 6.1 and 6.2. The figures include a two-dimensional section indicated by the dashed lines. The two dimensions are the downsizing process diagrammed in Figure 6.1 and the management hierarchy for downsizing depicted in Figure 6.2. To begin with, there are change factors in the external environment of agencies. These change factors influence agency leaders to make strategic decisions affecting their organizations. External environmental change factors can be categorized as political, economic, social, and technical.

One specific type of organizational change is downsizing. The downsizing process dimension is represented in the center of the first part of Figure 6.1 with the dashed lines surrounding it. The downsizing process consists of three components: process changes, personnel reduction strategies, and organizational reorientations. Process changes include reengineering, redesigning, restructuring, and streamlining actions that change organizational work processes; reduce functions, hierarchical levels, and units; realign functional activities; and maximize value-added steps. In some agencies, process changes result in the requirement for fewer personnel. Thus, process changes precede personnel reduction strategies. In other agencies, process changes are implemented jointly with personnel reduction strategies. In still other agencies, personnel reductions are followed by process changes in order to balance workloads with fewer employees. In most downsizing cases, there will probably be some overlap between process changes and personnel reduction strategies. Furthermore, both help to achieve organizational reorientations that are usually the drive toward fulfillment of a new mission, a change in culture, the use of businesslike practices, or other new ways of operating. In some cases, process changes and personnel reduction strategies naturally result in organizational reorientations. In other cases, the goal of achieving an organizational reorientation means that process changes and personnel reduction strategies are intentionally used as the means of achieving the reorientation. Together, the three events are elements of downsizing.

The area within the dashed lines also represents the management hierarchy for downsizing. Figure 6.2 refers to this dimension. Executives perform the primary role in managing downsizing. Executives manage with emphases on particular practices while utilizing particular competencies. How-

181

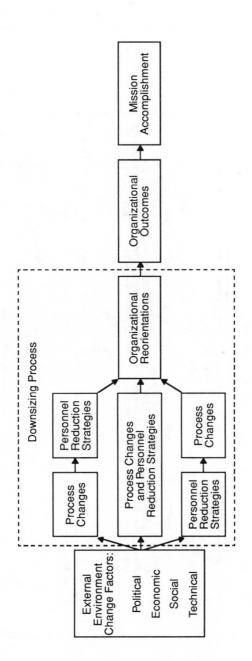

Figure 6.1 **Revised Theoretical Model for Executive Management of Downsizing in Federal Agencies**

182

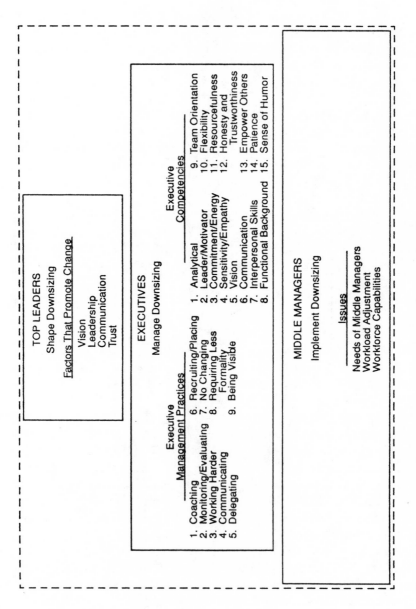

Figure 6.2 Theoretical Model of the Management Hierarchy for Downsizing

TOP LEADERS
Shape Downsizing

Factors That Promote Change

Vision
Leadership
Communication
Trust

EXECUTIVES
Manage Downsizing

Executive
Management Practices

1. Coaching
2. Monitoring/Evaluating
3. Working Harder
4. Communicating
5. Delegating
6. Recruiting/Placing
7. No Changing
8. Requiring Less Formality
9. Being Visible

Executive
Competencies

1. Analytical
2. Leader/Motivator
3. Commitment/Energy
4. Sensitivity/Empathy
5. Vision
6. Communication
7. Interpersonal Skills
8. Functional Background
9. Team Orientation
10. Flexibility
11. Resourcefulness
12. Honesty and Trustworthiness
13. Empower Others
14. Patience
15. Sense of Humor

MIDDLE MANAGERS
Implement Downsizing

Issues

Needs of Middle Managers
Workload Adjustment
Workforce Capabilities

ever, top leaders, who are either political appointees in civilian agencies or military commanders in defense agencies, influence executive management. These top leaders shape downsizing and promote change with the vision they provide, the leadership they demonstrate, the communication they exercise, and the trust they instill.

Executives, in turn, greatly influence implementation of downsizing actions by middle managers. The executives rely on the management practices and need the competencies listed in the center of Figure 6.2. Shown in the middle manager section at the bottom of the pyramid are three major issues that need to be acted upon by executive management practices using executive competencies. The three issues are central findings of the research and, if they are treated, will help to overcome downsizing's greatest challenges. First, the special needs of middle managers require attention. For example, middle managers have anxiety, mistrust, and career concerns that need to be allayed. Second, workload adjustment needs to be performed to balance human resources with workloads. Third, workforce capabilities need to be maintained and strengthened to ensure the capacity exists to accomplish organizational objectives and the mission. The three problems are firmly grounded in the case study data and are supported by strong, corroborated evidence. Chapter 7 will address relevant executive management practices and competencies for satisfying each of the three requirements.

The final stages after downsizing appear on the far right of Figure 6.1. Organizational outcomes follow the downsizing process. The outcomes are expected to be improved organizational effectiveness, efficiency, productivity, quality, and customer satisfaction. From this, mission accomplishment is expected to occur.

Hypotheses for Executive Management of Downsizing

The final part of this chapter goes one step beyond the theoretical model and proposes seven hypotheses for executive management of downsizing. These hypotheses are specified expectations about empirical reality reached after inductive analysis and theory generation. More specifically, the hypotheses state the expected relationships between variables in Figures 6.1 and 6.2. Each hypothesis is stated in two ways to indicate the different possible expected relations among variables in terms of directional causation. The hypotheses are designed to be testable in subsequent research. Accompanying each hypothesis are brief statements or information from the DLA, BOR, and FDA case studies that support the hypothesis. Of course, more detailed accounts and evidence are contained in the case chapters and the comparative analysis presented earlier in this chapter.

Hypothesis 1.

Change factors in agency external environment and timing, opportunity, and planning for downsizing:

a. The more agencies have fortuitous timing for downsizing, regard downsizing as an opportunity, and have a planned and organized approach to downsizing, the less difficulty and resistance there will be during downsizing.

b. The less agencies have fortuitous timing for downsizing, regard downsizing as an opportunity, and have a planned and organized approach to downsizing, the more difficulty and resistance there will be during downsizing.

Case Studies

DLA—Downsizing already under way has a planned and organized approach and makes further downsizing less difficult.

BOR—Downsizing is regarded as an opportunity to change the agency mission and transform the agency and includes extensive implementation plans that help the agency with downsizing.

FDA—Simultaneous timing for growth and downsizing is accompanied by little planning and organization for downsizing, a situation that causes downsizing difficulties and resistance.

MANAGING DOWNSIZING   185

Hypothesis 2.

Process changes and personnel reduction strategies:

a. The more executives reengineer, redesign, restructure, and streamline agency organizations and work processes before they implement personnel reduction strategies, the less difficulty and resistance there will be during downsizing.

b. The more executives implement personnel reduction strategies before they reengineer, redesign, restructure, and streamline agency organizations and work processes, the more difficulty and resistance there will be during downsizing.

Case Studies

DLA—Much reengineering, restructuring, and streamlining before personnel reductions make downsizing less difficult.

BOR—Reengineering, redesigning, and streamlining are occurring with personnel reductions, and there is difficulty and resistance to downsizing.

FDA—Personnel reductions are taking place prior to redesigning and streamlining and contribute to more difficulty and resistance.

Hypothesis 3.

Executive management practices to achieve middle manager buy-in during downsizing:

a. The more executives use the following management practices during downsizing, the more middle managers will buy in to the downsizing efforts:

b. The less executives use the following management practices during downsizing, the less middle managers will buy in to the downsizing efforts:

1. Coaching, mentoring, encouraging, and lifting morale
4. Communication
5. Delegation of authority and participatory style
8. Less formality and hierarchy
9. Visibility

Case Studies

DLA—See Table 3.10.
BOR—See Table 4.10.
FDA—See Table 5.6.

Hypothesis 4.

Executive competencies for downsizing:

a. The more executives have the following competencies, the more successful downsizing will be:

b. The less executives have the following competencies, the less successful downsizing will be:

Clearly Important with Greatest Case Consensus

1. Analytical
2. Leader and motivator through coaching, mentoring, and lifting morale
3. Commitment, energy, and inner strength
4. Sensitivity and empathy for people
5. Vision
6. Communication

Important with Case Consensus

7. Interpersonal skills
8. Background with functional/technical preparation
9. Team orientation
10. Flexibility
11. Resourcefulness
13. Empower others

Important without Case Consensus

12. Honesty and trustworthiness
14. Patience
15. Sense of humor

Case Studies

DLA—See Table 3.10.
BOR—See Table 4.10.
FDA—See Table 5.6.

Hypothesis 5.

Needs of middle managers during and after downsizing:

a. The more executives satisfy middle manager needs for assistance with change management, new roles, retraining, management systems, and other programs during and after downsizing, the fewer workforce problems there will be and the more downsizing goals will be achieved.

b. The less executives satisfy middle manager needs for assistance with change management, new roles, retraining, management systems, and other programs during and after downsizing, the more workforce problems there will be and the less downsizing goals will be achieved.

Case Studies

DLA—Personnel remaining need better assistance programs and adjustment mechanisms to counter fear and resistance and allow coping with change.

BOR—Agency is beginning to strengthen the focus on the needs of remaining personnel for assistance programs and adjustment mechanisms to deal with negative morale and motivation and intermittent efficiency and productivity shortcomings.

FDA—There are no formal agency-wide assistance programs and adjustment mechanisms to overcome attitudes of denial, disbelief, and confusion and to improve morale and motivation.

Hypothesis 6.

Workload adjustment during and after downsizing:

a. The more executives adjust middle manager workloads by reducing or eliminating workloads and modifying workload distribution during and after downsizing, the fewer workforce problems there will be and the more downsizing goals will be achieved.

b. The less executives adjust middle manager workloads by reducing or eliminating workloads and modifying workload distribution during and after downsizing, the more workforce problems there will be and the less downsizing goals will be achieved.

Case Studies

DLA—Workloads have not been adjusted much, and there are anxiety and low morale in the workforce.

BOR—There has been some elimination of overhead work, functions, positions, units, programs, reviews and approvals, and regulatory oversight that helps transform the agency.

FDA—Workload adjustments have been minor, and there are anxiety, low morale, and low motivation in the workforce.

Hypothesis 7.

Workforce capabilities during and after downsizing:

a. The more skillfully executives manage the internal recruitment, placement, retraining, and performance evaluation of middle managers during and after downsizing, the fewer workforce capability problems there will be and the more downsizing goals will be achieved.

b. The less skillfully executives manage the internal recruitment, placement, retraining, and performance evaluation of middle managers during and after downsizing, the more workforce capability problems there will be and the less downsizing goals will be achieved.

Case Studies

DLA—Executives place high management emphasis on the internal recruitment and placement of middle managers and on monitoring and evaluating their work and performance because there is uncertainty of future workforce capabilities.

BOR—Insufficient attention was given to placement and retraining of middle managers early in the downsizing process, resulting in uncertainty regarding future human resources capabilities.

FDA—Executives are aware of the importance of internal recruitment, placement, and skills balancing of middle managers to ensure a capable future workforce.

Summary

This chapter presents a comparative analysis of downsizing experiences in the Defense Logistics Agency, the Bureau of Reclamation, and the Food and Drug Administration case studies. Comparisons are made of factors and characteristics associated with agency downsizing processes. Next, lessons learned are determined for organizations and downsizing, middle managers and downsizing, executive views of downsizing, executive management practices during downsizing, and executive competencies for downsizing. Furthermore, the comparative analysis identifies "patience" as a new competency for consideration by OPM to include as a new competency in its Leadership Effectiveness Framework. Also, "leader and motivator through coaching, mentoring, and lifting morale" and "commitment, energy, and inner strength" are found to be important competencies that could be added as new dimensions in revised OPM competencies in the future. Most important, a revised theoretical model for executive management of downsizing is presented. The model represents the theory generated about downsizing phenomena, including its primary conceptual variables and the relationships among them. Finally, the theoretical model enables the formulation of seven empirically testable hypotheses.

Note

1. For a groundbreaking study of managerial competencies, see Boyatzis (1982). Also, for an excellent summary of job competence assessment methodology and findings from 286 competency studies, see Spencer and Spencer (1993).

7

Overcoming Downsizing's Greatest Challenges

The final chapter addresses how agencies can overcome downsizing's greatest challenges and manage with excellence in a downsizing environment. The research investigated executive management of downsizing in the Defense Logistics Agency, the Bureau of Reclamation, and the Food and Drug Administration required by the Clinton Administration's National Performance Review to reinvent government. The three case studies produced fresh perspectives and empirical evidence to support a theoretical model of executive management of downsizing. The research aims to be useful for practice and theory. Therefore, the chapter starts by highlighting downsizing's greatest challenges and how to overcome them. Next, fourteen management actions for effectively leading and managing change such as downsizing are summarized. Then, policy implications followed by theoretical implications are discussed. Finally, concluding remarks are made with some suggestions for future research.

Downsizing's Greatest Challenges

Downsizing presents a number of formidable challenges to executives and managers responsible for managing and implementing it. The hypotheses in chapter 6, derived from the DLA, BOR, and FDA case studies, point to the most intractable aspects of downsizing. Downsizing's greatest five challenges are listed in Table 7.1. The primary organizational objectives during downsizing are to minimize difficulties associated with the downsizing process, minimize resistance by employees to downsizing and related change, obtain middle manager buy-in to the downsizing process, achieve the goals of downsizing, and minimize potential workforce problems from downsizing.

Table 7.1

Downsizing's Greatest Challenges

1. Minimize difficulties associated with the downsizing process.
2. Minimize resistance by employees to downsizing and related change.
3. Obtain middle manager buy-in to the downsizing process.
4. Achieve the goals of downsizing.
5. Minimize potential workforce problems from downsizing.

Overcoming the Challenges

Despite the vexing nature of the downsizing challenges, they can be overcome by organizations. The actions required to achieve corresponding expected responses appear in the hypothesis statements in chapter 6. The hypotheses suggest seven steps for overcoming the challenges of downsizing. These appear in Table 7.2. Step 1 is to leverage any advantages that can come from fortuitous timing, any existing opportunities, and planning measures. Step 2 is to implement process changes before personnel reduction strategies as much as possible. This study identified nine executive management practices for step 3 to use to achieve middle manager buy-in. These practices appear in Table 6.6. Furthermore, the research resulted in fifteen competencies for step 4 for executives to lead with during downsizing. These competencies are outlined in Table 6.7. As previously discussed, three critical issues related to middle managers are the needs of middle managers, workloads, and workforce capabilities. Steps 5 through 7 are to satisfy the needs of middle managers, adjust workloads of employees, and ensure workforce capabilities, respectively. Table 7.2 includes specific executive management practices and executive competencies for use in exercising steps 5, 6, and 7 that are central to successfully overcoming downsizing's challenges.

Management Actions for Downsizing

Executives and middle managers perform critical roles in leading and managing downsizing and other change efforts. Downsizing is just one element of widespread organizational change sweeping across the federal government. Government reinvention brings changes in control, procurement, and personnel systems; management structures; organizational size; and the culture of the bureaucracy. Agencies are implementing numerous initiatives aimed at achieving improved performance and lasting change. Chapter 1 discussed the intrinsic roles of executives and middle managers in change affairs including downsizing. In summary, both executives and middle managers are essential. They are strategy, change, and information conduits. They manage different, but equally important, levels of organizational change. They make reinventing government

Table 7.2

Steps to Overcome Downsizing Challenges

1. Take advantage of timing, opportunity, and planning.
2. Implement process changes before personnel reduction strategies.
3. Use executive management practices to achieve middle manager buy-in.
4. Lead with executives who have competencies for downsizing.
5. Satisfy the needs of middle managers with:
   Executive management practices[a]
   1. More coaching, mentoring, encouraging, and lifting morale
   4. More communication
   5. More delegation of authority and participatory style
   8. Less formality and hierarchy
   9. More visibility
   Executive competencies[b]
   2. Leader and motivator through coaching, mentoring, and lifting morale
   3. Commitment, energy, and inner strength
   4. Sensitivity and empathy for people
   6. Communication
   7. Interpersonal skills
   9. Team orientation
   10. Flexibility
   12. Honesty and trustworthiness
   13. Empower others
   14. Patience
6. Adjust workloads of employees with:
   Executive management practices[a]
   2. More monitoring and evaluating work and performance
   3. More effort to accomplish more difficult work
   4. More communication
   Executive competencies[b]
   1. Analytical
   3. Commitment, energy, and inner strength
   4. Sensitivity and empathy for people
   5. Vision
   6. Communication
   8. Background with functional or technical preparation
   10. Flexibility
   11. Resourcefulness
7. Ensure workforce capabilities with:
   Executive management practices[a]
   2. More monitoring and evaluating work and performance
   3. More effort to accomplish more difficult work
   4. More communication
   6. More attention to internal recruitment and placement of personnel
   Executive competencies[b]
   1. Analytical
   3. Commitment, energy, and inner strength
   5. Vision

Table 7.2 *(continued)*

6. Communication
8. Background with functional or technical preparation
9. Team orientation
11. Resourcefulness
13. Empower others

[a]See Table 6.6; [b]See Table 6.7.

Table 7.3

Management Actions for Downsizing

1. Be less directive and controlling.
2. Reduce micromanagement.
3. Rely less on technical expertise and more on human resources management.
4. Increase employee empowerment.
5. Implement teaming.
6. Increase communication.
7. Facilitate, coach, and mentor.
8. Satisfy the needs of employees.
9. Jointly establish organizational vision.
10. Create and maintain a climate of trust.
11. Make workload adjustments.
12. Enhance workforce capabilities for the future.
13. Promote responsible risk taking, and reward innovations and creativity.
14. Develop a culture of cooperation, teamwork, and jointness.

---

work. As a result of the many changes affecting government organizations, the roles of executives and middle managers are changing also (Gore 1994; Ingraham and Jones, forthcoming). New or improved skills are necessary to effectively lead and manage change. Furthermore, actions are required that will increase the probability of agency success. Table 7.3 lists fourteen recommended management actions, derived from DLA, BOR, and FDA experiences with downsizing, for managing complex change. Each management action is explained in greater detail below.

1. *Be less directive and controlling.* Learn to give up power and control. It is essential that executives and middle managers let go of the previous hierarchical ways of doing business. Both levels of managers must shift from being "directors" or "chiefs" to being primarily "team leaders." By reducing methods of directing and controlling, executives and middle managers make it possible for other actions to occur such as empowerment of employees and teaming of employees.

2. *Reduce micromanagement.* Eliminate or reduce detailed oversight of employees and their work. Organizations have fewer people to perform the same amount of or more work. Micromanagement impedes work accomplishment.

3. *Rely less on technical expertise and more on human resources management.* Rely less on technical skills and rely more on human resources management skills. It is important that the right employees get placed in the right positions and have the right workplace environment.

4. *Increase employee empowerment.* Executives and middle managers will find greater organizational success if they increase employee involvement in work systems, decision-making processes, and problem solving. Let employees participate in organizational change processes and implement change.

5. *Implement teaming.* Implement teaming among employees. Teamwork generates higher levels of synergy, energy, and morale among employees. Teams can share resources, integrate the organization, and improve processes.

6. *Increase communication.* Raise the level of communication and share information and knowledge. Voluntarily loosen or abolish traditional managerial prerogatives and create new, nonhierarchical patterns of communication. Communicating vision to employees may be the most important communication item.

7. *Facilitate, coach, and mentor.* Facilitate the needs of empowered employees and workers in teaming arrangements. Coach employees through new experiences and challenging work conditions. Mentor subordinates, and have sensitivity and empathy for workers experiencing high levels of stress.

8. *Satisfy the needs of employees.* Recognize that employees have special needs that require attention. For example, allay the anxiety, apprehension, and career concerns of employees.

9. *Jointly establish organizational vision.* Know where the organization is headed. Executives, middle managers, and employees should work together to establish a clear mission and vision. All will better achieve organizational objectives if they share in the underlying values and goals of the organization.

10. *Create and maintain a climate of trust.* Earn the trust of employees. Then maintain the trust. Communicate confidence in the ability of employees to make greater contributions to the success of the organization. Exercising the previous nine actions will generate a climate of trust.

11. *Make workload adjustments.* Recognize that in many organizations employees experience workload increases that lead to increased anxiety. Make workload adjustments to balance human resources with workloads. Make decisions about what work or functions will be eliminated or reduced. At the very least, communicate to employees what the work priorities are.

12. *Enhance workforce capabilities for the future.* Be concerned about workforce capabilities and outcomes after the change process subsides. Maintain and strengthen workforce capabilities to ensure the capacity exists to accomplish organizational objectives and the mission. Take measures to

prevent excessive loss of experienced personnel, work skills imbalances, lack of resources and flexibility, and gaps in necessary experience. Provide your employees with reorientation training, education, management tools, and new techniques.

13. *Promote responsible risk taking, and reward innovations and creativity.* Let employees know it is acceptable to take risks within bounds. Then reward innovations and creativity.

14. *Develop a culture of cooperation, teamwork, and jointness.* Develop and foster a culture for a high performing organization. Ensure that cooperation, teamwork, and jointness are primary methods of doing business. Implementing many of the previous actions makes this accomplishment possible.

Policy Implications

Soundly conducted research with empirically supported findings should be of value to policy makers and practitioners. Policy makers and practitioners concerned with downsizing should be able to profit from this research. The findings of the study can improve decision making and provide guidance for action related to downsizing in the public sector. Policy implications are discussed in the following paragraphs for agency executives, human resources management specialists, and reinventing government policy makers.

Executives in federal agencies have the responsibility to lead and manage organizational change. Therefore, they are the chief engineers of downsizing, a process that is expected to continue at least until the end of the 1990s. The experiences of the three agencies in this study offer practical lessons learned for executives in federal agencies. The cross-case patterns identified in chapter 6 are valuable sources of knowledge for executives. For example, the lessons learned dealing with preparation for downsizing, personnel reduction strategies for downsizing, and downsizing process changes and reorientations tell what is common about downsizing in agencies. Also, lessons learned for middle managers and downsizing let executives benefit from eleven specific findings about middle managers, who are critical links in ensuring that downsizing succeeds. Another opportunity comes from knowing what views their executive peers hold about downsizing. Similarly, the executive management practices derived from the data analyses can be assets to executives managing downsizing. What works for some executives might work for others also. At the very least, practices identified in Table 6.6 might stimulate executives to think of variations of the listed practices and then to try them. For example, an executive might decide, because of "more delegation of authority and participatory style" and "less formality and hierarchy," that he should trust his managers more and reduce the amount of work subject to executive review. In addition, the executive competencies for downsizing that emerged from the study can assist executives. Because the competencies are those specifically identified as applicable to downsizing management situations, they should be appreciated by executives facing downsizing. As an example, an executive who takes note that "sensitivity and empathy for people" is one of the top competencies, and who is aware that she tends to be task oriented, might be guided to alter her approach during the downsizing process.

Human resources management specialists in agencies and at OPM will find important material in the study worthy of their attention. For specialists concerned with workplace issues such as morale and motivation, workload stress, employee relationships on teams, promotion systems, and many other related matters, the study should be of interest. From the findings and discussion of lessons learned, management practices, and management competencies, numerous topics can be gleaned for further investigation. In this way, human resources specialists can follow up on those issues of most importance to them. The following are just some of the many possible topics: types of communication during downsizing, techniques for empowering others, dealing with resistance to downsizing, managing with less control and more encouragement, and managing workplace environments with skills imbalances.

Policy makers at the executive branch level can gain from the study's findings. For any administration considering downsizing, policy makers ought to be careful architects of downsizing initiatives. There are three principal points that policy makers should be aware of. First, the across-the-board requirement for all agencies to downsize is not without flaws. Certainly every agency can get by with fewer employees somewhere in the agency. And while equitable distribution of personnel cuts may seem sensible in the name of fairness or consistency, it is not wise from the standpoint of program administration and execution. Some agencies, like BOR in this study, may need to downsize because their new missions require fewer personnel. Other agencies, such as FDA in this study, actually require more people to accomplish a complex mission. Second, requiring agencies to downsize without authorizing them to modify, reduce, or eliminate certain functions, programs, and services makes downsizing counterproductive. Fewer employees with the same amount of work places enormous strains on agencies. Although those conditions help force greater efficiencies in agencies, there are limits. In the long run, costs may increase due to workforce recruitment and retention problems, program mismanagement, and contracting out for work accomplishment (Hornestay 1996). Third, policy makers should be cognizant that downsizing has the potential to negatively affect the capabilities of workforces (Goldenkoff 1997). If necessary workforce skills are lost during downsizing and agencies are limited in rehiring, then capabilities to accomplish the mission suffer. For the above reasons, therefore, downsizing policies should be made judiciously to preserve effective program administration and protect the public interest.

Theoretical Implications

This study has theoretical implications also. The following discussion compares the concepts and theory developed in the study with some of the existing literature on downsizing, cutback and retrenchment, reinventing government, and leadership and management. Literature with similar findings as well as literature that conflicts with the study's theory are included.

Downsizing Literature

On the organizational level of analysis, the findings of the study are consistent with several other studies of downsizing. One of the major findings of the Cameron, Freeman, and Mishra (1993) study, one of the most extensive and systematic studies of downsizing, is supported. They identify three types of downsizing in their study: "workforce reduction," "organization redesign," and "systemic" (or cultural). Correspondingly, this study develops downsizing process categories that are "personnel reduction strategies," "process changes," and organizational "reorientations." The two sets of categories are analogous. Similar to the private sector firms in their study, the public sector agencies in this study used strategies from all three categories and differed in the extent to which they used them. Another similar finding was that more work required of remaining employees is related to some of the negative attributes associated with organizational decline. The overlapping dysfunctional attributes found in both studies were decreasing morale, resistance to change and downsizing, and loss of trust by employees.

In another comparison, a recent study by the U.S. General Accounting Office on workforce reduction strategies in seventeen private companies, five states, and three foreign governments has a number of common findings with this study (U.S. General Accounting Office 1995). Furthermore, the GAO's analysis is highly consistent with conceptual variables of the theoretical model constructed for this study. First, the importance of strategic and workforce planning in downsizing decision making was identified as an essential activity. Primary steps in planning consisted of eliminating work and redesigning work processes. Moreover, lack of planning was linked with downsizing difficulties. Second, multiple strategies for reducing workforce sizes were used. Also, involuntary separation programs or RIFs were used as a final strategy. Third, employees' personal concerns were emphasized in human resource management considerations. Vital parts of this variable included importance placed on communication, employee assistance, and employee training. Finally, a key lesson learned was the necessity for organizations to examine their functions and make structural and process changes prior to downsizing. It is noteworthy that the results of this study and the GAO study strongly agree with each other.

It is interesting to compare the study's results with the National Academy of Public Administration's (1995) compendium on effective downsizing for government agencies. The downsizing compendium was developed as part of NAPA's project to implement change in human resources management. In general, the findings and lessons learned from the study are consistent with many of the downsizing guidelines, best practices used successfully by organizations, and lessons learned contained in the compendium.

On the individual level of analysis, this study's findings are consistent with findings from some studies and contradictory to others. For example, the following dysfunctional consequences of downsizing were found in prior studies (Brockner 1988; Cascio 1993; Noer 1993; Wyatt 1993) and in this study: reduced morale, motivation, trust of management, and productivity under some circumstances, and increased stress and challenges for managers. However, reduced commitment and loyalty to agencies and their missions did not occur, although some studies found them for other organizations (Brockner and Wiesenfeld 1993; Wyatt 1993).

A comparison with Noer's (1993, 89–91) study of layoff survivor sickness reveals similar and conflicting findings. Noer identified sets of "feeling clusters" and coping strategies of remaining employees after downsizing. Evidence of some of them was found in the case studies. For example, Noer's "fear, insecurity, and uncertainty," "frustration, resentment, and anger," and "unfairness, betrayal, and distrust" feeling clusters were indicated in the three agencies to varying degrees. However, "sadness, depression, and guilt" were not evident. Additionally, in general, coping methods such as reduced risk taking, lowered productivity, and survivor blaming were found to exist only at moderate levels. There are three likely explanations for why the case studies may not show some of the Noer feeling clusters or coping strategies or why they may not exist at the same level of intensity. First, this study did not interview extensive numbers of middle managers, or any lower-level employees, to obtain their perceptions about these issues. Second, the investigation inquired about these issues at the middle manager and executive levels and not for the entire workforce.

Third, downsizing implementation was in its early stages in BOR and FDA. Some of Noer's (1993, 197–208) suggestions for new skill development for leadership competencies are consistent with this study. Comparable competencies are as follows, with this study's competencies in parentheses: "transition facilitation" ("analytical"), "visioning" ("vision"), "value congruence" ("honesty and trustworthiness"), "empowerment" ("empower others"), "process wisdom" ("analytical" and "flexibility"), and "interpersonal competence" ("interpersonal skills"). Noer also lists "self-understanding," for which this study had no counterpart, although one executive interviewed did mention this as a competency.

In a review of the scholarly literature on downsizing and organizational effectiveness, Druckman, Singer, and Van Cott (1997, 52–57) find discouraging results. They summarize with the statement that "many more negative than positive associations have been reported between downsizing and organizational effectiveness" (Druckman, Singer, and Van Cott 1997, 55). Although the study conducted with DLA, BOR, and FDA did not investigate organizational effectiveness after downsizing completion, there is substantial evidence that negative factors exist *during* downsizing. Furthermore, this study does agree with Druckman, Singer, and Van Cott that the manner in which downsizing is implemented significantly affects the outcomes of downsizing.

Finally, this study's theoretical model compares favorably with the downsizing conceptual framework of Kozlowski, Chao, Smith, and Hedlund (1993). They integrate three theoretically based themes that are the foundation for their framework. A common feature of this study's model and their framework is the emphasis on downsizing as a process with explicit consideration of its temporal nature.

Cutback and Retrenchment Literature

In comparing this study with the cutback and retrenchment literature, some differences exist. First, the earlier cutback and retrenchment literature tends not to be empirically based and is highly prescriptive with lessons learned from experience. Also, much of it considers political dimensions. In addition, some of it is in reference to state and local levels of government. Finally, much of it is atheoretical.

Some interesting results are discovered upon comparing this study's findings with the sixteen findings extracted from the Rubin (1985) study of cutbacks in five federal agencies (see Table 1.1). This study agrees with six of her findings (numbers 1, 4, 6, 9, 12, and 15) related to lowered employee morale and motivation and increased uncertainty and difficulties. Also, this study disagrees with four of her findings (numbers 3, 7, 13, and 14) primarily because downsizing is accompanied by more employee involvement than were cutbacks and because there were some differences in implementation policies. Downsizing has not progressed enough to determine if four of her findings (numbers 2, 5, 8, and 16) are true for downsizing. Finally, this study did not examine two areas to compare with her findings (numbers 10 and 11).

One source with some of the few studies on organizational aspects of cutting back is the Hirschhorn and Associates (1983) collection of case studies on retrenchment in human and community service organizations. They state that virtually no research addresses the problems and issues of retrenchment management from an organizational perspective. One of their case studies argues that the psychosocial dynamics of retrenchment can vary according to whether or not an organization undergoing retrenchment is overstaffed. They find that organizations cutting back do not react strongly to retrenchment actions when they are overstaffed. Similarly, this study finds that, to some degree, the level of resistance to downsizing is affected by the perception that employees have regarding the staffing level of the agency. For example, in DLA and BOR, there is a recognition that there are too many employees for their changing organizations. Thus, although some resistance exists, employees recognize personnel reductions are inevitable. For FDA, however, employees feel the agency is not overstaffed, do not believe downsizing should occur, and display stronger resistance to it. Another case study of retrenchment shows that retrenchment often exposes hidden weaknesses in management and organizational design that must be corrected before the organization moves ahead. Similarly, this study finds that agencies change some of their processes as part of downsizing with the intent of improving efficiencies.

Additionally, Levine, Rubin, and Wolohojian (1982) assert that retrenchment forces public organizations to conduct excessive oversight that stifles initiative, encourages errors, and in the long term makes them less effective and capable. To the contrary, evidence in this study indicates that downsized public organizations encourage risk taking, initiative, participation, and employee empowerment to make them more effective and capable. More research is necessary, though, to confirm whether agencies do become more effective and capable.

Finally, most of the literature on President Ronald Reagan's approach to the executive branch addresses issues associated with the responsiveness of civil servants to presidential leadership. Little of this literature addresses the management of cutbacks and the effects of cutbacks in agencies.

patterns in this study correspond with Kettl's (1994, 1995) appraisal of the National Performance Review. First, downsizing has some problems: (1) downsizing may shrink government in the wrong places since downsizing goals were not derived from careful analysis and this lack of analysis may affect capacity to perform; (2) the wrong employees may leave, causing skills imbalances; and (3) remaining employees have more work. Second, the NPR does not define what the government should do prior to downsizing. In this study, FDA's mission remains unchanged, its work is more complex, and it still is being asked to downsize. Third, middle managers must be a part of the change process. And fourth, capacity of federal government agencies to perform effectively is an underlying issue that needs to be addressed. Furthermore, the study supports the seven characteristics for the new job of the federal executive in a reinvented federal government (Gore 1994). The characteristics are developing a clear vision, creating a team environment, empowering employees, putting customers first (satisfying citizens), communicating with employees, cutting red tape (improving efficiency), and creating clear accountability (concentrating on performance and measuring results).

Leadership and Management Literature

This study's findings compare favorably with findings in the executive leadership and management literature. First, there is strong consistency between Mintzberg's (1973) manager roles and this study's findings. Seven of nine executive management practices during downsizing and eight of fifteen executive competencies for downsizing correspond with six of the ten Mintzberg manager roles.

Second, this study's findings correspond strongly with the Competing Values Model of leadership competency (Quinn and Rohrbaugh 1983; Quinn 1988; Quinn, Faerman, Thompson, and McGrath 1990). Ten of the fifteen executive competencies in this study correspond with all twenty-four competencies in the eight managerial/leadership roles in the competing values framework.

Third, the Burke-Litwin model of organizational performance and change is valuable for showing the interrelationships of organizational variables that affect change (Burke and Litwin 1992). This study provides support for the model's validity. At the executive level in federal agencies, political appointees represent "leadership" in the model and career SES executives represent "management practices" in the model. The BOR case study is the best example in this study of phenomena explained by the Burke-Litwin model.

executives represent "management practices" in the model. The BOR case study is the best example in this study of phenomena explained by the Burke-Litwin model.

Fourth, Nutt and Backoff (1993) suggest thirty propositions for key issues related to the theory and process of strategic management and leadership for transforming public organizations. This downsizing research supports some of the propositions. For example, proposition number 17 states, "The prospect of a successful transformation is influenced by the leadership practices of a strategic leader." The study finds that executives use specific management practices and competencies for downsizing. However, a study of organizational performance after downsizing would more completely determine which propositions were supported and to what extent.

Conclusion

The study of downsizing in DLA, BOR, and FDA makes important contributions in four key ways. The contributions relate to weaknesses in the literature, public sector downsizing, executives and downsizing, and a theoretical model of downsizing.

1. *Responds to weaknesses in the literature.* The study addresses four weaknesses in the literature. First, the study provides an analysis of public organizations, public management, and the influences of their institutional environments for organization theory literature (Rainey 1997). Second, it is an empirical study of the internal structure, behavior, and management in the bureaucracy for public bureaucracy literature (Rainey 1997). Third, because few empirical studies and little theory exist on downsizing, it produces an empirical study with a theoretical model of downsizing (Cameron, Freeman, and Mishra 1991, 1993; Freeman and Cameron 1993; Kozlowski, Chao, Smith, and Hedlund 1993; Druckman, Singer, and Van Cott 1997). Fourth, it offers an empirical investigation, rather than a normatively based discourse, of a government reinvention activity (Overman and Boyd 1994).

2. *Addresses public sector downsizing.* The study contributes a comparative case study analysis of the organizational change process internal to public sector organizations. More specifically, it contributes to a deeper understanding of downsizing change processes in federal government agencies. It heightens insight into the interrelationships among external environmental factors, process changes, personnel reduction strategies, reorientations, executives, and middle managers.

3. *Studies the role of executives in downsizing.* Greater knowledge of the role of executives in downsizing is acquired from the study. In particular, the study presents findings and lessons learned on executive views of down-

sizing (Table 6.5), executive management practices during downsizing (Table 6.6), and executive competencies for downsizing (Table 6.7). Furthermore, it proposes a new competency and two competency dimensions for OPM's SES Leadership Effectiveness Framework.

4. *Generates a theoretical model.* A major result of the study is a theoretical model for executive management of downsizing (Figures 6.1 and 6.2). The theoretical model illuminates conceptual variables and relationships among them and expands the explanation of downsizing phenomena. Accompanying the model are seven hypotheses for executive management of downsizing (see chapter 6).

Congressional legislation requires that the federal government continue to reduce its workforce through fiscal year 1999. The mandated reduction of full-time-equivalent positions by 12 percent means almost every agency will have to implement downsizing at some level during some time in this decade. Furthermore, since many of the cuts will consist of supervisory and management control positions, organizational challenges are exacerbated for agencies. Many states and local governments are also undergoing downsizing. For these reasons, scholars should continue to conduct research on downsizing in the public sector. As in this study, increased focus on managerial and organizational aspects will help overcome shortcomings in the literature. The following are areas where more research would extend the work accomplished in this study and further advance our knowledge of downsizing. It is suggested that future studies be concentrated here.

1. *Study middle managers.* More research needs to be conducted on middle manager experiences with downsizing. Because middle managers are in the middle of their careers or beyond, important links in agency operations, and key targets of downsizing, they are particularly affected by downsizing. How do middle managers cope during downsizing? How do they adjust in postdownsized organizations? How have their roles and jobs changed after downsizing? What are the new career patterns for them? How do they manage their organizations toward successful mission accomplishment?

2. *Examine workforce issues.* More investigation should be made into workforce issues in downsized organizations. What are the new working conditions for employees? How are teams managed, and how are they performing? What changes in workloads occurred, and what processes were used to make the changes? What is the capability of the workforce to execute programs and accomplish agency missions?

3. *Concentrate on organizational performance.* Many of the most interesting and critical issues surrounding downsizing concern organizational performance. It is important that studies examine the effects of downsizing on organizational performance. Answers to key questions can help agencies

adjust their downsizing programs to improve organizational performance. How do factors related to the public sector environment, such as congressional oversight, public scrutiny, budget limitations, and personnel laws, make downsizing difficult to implement? What and how do organizational changes in conjunction with downsizing enhance or inhibit positive organizational effectiveness? How effectively are programs being administered? What efficiencies have been achieved because of downsizing? How have costs decreased or increased as a result of downsizing? How has organizational productivity changed since downsizing was initiated? What are the ways that mission accomplishment is inhibited or enhanced?

4. *Investigate successful and failed downsizing.* Another recommended avenue for research is to conduct studies of agencies judged to have "succeeded" or "failed" with downsizing implementation. The research in this area should investigate the variables associated with successful and failed downsizing. How is successful and failed downsizing determined? What are the relationships among reengineering, redesigning, restructuring, streamlining, personnel reduction strategies, organizational reorientations, and success or failure with downsizing? What executive management practices are related to successful and failed downsizing efforts?

Downsizing and other reinventing government initiatives are opportunities to bring needed change to the federal government. Unfortunately, the change is difficult and painful. Career civil servants face tremendous challenges associated with high levels of organizational change now under way. According to the theory generated in this study, if executive management of downsizing takes care of middle manager needs, adjusts workloads, and strengthens workforce capabilities, then employees will take care of mission accomplishment. The federal career Senior Executive Service leaders and managers in this study remain optimistic that the federal workforce will respond to meet the challenges.

Appendix A

Definitions of Competencies in the Office of Personnel Management Leadership Effectiveness Framework (LEF)

1. Conflict Management—Anticipates and seeks to resolve confrontations, disagreements, and complaints in a constructive manner.

2. Creative Thinking—Develops insights and solutions; fosters innovation among others.

3. Customer Orientation—Actively seeks customer input; ensures customer needs are met; continuously seeks to improve the quality of services, products, and processes.

4. Decisiveness—Takes action and risks when needed; makes difficult decisions when necessary.

5. External Awareness—Stays informed on laws, policies, politics, Administration priorities, trends, special interests, and other issues; considers external impact of statements or actions; uses information in decision making.

6. Financial Management—Prepares and justifies budget; monitors expenses; manages procurement and contracting.

7. Flexibility—Adapts to change in the work environment; effectively copes with stress.

8. Human Resources Management—Ensures effective recruitment, selection, training, performance appraisal, recognition, and corrective/disciplinary action; promotes affirmative employment, good labor relations, and employee well-being.

9. Influencing/Negotiating—Networks with, and provides information to, key groups and individuals; appropriately uses negotiation, persuasion, and authority in dealing with others to achieve goals.

10. Interpersonal Skills—Considers and responds appropriately to the needs, feelings, capabilities and interests of others; provides feedback; treats others equitably.

11. Leadership—Demonstrates and encourages high standards of behavior; adapts leadership style to situations and people; empowers, motivates, and guides others.

12. Management Controls/Integrity—Ensures the integrity of the organization's processes; promotes ethical and effective practices.

13. Managing Diverse Workforce—Recognizes the value of cultural, ethnic, gender, and other individual differences; provides employment and development opportunities for a diverse workforce.

14. Oral Communication—Listens to others; makes clear and effective oral presentations to individuals and groups.

15. Planning and Evaluating—Establishes policies, guidelines, plans, and priorities; identifies required resources; plans and coordinates with others; monitors progress and evaluates outcomes; improves organizational efficiency and effectiveness.

16. Problem Solving—Recognizes and defines problems; analyzes relevant information; encourages alternative solutions and plans to solve problems.

17. Self-Direction—Realistically assesses own strengths, weaknesses, and impact on others; seeks feedback from others; works persistently toward a goal; demonstrates self-confidence; invests in self-development; manages own time effectively.

18. Team Building—Fosters cooperation, communication, and consensus among groups.

19. Technical Competence—Demonstrates technical proficiency and an understanding of its impact in areas of responsibility.

20. Technology Management—Encourages staff to stay informed about new technology; applies new technologies to organizational needs; ensures staff are trained and capable.

21. Vision—Creates a shared vision of the organization; promotes wide ownership; champions organizational change.

22. Written Communication—Communicates effectively in writing; reviews and critiques others' writing.

Source: Guide to SES Qualifications, U.S. Office of Personnel Management, Office of Executive Resources, Human Resources Development Group, SES-94-01 (Washington, DC: U.S. Office of Personnel Management, August 1994), 20–21.

Appendix B

Definitions of Senior Executive Service (SES) Executive Core Qualifications (ECQ)

1. Strategic Vision—The ability to ensure that key national and organizational goals, priorities, values, and other issues are considered in making program decisions and exercising leadership to implement and to ensure that the organization's mission and strategic vision are reflected in the management of its people.

2. Human Resources Management—The ability to design human resource strategies to meet the organization's mission, strategic vision, and goals and to achieve maximum potential of all employees in a fair and equitable manner.

3. Program Development and Evaluation—The ability to establish program/policy goals and the structure and processes necessary to implement the organization's mission and strategic vision. Inherent in this process is ensuring that programs and policies are being implemented and adjusted as necessary, that the appropriate results are being achieved, and that a process for continually examining the quality of program activities is in place.

4. Resource Planning and Management—The ability to acquire and administer financial, material, and information resources. It also involves the ability to accomplish the organization's mission, support program policy objectives, and promote strategic vision.

5. Organizational Representation and Liaison—The ability to explain, advocate, and negotiate with individuals and groups internally and externally. It also involves the ability to develop an expansive professional network with other organizations and organizational units.

Source: Guide to SES Qualifications, U.S. Office of Personnel Management, Office of Executive Resources, Human Resources Development Group, SES-94-01 (Washington, DC: U.S. Office of Personnel Management, August 1994), 4.

Appendix C

Executive Interview Protocol

INTERVIEW GROUND RULES

1. Interview at least 30 percent of the SES executives in the agency (less in FDA).

2. Interview only career SES executives.

3. Tape-record the interviews if the executive grants permission.

4. Some SES executives should be from headquarters and some from field locations.

5. SES executives should be from organizational units experiencing downsizing, not growth.

6. Interview SES executives in a neutral environment away from job requirements (if possible) to obtain full participation.

7. Each interview should last between one and two hours.

8. SES executives should have experienced some management activities, situations, incidents, and other involvements with downsizing actions, matters, and issues.

9. Statements from executives will not be attributed to executives by name when confidentiality is preferred.

10. Interview methodology:

Part I.

Interviews will use Critical Incident/Behavior Interview methodology. The following briefly overviews the expectations of the executives regarding *downsizing* incidents/situations:

a. Focus on "high points" and "low points" from past incidents.

b. Recall and express in detail what he/she did and said in critical situations.

c. Recall and express what he/she was thinking about and feeling during the situation itself.

210

d. Talk and talk and talk (the interviewer will probe and ask short follow-up questions to stimulate more detail from the executive).

e. Cover approximately three situations (two high and one low).

f. What the interviewer will want to know about each situation:

(1) the background of the situation (personnel involved, etc.)

(2) the time line for the situation

(3) the person's thoughts

(4) the person's feelings

(5) the person's behavior

(6) dialogue between the person and others

(7) the outcome of the situation

(8) details

Part II.

Interviews will follow a semistructured question format.

a. The interviewer will ask a predetermined set of twenty questions pertaining to downsizing events and management during downsizing.

b. The predetermined questions will be the same for all executives.

c. The researcher will use probes that are not predefined to induce further information.

Part III.

The one-page form requests demographic and employment-related background information. The executive should complete the form before the interview and give it to the researcher at the interview. If the executive does not complete it before the interview, he/she may complete it after the interview and mail it.

INTERVIEW PACKET

Downsizing the Federal Government
Case Studies of Senior Executive Service (SES) Management in the Defense Logistics Agency, the Bureau of Reclamation, and the Food and Drug Administration

Interview Number: _____

Name of Interviewee: _____

Agency: _____

Location: _____

Organization Chart: _____

Date: _____

Start Time: _____

Finish Time: _____

Notes:

_____
_____
_____
_____
_____
_____
_____
_____
_____
_____

Components of the Interview

A. Introduction
(5 minutes)
- Brief the person about the interview.
- Establish a comfortable atmosphere.

B. Part I - Job Background Information
(5 minutes)
- Get overview of person's major duties and responsibilities.

C. Part I - Critical Incidents
(36 minutes)
- Find out what person did to achieve specific accomplishments and deal with difficulties.
- Incident 1: High Point
- Incident 2: Low Point
- Incident 3: High Point

D. Part I - Key Characteristics and Capabilities
(5 minutes)
- Get examples of those required to perform job and manage during downsizing.

E. Part II - Questions
(40 minutes)
- Get answers to 20 questions on downsizing.
- Priority questions: 2, 3, 4, 6, 8, 12, 16, 17, 18, 19

F. Part III - Executive Background Information Questionnaire
(0 minutes)
- Receive form from person.

A. Introduction
(5 minutes)
1. Choose a comfortable seating arrangement for taping and writing.

2. Establish a comfortable, relaxed tone. Start with small talk.

I'll begin by first asking if you received my letter introducing my research and the format of the interview? _____

Before we start, do you have any questions or concerns?

_____

_____

_____

_____

As background, I want to explain the contact I've already had with the Bureau of Reclamation. On June 2 and July 18, I met with _____, Director, Policy and External Affairs, to explain my research and to seek permission for Reclamation to be one of my case studies. He granted me permission. Since then, I have met with _____ on August 26 to obtain specific information about Reclamation's downsizing programs. Additionally, I've been in touch with the Public Affairs Office.

3. Open by explaining purpose:

The purpose of this interview is to get a picture of what is involved in being an executive managing in an organization experiencing downsizing. Since you are currently in this position, you are the best person to tell me about the details on a day-to-day basis. In the time we have together I would like to cover as many of your experiences in this role as possible. Most of our time will involve your recalling specific situations in your work during the last year, or recently, that relate to downsizing.

4. Briefly outline interview:

Job Background Information (5 minutes)
3 Critical Incidents (36 minutes)
Key Characteristics/Capabilities (5 minutes)
Twenty Specific Questions (40 minutes)

5. Ask for permission to record the interview:

With your permission, I would like to tape-record our interview to get a complete record of what you say, since the notes I take will not be as complete as I will need. No one in your agency will hear anything that you tell me. Only I will have access to the data. Research results will report what you and other people have said primarily in summary form. No responses will be attributed to you by name.

(If the person is concerned, let him/her know that the tape recorder can be turned off at any time if sensitive issues are discussed.)

Person's stipulations:

_____
_____
_____
_____
_____
_____

B. Part I - Job Background Information
(5 minutes)

1. Start with the following:

I would like to begin by asking you about your job to help me understand more about you and your present position. The main questions are about your superior, whom you supervise, and what your primary duties and responsibilities are.

2. Review the person's present job with questions designed to tell me about the *activities* currently involved in:

- What is your full job title?

_____

- Who is your superior? What is his/her title?

_____

- Whom do you supervise?

_____
_____

- What are they responsible for doing?

_____
_____

• What are the major duties and responsibilities in
your present position?

_____

_____

3. Ask the person for details about the above: activities and examples of activities.

_____

_____

_____

_____

_____

_____

4. If the person held another job:

If you held another position until recently, please answer the same questions for that position.

_____

_____

_____

_____

_____

5. Watch the time and do not get too far behind with this section!

6. Transition to the Critical Incidents section of the interview:

That gives me a good overview of the sorts of activities you do in your job. With that background, I would like to move into the next part of the interview, dealing in more depth with some of the specific incidents or situations you have been involved in regarding downsizing.

C. Part I - Critical Incidents
(36 minutes)

1. I now have a good introduction to what you have been doing in your present position. Now, in this next part of the interview, let's shift to talking about some specific incidents or situations in detail that pertain in any way to downsizing. For each situation, what I want you to do is to tell me what happened in as much detail as possible. Tell me the story—how you got involved, what you were trying to

accomplish and what you did, what you said, and what you thought about at each step along the way—almost as if I had followed you around with a videotape recorder, but was also able to know what you were thinking.

2. *Incident 1: High Point.*

Tell me about a time or incident that was a real "high point" for you: a time when you were able to accomplish something you felt really good about, or a time when you felt especially pleased with something you did. First, give me a brief overview of the situation so that I know what you're going to be telling me about, and then we'll go back for the details.

3. Let the person think and begin to tell about it.

4. Follow-up questions to get the incident in general:

- What about that situation was the real "high point" for you?
- Can you tell me exactly what in the situation was the "high point" for you?
- Could you tell me a bit more about the situation?

5. Get the full story + person's involvement + probe for details:

That sounds like a good situation. What I'd like to do is go back and get the whole story as it happened. So, would you please go back to the beginning of the story, where you first got involved, and tell me how it started.

- What the background is?
- What led up to the situation?
- What the time frame was?
- What the person actually did?
- What the person actually said?
- What the person's thoughts were?
- What the person's feelings were?
- How the situation turned out; results; outcome?

_____

_____

_____

_____

6. Good. That was exactly the kind of detail I needed to understand the part you played in that situation.

OR

Good. That was a good first situation. Now, for the next situation, I would like you to choose something where you can describe more of the details, perhaps something that happened recently where you can tell me more of what happened.

7. *Incident 2: Low Point.*

In this second incident, I would like you to talk about a situation that was a "low point" for you. Remember, any situation related to downsizing is what we need: a time when you were not able to accomplish what you wanted, you were displeased with something you accomplished, you were blocked in your attempts to accomplish something, or you felt frustrated.

8. Follow-up questions to get the incident in general:

- What about that situation was the real "low point" for you?
- Can you tell me exactly what in the situation was the "low point" for you?
- Could you tell me a bit more about the situation?

9. Get the full story + person's involvement + probe for details:

- What the background is?
- What led up to the situation?
- What the time frame was?
- What the person actually did?
- What the person actually said?
- What the person's thoughts were?
- What the person's feelings were?
- How the situation turned out; results; outcome?

_____

_____

_____

10. *Incident 3: High Point.*

Now, for our last situation, I would like you to tell me about another situation that was a "high point" for you. You can use this last situation to round out the picture of the downsizing things you have been involved in and what you have done. Again, think about an incident or situation when you were able to accomplish something that you were especially pleased with.

11. Follow-up questions to get the incident in general:

- What about that situation was the real "high point" for you?

- Can you tell me exactly what in the situation was the "high point" for you?
- Could you tell me a bit more about the situation?

12. Get the full story + person's involvement + probe for details:

- What the background is?
- What led up to the situation?
- What the time frame was?
- What the person actually did?
- What the person actually said?
- What the person's thoughts were?
- What the person's feelings were?
- How the situation turned out; results; outcome?

_____

_____

_____

D. Part I - Key Characteristics and Capabilities
(5 minutes)

1. In this final section of Part I, the person's expert knowledge will be emphasized by asking for a description of "what it takes to do this job." In addition, by asking for a list of characteristics and capabilities, the interviewer will be able to ask for examples of any particular capabilities that are included as being important, but were not in evidence in any of the situations provided.

We've covered a lot of ground in the time up to this point in the interview. Right now, I would like you to think about what qualities, characteristics, or capabilities you would look for if you were going to select someone to fill your job. In particular, what are the qualities, characteristics, and capabilities needed to perform those aspects of your position related to downsizing?

2. List of capabilities:

(1)_____

(2)_____

(3)_____

(4)_____

(5)_____

(6)_____

(7)_____

(8)_____

(9)_____

(10)_____

E. Part II - Questions
(40 minutes)

1. We've obtained some very good incidents and a very useful list of capabilities from Part I of the interview. Thank you for recalling those situations and giving me your insights. The second half of the interview is Part II, in which I will ask you specific questions regarding downsizing in your agency. For each question, please indicate whether your answers are in reference to the unit you head or to your agency.

2. Ask the twenty questions with follow-up questions as necessary.

3. If time runs low, ask the priority questions, which are: 2, 3, 4, 6, 8, 12, 16, 17, 18, 19

Interview Questions

1. How do you view downsizing in your agency?

2. What are the general reactions by middle managers (GS 13–15) and SES executives to downsizing in your agency?

3. What have been the impacts of downsizing on middle managers in your agency?

4. What are the concerns of middle managers regarding downsizing in your agency?

5. What are the general reactions by employees below the management levels to downsizing in your agency?

6. How well prepared for downsizing is your agency?

7. How did your agency go about initiating and implementing downsizing?

8. What are the general downsizing strategies being used by your agency?

9. How are those who are leaving your agency treated in the downsizing process?

10. How is attention being paid to employees who remain with your agency?

11. How are any of the following activities occurring as part of the downsizing process in your agency?
   a. reduction or elimination of workloads or functions
   b. elimination of positions or groups of positions
   c. elimination of management layers
   d. elimination of organizational units
   e. implementation of cost-containment strategies

12. How is downsizing affecting any of the following in your agency?
   a. morale
   b. motivation
   c. commitment
   d. loyalty
   e. risk taking
   f. quality of work
   g. productivity

13. Please describe any instances of resistance to change associated with or caused by downsizing in your agency.

14. Please describe any instances of using downsizing to bring about other change in your agency.

15. What are the expected benefits of downsizing, and are they being achieved in your agency.

16. How are you managing during downsizing in your agency.

17. What new management challenges have emerged for you as a result of downsizing in your agency.

18. What new management styles, tactics, and strategies are you using for managing during downsizing in your agency.

19. What managerial competencies and skills do you believe are important for SES executives to exercise in managing during downsizing.

20. What else would you like to tell me about the downsizing process or managing during downsizing in your agency.

F. Part III - Executive Background Information Questionnaire
(0 minutes)

1. If you have had a chance to complete the questionnaire I sent you regarding your background, you can give that to me at this time.

2. Give the person a self-addressed envelope to mail it to me if he/she did not complete it and does not have time to complete it at the interview.

Closing Remarks

We have now completed the interview. I greatly appreciate the time you spent with me today. The information you have shared with me has been very valuable. Your participation has been very important to my research on downsizing in the federal government. Without the willingness of you and your SES colleagues in the Bureau of Reclamation and the other agencies to share your experiences, this research would not be possible. Thank you very much.

Do you have any questions for me about the research?

Part III - Executive Background Information Form
(Please complete this part before the interview)

This part requests demographic and employment-related information. The answers you provide will be used to describe the sample of executives interviewed. No data will be reported for specific individuals. Your responses to these background items will allow the researcher to analyze the interviews more effectively.

1. Name: _____

2. Age: _____

3. What is your current position's occupational series number? _____

4. For how many years have you been a member of the Senior Executive Service? _____

5. For how many years have you worked for your present agency? _____

6. For how many years have you been in your present position? _____

7. If your agency reorganized in the past one–two years, how many years were you in your previous position? _____

8. For how many departments or independent agencies have you worked during your federal career? _____

9. How many total years of federal service do you have (excluding military service)? _____

10. How many total years of federal supervisory/managerial job experience do you have (excluding military service)? _____

11. How many total years of nonfederal supervisory/managerial job experience do you have? _____

12. How many total years of work experience do you have in the private sector? _____

13. How many employees are in the organizational unit that you head? _____

14. How many first-line or higher-level supervisors report to you directly? _____

15. What is your present pay level? (Indicate 1 through 6) _____

16. What is your highest level of education? (Indicate degree earned and/or extent of education) _____

17. What is the field of concentration for your highest degree or highest educational level? _____

Thank you for your participation!

Appendix D

Critical Incident and Behavior Interview Steps and Techniques

The Approach

1. Begins with a competency model that serves as a framework for designing the interview.
2. Is a systematic procedure that is applied consistently across interviewees.
3. Is an efficient method for gathering information.
4. The interviewer suspends making judgments until the interview is over.
5. The information gathered is highly detailed and specific.

Steps

1. Define the situation.
2. Establish the time line for the situation.
3. Get the full story of what happened:
   a. Background to the situation
   b. Person's thoughts
   c. Person's feelings
   d. Person's behavior
   e. Dialogue
   f. Outcome of the situation
4. Keep the person moving through the story.
5. Get sufficient information from each situation.

Techniques

1. Get an overview and a clear identification of the high or low point.
2. Follow the story from start to finish.

3. Keep the probing questions short, direct, in past tense, and focused on the person's behavior in the situation.

4. Choose depth over range.

5. Be sure to get all the important parts of the story.

6. Use all the time available to get additional stories.

Questions to Avoid

1. Avoid leading questions.
2. Avoid "yes" or "no" questions.
3. Avoid "should" or "would" questions.
4. Avoid "why" questions"
5. Avoid "double-barreled" questions.
6. Avoid asking for "usual" behavior.
7. Avoid asking speculation questions.
8. Avoid going off on tangents.
9. Avoid paraphrasing.
10. Avoid drawing conclusions.

Appendix E

Summary of Defense Logistics Agency Interviews

Interview	Location	Years[a] in SES	Number of Employees	Length of Interview (Minutes)	Transcription Page Length (Single-Spaced)
DLA 1	Field	> 5	4,500	80	17
DLA 2	Headqtrs	> 5	65	85	13
DLA 3	Headqtrs	> 5	200	90	23
DLA 4	Headqtrs	> 5	200	100	16
DLA 5	Headqtrs	> 5	146	75	13
DLA 6	Headqtrs	> 5	2,000	105	21
DLA 7	Field	> 5	300	90	13
DLA 8	Headqtrs	> 5	200	60	14
Total				685	130
Mean				86	16

[a]Greater than five years (" > 5") or less than five years (" < 5").

Appendix F

Summary of Bureau of Reclamation Interviews

Interview	Location	Years[a] in SES	Number of Employees	Length of Interview (Minutes)	Transcription Page Length (Single-Spaced)
BOR 1	Headqtrs	>5	5,000	65	10
BOR 2	Headqtrs	>5	25	95	10
BOR 3	Field	<5	330	60	17
BOR 4	Field	<5	1,650	98	14
BOR 5	Field	<5	250	115	20
BOR 6	Field	<5	100	270	25
BOR 7	Field	<5	830	110	18
Total				813	114
Mean				116	16

[a]Greater than five years (" > 5") or less than five years (" < 5").

Appendix G

Summary of Food and Drug Administration Interviews

Interview	Location	Years[a] in SES	Number of Employees	Length of Interview (Minutes)	Transcription Page Length (Single-Spaced)
FDA 1	Headqtrs	< 5	117	100	22
FDA 2	Headqtrs	> 5	665	90	20
FDA 3	Center	< 5	83	80	13
FDA 4	Center	> 5	1,660	90	16
FDA 5	Center	> 5	30	80	10
FDA 6	Center	> 5	140	90	13
FDA 7	Center	> 5	90	48	12
FDA 8	Center	< 5	160	75	16
Total				653	122
Mean				82	15

[a]Greater than five years (" > 5") or less than five years (" < 5").

Note: Interviews were conducted in the Office of the Commissioner, ORA, CBER, CDER, and CFSAN. Although centers are considered part of the headquarters, they are not at the highest level of FDA.

Appendix H

Middle Manager Interview Questions

Part I—Middle Manager Background Information

This form requests demographic and employment-related information. The answers you provide will be used to describe the sample of middle managers interviewed. No data will be reported for specific individuals. Your responses to these background items will allow the researcher to analyze the interviews more effectively.

    1. Name: _____

    2. Age: _____

    3. Grade: _____

    4. What is your current position's occupational series number? ____

    5. For how many years have you worked for the federal government (excluding military service)? ____

    6. For how many years have you worked for your present agency? ____

    7. For how long have you been in your present position? ____

    8. If your agency reorganized recently, for how long were you in your previous position? ____

    9. For how many federal departments or independent agencies have you worked for during your federal career? ____

    10. How many total years of federal supervisory/managerial job experience do you have? ____

    11. How many total years of work experience do you have in the private sector? ____

    12. How many employees are in the organizational unit that you head? ____

    13. What is the name of the first Senior Executive Service (SES) member in your chain-of-command? _____

    14. What is your highest level of education? (Indicate degree earned and/or extent of education.) _____

15. What is the field of concentration for your highest degree or highest educational level? _____

Thank you for your participation!

Part II—Interview Questions

Job Background

1. What is your full job title?
2. Who is your superior, and what is his/her title?
3. Whom do you supervise? (General description)
4. What are they responsible for doing?
5. What are your major duties and responsibilities in your present position?

Downsizing

1. Please provide an overview of the downsizing events and processes that have occurred in your agency.
2. How do you view downsizing in your agency?
3. What are the general reactions by middle managers (GS-14 and GS-15) to downsizing in your agency?
4. What have been the impacts of downsizing on middle managers in your agency?
5. What are the concerns of middle managers regarding downsizing in your agency?
6. What are the general reactions by employees below the management levels to downsizing in your agency?
7. How are those who are leaving your agency treated in the downsizing process?
8. How is attention being paid to middle managers who remain with your agency?
9. How are any of the following activities occurring as part of the downsizing process in your agency?
   a. reduction or elimination of workloads or functions
   b. elimination of positions or groups of positions
   c. elimination of management layers
   d. elimination of organizational units
10. How is downsizing affecting any of the following for middle managers in your agency?
    a. morale
    b. motivation
    c. commitment
    d. loyalty

    e. risk taking

    f. quality of work

    g. productivity

11. What are the needs of middle managers during and after downsizing in your agency?

12. Please describe any instances of resistance to change associated with or caused by downsizing in your agency.

13. Please describe any instances of using downsizing to bring about other change in your agency.

14. How has the job of the middle manager changed as a result of the downsizing in your agency?

15. Please tell me about the new role of middle managers as "team chiefs" or "team leaders."

16. What strategies are middle managers employing to achieve change in your agency?

17. Please tell me about workloads during and after downsizing in your agency.

18. Please tell about workforce capabilities during and after downsizing in your agency.

19. Did any of the "wrong" workers leave the agency? (personnel not expected to leave or personnel in critical functions)

20. Has empowerment of middle managers, field employees, and lower-level employees really occurred?

21. What management practices for downsizing have you observed in Senior Executive Service (SES) leaders in your agency?

22. What managerial competencies for downsizing do you believe are important for Senior Executive Service (SES) leaders in your agency to have?

23. What else would you like to tell me about the downsizing process or middle managers and downsizing in your agency?

Appendix I

Coding Scheme for Interview Analysis

Guidelines

1. The coding scheme uses the seventy-two codes for the categories and sub-categories on the following pages.

2. The coding scheme is used to code interview transcripts (including the critical incidents and answers to questions), documents, and field notes.

3. Codes are used to mark words, phrases, sentences, paragraphs, and other data, and codes refer to concepts, themes, and variables contained in the words, phrases, sentences, paragraphs, and other data.

4. Codes are marked in the margins of interview transcripts (including the critical incidents and answers to questions), documents, and field notes along with any additional notes.

5. A word, phrase, sentence, paragraph, or other data may be given more than one code.

6. Codes may overlap.

7. Codes may be nested within other codes.

8. Use the following code suffixes when appropriate:

   a. Add "+" after a code to refer to a positive effect. For example, "MBM +" means morale increased.

   b. Add "–" after a code to refer to a negative effect. For example, "MBV –" means motivation decreased.

   c. Add "–opp" after a code to represent the opposite orientation. For example, "XML-opp" means more formality and hierarchy.

Organizations (O)

Organizational preparation for downsizing (OP)

    1. Prepared: Experienced (OPE)
    2. Prepared: Programs and systems in place (OPP)

3. Not prepared: In denial   (OPD)
4. Not prepared: Few programs and systems in place   (OPO)
5. Not prepared: Never can do enough   (OPN)

Organizational strategies for downsizing   (OS)

   1. Attrition   (OSA)
   2. Buyouts   (OSB)
   3. Philosophy or principles for downsizing   (OSH)
   4. Management layers   (OSL)
   5. Positions   (OSP)
   6. Reduction-in-force (RIF)   (OSR)
   7. Early retirements or separations   (OST)
   8. Organizational units   (OSU)
   9. Workloads or functions   (OSW)

Organizational use of downsizing in conjunction with other change   (OC)

   1. Change to become more businesslike, leaner, and efficient   (OCB)
   2. Change of culture   (OCC)
   3. Change of mission   (OCM)
   4. Change of personnel to place right people in right jobs   (OCP)

Middle Managers M

Middle manager reactions to and concerns about downsizing   (MM)

   1. No sense of control and tired of change   (MMC)
   2. Disbelief and "why us?" reaction   (MMD)
   3. Concern for workload and work efficiency,   (MME)
      performance, and productivity
   4. Health and family problems   (MMH)
   5. Loss of talent and resources   (MML)
   6. Concern for mission accomplishment   (MMM)
   7. Negative reaction such as disfranchisement and frustration   (MMN)
   8. Positive reaction such as recognition of opportunities   (MMP)
   9. Reduced career advancement, promotions, and professional standing   (MMR)
  10. Feelings of being threatened and challenged   (MMT)
      and having energy diverted

Treatment of middle managers during downsizing   (MT)

   1. Actions implemented   (MTI)
   2. Actions in need of implementation   (MTN)

Downsizing effects on middle manager behavior   (MB)

   1. Commitment or "buy-in"   (MBC)
   2. Loyalty   (MBL)
   3. Morale   (MBM)
   4. Productivity and efficiency   (MBP)
   5. Quality of work   (MBQ)
   6. Risk taking   (MBR)
   7. Motivation   (MBV)

Conditions for resistance to change and downsizing by middle managers   (MR)

   1. When unable to recognize value of change   (MRB)
   2. When failure to recognize the reality of change   (MRF)
   3. When at higher organizational levels   (MRH)
   4. When implementation processes are viewed as flawed   (MRI)
   5. When managers are more senior   (MRO)
   6. When reorganizing and restructuring   (MRR)
   7. When preference for stability exists and experience is (MRS)
      painful or uncomfortable
   8. When viewed as a threat and unable to cope with change (MRT)
   9. When uncertain of new roles   (MRU)

Executives   (X)

Executive views of downsizing   (XV)

   1. Negative   (XVN)
   2. Positive   (XVP)

Executive management during downsizing   (XM)

   1. More communication   (XMC)
   2. More effort to accomplish more difficult work   (XMD)
   3. More coaching, mentoring, encouraging, and lifting morale (XME)
   4. Less formality and hierarchy   (XML)
   5. More retraining, workplace tools, monitoring, and evaluating
      work and performance   (XMM)
   6. No change   (XMO)
   7. More delegation and participatory style   (XMP)
   8. More attention to recruitment and placement of personnel (XMR)
   9. More visibility   (XMV)

Executive competencies for downsizing   (XC)

   1. Analytical   (XCA)
   2. Background with functional or technical preparation   (XCB)
   3. Communication   (XCC)
   4. Commitment, energy, and inner strength   (XCE)
   5. Flexibility   (XCF)
   6. Honesty and trustworthiness   (XCH)
   7. Interpersonal skills   (XCI)
   8. Leadership through coaching, mentoring, motivating,   (XCL)
      and increasing "buy-in"
   9. Empower others   (XCO)
 10. Patience   (XCP)
 11. Resourcefulness   (XCR)
 12. Sensitivity, concern, compassion, empathy for people   (XCS)
 13. Team orientation   (XCT)
 14. Sense of humor   (XCU)
 15. Vision   (XCV)

Appendix J

Within-Case and Cross-Case Analysis Procedures

Within-Case Analysis

Extensive within-case analysis was performed for each of the three cases in order to become intimately familiar with each case before advancing to the cross-case comparison. The analysis consisted of reviewing and summarizing the data, coding the data in a series of iterative steps, and then identifying themes and patterns. The primary source of data was the interviews. Appendices C through H provide details of the interviews. To conduct accurate and thorough analysis, the interview tapes were transcribed. The transcripts were placed on computer disks for analysis of the data. Additionally, copies of the transcripts were printed for use in analysis. Copies of documents and archival records, field notes about documents and archival records, and field notes on direct observations also provided sources of data.

The first step in the analysis was to review and summarize the data from interviews. The case chapters discuss the interviews. In addition, Appendices E, F, and G summarize the interviews for each case.

The second step in the analysis consisted of performing an iterative process of coding the data collected in Part I, Critical Incident and Behavior, and Part II, Interview Questions, of the interviews. The following sequence was used for the coding process:

1. Read the interview transcripts and summarize the data.

2. Identify concepts embedded in the descriptions of the critical incidents and answers to the twenty interview questions.

3. Identify an initial set of codes to represent concepts, conditions, interactions, strategies, activities, meanings, relationships, perspectives, processes, events, participations, and settings.

4. Read the transcripts again and attach codes to words, phrases, sentences, and paragraphs and in the process modify the codes.

5. Categorize the codes into an operative coding scheme with conceptual and structural order and with codes related coherently to each other.

6. Write analytical notes and memoranda addressing potential relationships and linkages.

The outcome of the coding process is a coding scheme centered around the general categories of organizations, middle managers, and executives. Furthermore, the coding scheme consists of seventy-two codes in ten subcategories. Appendix I lists the codes with operational definitions.

The third step in the analysis identified themes and patterns, aggregated the data, and generated findings. The following sequence was followed:

1. Examine the coding scheme and coded data to identify themes and patterns.

2. Create matrix data displays to present information and communicate themes and patterns systematically.

3. Generate meaning and findings from the data.

4. Confirm the findings.

5. Create a causal network to represent explanation and causality of downsizing.

In the third step, a deeper examination of the coded data resulted in the identification of specific, well-grounded themes and patterns. The techniques in Miles and Huberman (1994) for displaying data and generating meanings from the data were relied upon for this stage of the analysis.

Cross-Case Analysis

After the three within-case analyses were completed, a systematic process was conducted for a comparative analysis. Cross-case comparisons and patterns in chapter 6 were recognized through the following highly iterative series of steps:

1. Determine themes and patterns represented by downsizing aspects and characteristics for the DLA case.

2. Determine themes and patterns represented by downsizing aspects and characteristics for the BOR case.

3. Look for similarities and differences between the DLA and BOR themes and patterns.

4. Repeat steps 1, 2, and 3 for the DLA and FDA cases.

5. Repeat steps 1, 2, and 3 for the BOR and FDA cases.

6. Identify cross-case comparison factors and patterns of the DLA, BOR, and FDA cases by examining the results of steps 3, 4, and 5.

7. In each step above, ensure data from interview critical incidents, interview answers to questions, and documents provide evidence to support the cross-case comparisons and patterns.

Formalized Procedures

The study used a highly formalized set of procedures to improve the quality of the research. The following seventeen procedures helped to increase the study's reliability and validity:

1. Standardized operations to facilitate data analysis in a multiple-case study.

2. Used a systematic approach.

3. Conducted theoretical sampling of cases.

4. Followed interview protocols.

5. Tape-recorded and transcribed all interviews and took field notes during interviews.

6. Relied on multiple sources of evidence to improve internal validity.

7. Achieved convergence or triangulation among data sources and methods to improve internal validity.

8. Established chains of evidence to improve internal validity.

9. Performed coding checks.

10. Conducted cross-case comparisons by analyzing in many divergent ways.

11. Executed a highly iterative data analysis.

12. Ensured anonymity of executive quotes.

13. Displayed data in matrices and networks for an organized and compressed assembly of information to permit conclusion drawing.

14. Preserved a documentation and data analysis trail.

15. Acquired informant feedback to verify accuracy of facts and check that concepts and the theoretical model correspond with observations and realities, steps that improve construct validity.

16. Avoided conflicts of interests with agencies.

17. Stated procedures explicitly.

Bibliography

Abramson, Mark A., and Schmidt, Richard E. 1984. "Implementing the Civil Service Reform Act in a Time of Turbulence." In *Legislating Bureaucratic Change: The Civil Service Reform Act of 1978*, ed. Patricia W. Ingraham and Carolyn Ban, 245–53. Albany, NY: State University of New York Press.

Agranoff, Robert, and Radin, Beryl A. 1991. "The Comparative Case Study Approach in Public Administration." In *Research in Public Administration: A Research Annual*, vol. 1, ed. James L. Perry, 203–31. Greenwich, CT: JAI Press.

Aldrich, Howard E. 1979. *Organizations and Environments*. Englewood Cliffs, NJ: Prentice-Hall.

Aldrich, Howard E., and Pfeffer, Jeffrey. 1976. "Environments of Organizations." In *Annual Review of Sociology*, vol. 2, ed. Alex Inkeles, James Coleman, and Neil Smelser, 79–105. Palo Alto, CA: Annual Reviews.

Arnold, Peri E. 1995. "Reform's Changing Role." *Public Administration Review* 55, no. 5 (September/October): 407–17.

Augustine Report. 1990. *Report of the Advisory Committee on the Future of the U.S. Space Program*. Washington, DC: U.S. Government Printing Office.

Ban, Carolyn. 1995. "Unions, Management, and the NPR." In *Inside the Reinvention Machine: Appraising Governmental Reform*, ed. Donald F. Kettl and John J. DiIulio Jr., 131–51. Washington, DC: Brookings Institution.

Barnard, Chester I. 1938. *The Functions of the Executive*. Cambridge, MA: Harvard University Press.

Barzelay, Michael. 1992. *Breaking through Bureaucracy: A New Vision for Managing in Government*. Berkeley, CA: University of California Press.

Baxter, Vern. 1989. "The Process of Change in Public Organizations." *Sociological Quarterly* 30, no. 2 (Summer): 283–304.

Behn, Robert D. 1978a. "How to Terminate a Public Policy: A Dozen Hints for the Would-Be Terminator." *Policy Analysis* 4, no. 3 (Summer): 393–413.

———. 1978b. "Closing a Government Facility." *Public Administration Review* 38, no. 4 (July/August): 332–38.

———. 1980a. "Can Public Policy Termination Be Increased by Making Government More Businesslike?" In *Fiscal Stress and Public Policy*, ed. Charles H. Levine and Irene Rubin, 249–80. Beverly Hills, CA: Sage.

———. 1980b. "Leadership for Cut-Back Management: The Use of Corporate Strategy." *Public Administration Review* 40, no. 6 (November/December): 613–20.

———. 1988. "The Fundamentals of Cutback Management." In *Readings in Organizational Decline: Frameworks, Research, and Prescriptions*, ed. Kim S. Cameron, Robert I. Sutton, and David A. Whetten, 347–56. Cambridge, MA: Ballinger.

————. 1991. *Leadership Counts: Lessons for Public Managers from the Massachusetts Welfare, Training, and Employment Program*. Cambridge, MA: Harvard University Press.

Berne, Robert, and Stiefel, Leanna. 1993. "Cutback Budgeting: The Long-Term Consequences." *Journal of Policy Analysis and Management* 12, no. 4 (Fall): 664–84.

Biller, Robert P. 1980. "Leadership Tactics for Retrenchment." *Public Administration Review* 40, no. 6 (November/December): 604–9.

Bilstein, Roger E. 1989. *Orders of Magnitude: A History of the NACA and NASA, 1915–1990*. NASA SP-4406. Washington, DC: National Aeronautics and Space Administration.

Blau, Peter M. 1955. *The Dynamics of Bureaucracy*. Chicago: University of Chicago Press.

Bogdan, Robert C., and Biklen, Sari Knopp. 1992. *Qualitative Research for Education: An Introduction to Theory and Methods*. 2d ed. Boston: Allyn and Bacon.

Boulding, Kenneth E. 1975. "The Management of Decline." *Change* 7, no. 5 (June): 8–9, 64.

Bourgeois, L.J. III. 1985. "Strategic Goals, Perceived Uncertainty, and Economic Performance in Volatile Environments." *Academy of Management Journal* 28, no. 3 (September): 548–73.

Boyatzis, Richard E. 1982. *The Competent Manager: A Model for Effective Performance*. New York: John Wiley & Sons.

Bozeman, Barry, and Slusher, E. Allen. 1979. "Scarcity and Environmental Stress in Public Organizations: A Conjectural Essay." *Administration and Society* 11, no. 3 (November): 335–55.

Brecher, Charles, and Horton, Raymond D. 1985. "Retrenchment and Recovery: American Cities and the New York Experience." *Public Administration Review* 45, no. 2 (March/April): 267–74.

Brewer, Gary D. 1978. "Termination: Hard Choices—Harder Questions." *Public Administration Review* 38, no. 4 (July/August): 338–44.

Brockner, Joel. 1988. "The Effects of Work Layoffs on Survivors: Research, Theory, and Practice." In *Research in Organizational Behavior: An Annual Series of Analytical Essays and Critical Reviews*, vol. 10, ed. Barry M. Staw and L.L. Cummings, 213–55. Greenwich, CT: JAI Press.

————. 1992. "Managing the Effects of Layoffs on Survivors." *California Management Review* 34, no. 2 (Winter): 9–28.

Brockner, Joel, and Greenberg, Jerald. 1990. "The Impact of Layoffs on Survivors: An Organizational Justice Perspective." In *Applied Social Psychology and Organizational Settings*, ed. John S. Carroll, 45–75. Hillsdale, NJ: Lawrence Erlbaum Associates.

Brockner, Joel, and Wiesenfeld, Batia. 1993. "Living on the Edge (of Social and Organizational Psychology): The Effects of Job Layoffs on Those Who Remain." In *Social Psychology in Organizations: Advances in Theory and Research*, ed. J. Keith Murnighan, 119–40. Englewood Cliffs, NJ: Prentice-Hall.

Bromiley, Philip. 1991. "Testing a Causal Model of Corporate Risk Taking and Performance." *Academy of Management Journal* 34, no. 1 (March): 37–59.

Bureau of Reclamation. 1987. *Assessment '87 . . . A New Direction for the Bureau of Reclamation*. 10 September. Washington, DC: Bureau of Reclamation.

Bureau of Reclamation. 1992. *Reclamation's Strategic Plan: A Long-Term Framework for Water Resources Management, Development and Protection*. June. Washington, DC: Bureau of Reclamation.

Bureau of Reclamation. 1993a. *Report of the Commissioner's Program and Organization Review Team (CPORT)*. 6 August. Washington, DC: Bureau of Reclamation.

Bureau of Reclamation. 1993b. *Blueprint for Reform: The Commissioner's Plan for Reinventing Reclamation.* 1 November. Washington, DC: Bureau of Reclamation.

Bureau of Reclamation. 1997. *Bureau of Reclamation's Strategic Plan: 1997–2002.* Washington, DC: Bureau of Reclamation.

Burke, W. Warner, and Litwin, George H. 1992. "A Causal Model of Organizational Performance and Change." *Journal of Management* 18, no. 3 (September): 523–45.

Caiden, Gerald E. 1991. "What Really Is Public Maladministration?" *Public Administration Review* 51, no. 6 (November/December): 486–93.

Cameron, Kim S. 1983. "Strategic Responses to Conditions of Decline: Higher Education and the Private Sector." *Journal of Higher Education* 54, no. 4 (July/August): 359–80.

Cameron, Kim S.; Freeman, Sarah J.; and Mishra, Aneil K. 1991. "Best Practices in White-Collar Downsizing: Managing Contradictions." *Academy of Management Executive* 5, no. 3 (August): 57–73.

———. 1993. "Downsizing and Redesigning Organizations." In *Organizational Change and Redesign: Ideas and Insights for Improving Performance*, ed. George P. Huber and William H. Glick, 19–63. New York: Oxford University Press.

Cameron, Kim S.; Kim, Myung U.; and Whetten, David A. 1987. "Organizational Effects of Decline and Turbulence." *Administrative Science Quarterly* 32, no. 2 (June): 222–40.

Cameron, Kim S.; Sutton, Robert I.; and Whetten, David A., eds. 1988. *Readings in Organizational Decline: Frameworks, Research, and Prescriptions.* Cambridge, MA: Ballinger.

Cameron, Kim S.; Whetten, David A.; and Kim, Myung U. 1987. "Organizational Dysfunctions of Decline." *Academy of Management Journal* 30, no. 1 (March): 126–38.

Carnevale, David G. 1995. *Trustworthy Government.* San Francisco: Jossey-Bass.

Carroll, James D. 1995. "The Rhetoric of Reform and Political Reality in the National Performance Review." *Public Administration Review* 55, no. 3 (May/June): 302–12.

———. 1996. "Introduction." *Public Administration Review* 56, no. 3 (May/June): 245–6.

Cascio, Wayne F. 1993. "Downsizing: What Do We Know? What Have We Learned?" *Academy of Management Executive* 7, no. 1 (February): 95–104.

Champy, James. 1995. *Reengineering Management: The Mandate for New Leadership.* New York: Harper Collins.

Child, John. 1972. "Organizational Structure, Environment, and Performance: The Role of Strategic Choice." *Sociology* 6, no. 1 (January): 1–22.

Clark, Timothy B. 1995. "The Innovators." *Government Executive* 27, no. 11 (December): 14–16.

Cole, Roger L., and Pace, Larry A. 1991. "Power to Change: The Case of TVA." *Training and Development* 45, no. 8 (August): 59–64.

Colvard, James E. 1994. "In Defense of Middle Management." *Government Executive* 26, no. 5 (May): 57–58.

Conant, James. 1986. "Reorganization and the Bottom Line." *Public Administration Review* 46, no.1 (January/February): 48–56.

Corbin, Lisa. 1992a. "DOD Inc." *Government Executive* 24, no. 6 (June): 36–39.

———. 1992b. "Winning the Paper Chase." *Government Executive* 24, no. 9 (September): 31–37.

———. 1995a. "Going Leaner and Greener." *Government Executive* 27, no. 11 (December): 35–36.

———. 1995b. "Retooling the Supply Chain." *Government Executive* 27, no. 11 (December): 23–24.

Corts, Daniel B., and Gowing, Marilyn K. 1992. *Dimensions of Effective Behavior: Executives, Managers, and Supervisors*. Report PRD-92–05. January. Washington, DC: U.S. Office of Personnel Management.

Creswell, John W. 1994. *Research Design: Qualitative and Quantitative Approaches*. Thousand Oaks, CA: Sage.

Cyert, Richard M. 1978. "The Management of Universities of Constant or Decreasing Size." *Public Administration Review* 38, no. 4 (July/August): 344–49.

Daft, Richard L., and Lewin, Arie Y. 1993. "Where Are the Theories for the 'New' Organizational Forms? An Editorial Essay." *Organization Science* 4, no. 4 (November): i–vi.

D'Aunno, Thomas, and Sutton, Robert I. 1992. "The Responses of Drug Abuse Treatment Organizations to Financial Adversity: A Partial Test of the Threat-Rigidity Thesis." *Journal of Management* 18, no. 1 (March): 117–31.

D'Aveni, Richard A. 1989. "The Aftermath of Organizational Decline: A Longitudinal Study of the Strategic and Managerial Characteristics of Declining Firms." *Academy of Management Journal* 32, no. 3 (September): 577–605.

Defense Logistics Agency. 1993a. *The Roadmap to Transition: Headquarters Defense Logistics Agency*. January. Alexandria, VA: Defense Logistics Agency.

Defense Logistics Agency. 1993b. *Defense Logistics Agency: Base Realignment and Closure Detailed Analysis*. 12 March. Alexandria, VA: Defense Logistics Agency.

Defense Logistics Agency. 1993c. *Participant's Guide: Restructuring of HQ DLA*. June. Alexandria, VA: Defense Logistics Agency.

Defense Logistics Agency. 1994a. *Defense Logistics Agency Transition Book Prepared for Secretary of Defense Designate Dr. William J. Perry*. Draft, January. Alexandria, VA: Defense Logistics Agency.

Defense Logistics Agency. 1994b. *Defense Logistics Agency: Performance Plan Fiscal Year 1994*. March. Alexandria, VA: Defense Logistics Agency.

Defense Logistics Agency. 1994c. *Defense Logistics Agency: Performance Report Fiscal Year 1994*. June 1995. Alexandria, VA: Defense Logistics Agency.

Defense Logistics Agency. 1995a. *Defense Logistics Agency: Performance Plan Fiscal Year 1995*. November 1994. Alexandria, VA: Defense Logistics Agency.

Defense Logistics Agency. 1995b. *DLA Reinvention Journal*. October. Fort Belvoir, VA: Defense Logistics Agency.

Defense Logistics Agency. 1995c. *Defense Logistics Agency: Performance Report Fiscal Year 1995*. June 1996. Fort Belvoir, VA: Defense Logistics Agency.

Defense Logistics Agency. 1996a. *Defense Logistics Agency: Performance Plan Fiscal Year 1996*. April 1995. Alexandria, VA: Defense Logistics Agency.

Defense Logistics Agency. 1996b. *Defense Logistics Agency: Performance Report Fiscal Year 1996*. June 1997. Fort Belvoir, VA: Defense Logistics Agency.

Denhardt, Robert B. 1993. *The Pursuit of Significance: Strategies for Managerial Success in Public Organizations*. Belmont, CA: Wadsworth.

Dering, Robert Scott. 1996. "The Politics of Military Base Closures, 1988 to 1995." Ph.D. diss., University of Kansas.

DiIulio, John J. Jr., ed. 1994. *Deregulating the Public Service: Can Government Be Improved?* Washington, DC: Brookings Institution.

———.1995. "Works Better and Costs Less? Sweet and Sour Perspectives on the NPR." In *Inside the Reinvention Machine: Appraising Governmental Reform*, ed. Donald F. Kettl and John J. DiIulio Jr., 1–6. Washington, DC: Brookings Institution.

DiIulio, John J. Jr.; Garvey, Gerald; and Kettl, Donald F. 1993. *Improving Government Performance: An Owner's Manual*. Washington, DC: Brookings Institution.

Downs, Anthony. 1967. *Inside Bureaucracy*. Boston: Little, Brown.

Downs, George W., and Larkey, Patrick D. 1986. *The Search for Government Efficiency: From Hubris to Helplessness.* Philadelphia: Temple University Press.

Druckman, Daniel; Singer, Jerome E.; and Van Cott, Harold. 1997. *Enhancing Organizational Performance.* Washington, DC: National Academy Press.

Eisenhardt, Kathleen M. 1989. "Building Theories from Case Study Research." *Academy of Management Review* 14, no. 4 (October): 532–50.

Epstein, Paul D. 1993. "Reinventing Government Is Not Enough: Invest in Government Productivity Growth." *Public Productivity and Management Review* 16, no. 4 (Summer): 357–69.

Federal Personnel Guide. 1997. Washington, DC: Key Communications Group.

Feldt, James A., and Andersen, David F. 1982. "Attrition Versus Layoffs: How to Estimate the Costs of Holding Employees on Payroll When Savings Are Needed." *Public Administration Review* 42, no. 3 (May/June): 278–82.

Fiegenbaum, Avi, and Thomas, Howard. 1988. "Attitudes Toward Risk and the Risk-Return Paradox: Prospect Theory Explanations." *Academy of Management Journal* 31, no. 1 (March): 85–106.

Flanagan, John C. 1954. "The Critical Incident Technique." *Psychological Bulletin* 51, no. 4 (July): 327–58.

Food and Drug Administration. 1987. *All about FDA: An Orientation Handbook.* September. Rockville, MD: Food and Drug Administration.

Food and Drug Administration. 1989. *Requirements of Laws and Regulations Enforced by the U.S. Food and Drug Administration.* DHHS Pub. (FDA) 89-1115. Rockville, MD: Food and Drug Administration.

Food and Drug Administration. 1994a. *FDA Almanac: Fiscal Year 1994.* DHHS Pub. (FDA) 95-1193, November. Rockville, MD: Food and Drug Administration.

Food and Drug Administration. 1994b. *FDA Today* 23, no. 3 (December). Rockville, MD: Food and Drug Administration.

Food and Drug Administration. 1995a. *FDA Backgrounder.* BG 95-13, 19 April. Rockville, MD: Food and Drug Administration.

Food and Drug Administration. 1995b. *FDA Almanac: Fiscal Year 1995.* DHHS Pub. (FDA) 96-1193, Fall. Rockville, MD: Food and Drug Administration.

Food and Drug Administration. 1996. *FDA Almanac: Fiscal Year 1996.* DHHS Pub. (FDA) 96-1254, July. Rockville, MD: Food and Drug Administration.

Ford, Jeffrey D., and Baucus, David A. 1987. "Organizational Adaptation to Performance Downturns: An Interpretation-Based Perspective." *Academy of Management Review* 12, no. 2 (April): 366–80.

Foreman, Christopher H. Jr. 1995a. "Reinventing Capitol Hill? The NPR Meets Congress." *Brookings Review* 13, no. 1 (Winter): 35–37.

———. 1995b. "Reinventing Politics?: The NPR Meets Congress." In *Inside the Reinvention Machine: Appraising Governmental Reform,* ed. Donald F. Kettl and John J. DiIulio Jr., 152–68. Washington, DC: Brookings Institution.

Frederickson, H. George. 1992. "Painting Bull's-Eyes around Bullet Holes." *Governing* 6, no. 1 (October): 13.

———. 1996. "Comparing the Reinventing Government Movement with the New Public Administration." *Public Administration Review* 56, no. 3 (May/June): 263–70.

Freeman, Sarah J., and Cameron, Kim S. 1993. "Organizational Downsizing: A Convergence and Reorientation Framework." *Organization Science* 4, no. 1 (February): 10–29.

Friedman, Michael A. 1997. Statement by the Lead Deputy Commissioner, Food and Drug Administration, before the Subcommittee on Health and the Environment, Committee on Commerce, U.S. House of Representatives, 23 April.

Garvey, Gerald. 1993. *Facing the Bureaucracy: Living and Dying in a Public Agency.* San Francisco: Jossey-Bass.

———. 1995. "False Promises: The NPR in Historical Perspective." In *Inside the Reinvention Machine: Appraising Governmental Reform,* ed. Donald F. Kettl and John J. DiIulio Jr., 87–106. Washington, DC: Brookings Institution.

Gawthrop, Louis C. 1969. *Bureaucratic Behavior in the Executive Branch: An Analysis of Organizational Change.* New York: Free Press.

———. 1984. *Public Sector Management, Systems, and Ethics.* Bloomington, IN: Indiana University Press.

Glaser, Barney G., and Strauss, Anselm L. 1967. *The Discovery of Grounded Theory: Strategies for Qualitative Research.* Chicago: Aldine.

Goldenkoff, Robert. 1997. "Report Card on Downsizing." *Government Executive* 29, no. 2 (February): 49–50.

Goldstein, Mark L. 1989. "Hollow Government." *Government Executive* 21, no. 10 (October): 12–22.

———. 1992. *America's Hollow Government: How Washington Has Failed the People.* Homewood, IL: Business One Irwin.

———. 1993. "Hollow Government Welcomes Clinton." *Public Manager* 21, no. 4 (Winter): 55–57.

Goldstein, Mark L., and Clark, Timothy B. 1992. "Hollow Government II." *Government Executive* 24, no. 2 (February): 10–14.

Goodsell, Charles T. 1993. "Reinvent Government or Rediscover It?" *Public Administration Review* 53, no. 1 (January/February): 85–87.

———. 1994. *The Case for Bureaucracy: A Public Administration Polemic.* 3d ed. Chatham, NJ: Chatham House.

Gore, Al Jr. 1994. "The New Job of the Federal Executive." *Public Administration Review* 54, no. 4 (July/August): 317–21.

Gormley, William T. Jr. 1989. *Taming the Bureaucracy: Muscles, Prayers, and Other Strategies.* Princeton, NJ: Princeton University Press.

Gowan, M.A., and Gatewood, R.D. 1992. "A Causal Model of the Activity Level of Individuals Following Involuntary Job Loss." *Best Paper Proceedings.* Las Vegas: Academy of Management Meetings.

Grace Commission. 1984. *War on Waste: The President's Private Sector Survey on Cost Control.* New York: Macmillan.

Greenhalgh, Leonard. 1983. "Organizational Decline." In *Research in the Sociology of Organizations,* vol. 2, ed. Samuel B. Bacharach, 231–76. Greenwich, CT: JAI Press.

Greenhalgh, Leonard; Lawrence, Anne T.; and Sutton, Robert I. 1988. "Determinants of Work Force Reduction Strategies in Declining Organizations." *Academy of Management Review* 13, no. 2 (April): 241–54.

Greenhalgh, Leonard, and McKersie, Robert B. 1980. "Cost-Effectiveness of Alternative Strategies for Cutback Management." *Public Administration Review* 40, no. 6 (November/December): 575–84.

Greiner, Larry E. 1967. "Patterns of Organization Change." *Harvard Business Review* 45, no. 3 (May/June): 119–30.

Hale, Sandra J. 1991. "Reinventing Government the Minnesota Way." *Public Productivity Review* 15, no. 2 (Winter): 123–31.

Hall, Douglas T., and Mansfield, Roger. 1971. "Organizational and Individual Response to External Stress." *Administrative Science Quarterly* 16, no. 4 (December): 533–47.

Hall, Richard H. 1991. *Organizations: Structures, Processes, and Outcomes.* 5th ed. Englewood Cliffs, NJ: Prentice-Hall.

Hammer, Michael. 1996. *Beyond Reengineering: How the Process-Centered Organization Is Changing Our Work and Our Lives.* New York: HarperCollins.

Hammer, Michael, and Champy, James. 1993. *Reengineering the Corporation: A Manifesto for Business Revolution.* New York: HarperCollins.

Hannan, Michael T., and Freeman, John. 1984. "Structural Inertia and Organizational Change." *American Sociological Review* 49, no. 2 (April): 149–64.

Hardy, Cynthia. 1985. "Fighting Cutbacks: Some Issues for Public Sector Administrators." *Canadian Public Administration* 28, no. 4 (Winter): 531–49.

———. 1987. "Effective Retrenchment: Human Resource Implications." *Journal of General Management* 12, no. 3 (Spring): 76–92.

———. 1989. *Strategies for Retrenchment and Turnaround: The Politics of Survival.* New York: Walter de Gruyter.

Harper, Kirke. 1992. "The Senior Executive Service after One Decade." In *The Promise and Paradox of Civil Service Reform*, ed. Patricia W. Ingraham and David H. Rosenbloom, 267–82. Pittsburgh, PA: University of Pittsburgh Press.

Harris, Michael M.; Heller, Tamar; and Braddock, David. 1988. "Sex Differences in Psychological Well-Being during a Facility Closure." *Journal of Management* 14, no. 3 (September): 391–402.

Hirschhorn, Larry, and Associates. 1983. *Cutting Back: Retrenchment and Redevelopment in Human and Community Services.* San Francisco: Jossey-Bass.

Hodge, Scott A. 1996. "Reinvention Has Not Ended the 'Era of Big Government.' " Heritage Foundation Backgrounder Paper no. 1095, 15 October. Washington, DC: Heritage Foundation.

Hood, Christopher. 1974. "Administrative Diseases: Some Types of Dysfunctionality in Administration." *Public Administration* 52 (Winter): 439–54.

Hornestay, David. 1996. "Reconsidering Downsizing." *Government Executive* 28, no. 7 (July): 50.

Hrebiniak, Lawrence G., and Joyce, William F. 1985. "Organizational Adaptation: Strategic Choice and Environmental Determinism." *Administrative Science Quarterly* 30, no. 3 (September): 336–49.

Huber, George P. 1984. "The Nature and Design of Post-Industrial Organizations." *Management Science* 30, no. 8 (August): 928–51.

Huber, George P., and Glick, William H., eds. 1993. *Organizational Change and Redesign: Ideas and Insights for Improving Performance.* New York: Oxford University Press.

Huber, George P.; Sutcliffe, Kathleen M.; Miller, C. Chet; and Glick, William H. 1993. "Understanding and Predicting Organizational Change." In *Organizational Change and Redesign: Ideas and Insights for Improving Performance*, ed. George P. Huber and William H. Glick, 215–54. New York: Oxford University Press.

Huddleston, Mark W. 1991. "The Senior Executive Service: Problems and Prospects for Reform." In *Public Personnel Management: Current Concerns—Future Challenges*, ed. Carolyn Ban and Norma M. Riccucci, 175–89. White Plains, NY: Longman.

Huff, S.; Lake, D.; and Schaalman, M.L. 1982. *Principal Differences.* A Report to the Florida Council on Educational Management. Tallahassee: Department of Education.

Ingraham, Patricia W. 1992. "Commissions, Cycles, and Change: The Role of Blue-Ribbon Commissions in Executive Branch Change." In *Agenda for Excellence: Public Service in America*, ed. Patricia W. Ingraham and Donald F. Kettl, 187–207. Chatham, NJ: Chatham House.

Ingraham, Patricia W., and Ban, Carolyn, eds. 1984. *Legislating Bureaucratic Change: The Civil Service Reform Act of 1978.* Albany, NY: State University of New York Press.

Ingraham, Patricia W., and Barrilleaux, Charles. 1983. "Motivating Government Managers for Retrenchment: Some Possible Lessons from the Senior Executive Service." *Public Administration Review* 43, no. 5 (September/October): 393–402.

Ingraham, Patricia W., and Jones, Vernon Dale. Forthcoming. "The Pain of Organizational Change: Managing Reinvention." In *Public Management Reform and Innovation: Research, Theory, and Application*, ed. H. George Frederickson and Jocelyn Johnston. Tuscaloosa, AL: University of Alabama Press.

Ingraham, Patricia W., and Romzek, Barbara S. 1994. "Issues Raised by Current Reform Efforts." In *New Paradigms for Government: Issues for the Changing Public Service*, ed. Patricia W. Ingraham, Barbara S. Romzek, and Associates, 1–14. San Francisco: Jossey-Bass.

Janssen, Wallace F. 1992. *The U.S. Food and Drug Law: How It Came, How It Works*. Reprint from *FDA Consumer*. DHHS Pub. (FDA) 92-1054, May. Rockville, MD: Food and Drug Administration.

Jick, Todd D., and Murray, Victor V. 1982. "The Management of Hard Times: Budget Cutbacks in Public Sector Organizations." *Organization Studies* 3, no. 2: 141–69.

Jones, L.R. 1992. "Minding the Pentagon's Business." *Government Executive* 24, no. 10 (October): 40–45.

Jones, Vernon Dale, and Mathews, Kay. 1997. "Trusting the 'Nonessential': Is It Essential to Reinventing Federal Government Agencies?" *Public Integrity Annual* 2 (April): 61–75.

Kam, Allan J., and Shaw, G. Jerry. 1994. "Managers and Top Professionals Band Together." *Public Manager* 22, no. 4 (Winter): 7–10.

Kamensky, John M. 1996. "Role of the 'Reinventing Government' Movement in Federal Management Reform." *Public Administration Review* 56, no. 3 (May/June): 247–55.

Kanter, Rosabeth Moss. 1983. *The Change Masters: Innovation and Entrepreneurship in the American Corporation*. New York: Simon & Schuster.

Katz, Daniel, and Kahn, Robert L. 1978. *The Social Psychology of Organizations*. Rev. ed. New York: John Wiley & Sons.

Kaufman, Herbert. 1971. *The Limits of Organizational Change*. University, AL: University of Alabama Press.

———. 1976. *Are Government Organizations Immortal?* Washington, DC: Brookings Institution.

———. 1981. *The Administrative Behavior of Federal Bureau Chiefs*. Washington, DC: Brookings Institution.

Kaufman, Leslie. 1994a. "Reinvention Reality Check." *Government Executive* 26, no. 4 (April): 19–22.

———. 1994b. "Defense Logistics Agency: Supply Budget Bucks Downward Trend." *Government Executive* 26, no. 8 (August): 113–14.

Ketchum, Robert H. 1982. "Retrenchment: The Uses and Misuses of LIFO in Downsizing an Organization." *Personnel* 59 (November–December): 25–30.

Kettl, Donald F. 1993. *Sharing Power: Public Governance and Private Markets*. Washington, DC: Brookings Institution.

———. 1994. *Reinventing Government?: Appraising the National Performance Review*. A report of Brookings Institution's Center for Public Management, CPM Report 94-2, August. Washington, DC: Brookings Institution.

———. 1995. "Building Lasting Reform: Enduring Questions, Missing Answers." In *Inside the Reinvention Machine: Appraising Governmental Reform*, ed. Donald F. Kettl and John J. DiIulio Jr., 9–83. Washington, DC: Brookings Institution.

Kimberly, John R., and Quinn, Robert E. 1984. "The Challenge of Transition Management." In *New Futures: The Challenge of Managing Corporate Transitions*, ed. John R. Kimberly and Robert E. Quinn, 1–8. Homewood, IL: Dow Jones-Irwin.

Koberg, Christine S. 1987. "Resource Scarcity, Environmental Uncertainty, and Adaptive Organizational Behavior." *Academy of Management Journal* 30, no. 4 (December): 798–807.

Kotter, John P. 1990. *A Force for Change: How Leadership Differs from Management.* New York: Free Press.

———. 1996. *Leading Change*. Boston, MA: Harvard Business School Press.

Kozlowski, Steve W. J.; Chao, Georgia T.; Smith, Eleanor M.; and Hedlund, Jennifer. 1993. "Organizational Downsizing: Strategies, Interventions, and Research Implications." In *International Review of Industrial and Organizational Psychology*, vol. 8, ed. C.L. Cooper and I.T. Robertson, 263–332. New York: John Wiley & Sons.

Latack, Janina C. 1990. "Organizational Restructuring and Career Management: From Outplacement and Survival to Inplacement." In *Research in Personnel and Human Resources Management*, vol. 8, ed. Gerald R. Ferris and Kendrith M. Rowland, 109–39. Greenwich, CT: JAI Press.

Laurent, Anne. 1996. "Time to Get Cooking on GPRA." *Government Executive* 28, no. 7 (July): 51–52.

Lawler, Edward E. III; Mohrman, Allan M. Jr.; Mohrman, Susan A.; Ledford, Gerald E. Jr.; Cummings, Thomas G.; and Associates. 1985. *Doing Research That Is Useful for Theory and Practice*. San Francisco: Jossey-Bass.

Lawrence, Paul R., and Lorsch, Jay W. 1967. *Organization and Environment.* Cambridge, MA: Harvard University Press.

Leana, Carrie R., and Feldman, Daniel C. 1991. "Gender Differences in Response to Unemployment." *Journal of Vocational Behavior* 38, no. 1 (February): 65–77.

Ledford, Gerald E. Jr.; Mohrman, Susan Albers; Mohrman, Allan M. Jr.; and Lawler, Edward E. III. 1989. "The Phenomenon of Large-Scale Organizational Change." In *Large-Scale Organizational Change*, ed. Allan M. Mohrman Jr., Susan Albers Mohrman, Gerald E. Ledford Jr., Thomas G. Cummings, Edward E. Lawler III, and Associates, 1–32. San Francisco: Jossey-Bass.

Lee, Lawrence B. 1980. *Reclaiming the American West: An Historiography and Guide.* Santa Barbara, CA: ABC-Clio Press.

Levine, Charles H. 1978. "Organizational Decline and Cutback Management." *Public Administration Review* 38, no. 4 (July/August): 316–25.

———. 1979. "More on Cutback Management: Hard Questions for Hard Times." *Public Administration Review* 39, no. 2 (March/April): 179–83.

———. 1980. "The New Crisis in the Public Sector." In *Managing Fiscal Stress: The Crisis in the Public Sector*, ed. Charles H. Levine, 3–12. Chatham, NJ: Chatham House.

Levine, Charles H., and Kleeman, Rosslyn S. 1992. "The Quiet Crisis in the American Public Service." In *Agenda for Excellence: Public Service in America*, ed. Patricia W. Ingraham and Donald F. Kettl, 208–73. Chatham, NJ: Chatham House.

Levine, Charles H.; Rubin, Irene S.; and Wolohojian, George G. 1981a. *The Politics of Retrenchment: How Local Governments Manage Fiscal Stress*. Beverly Hills, CA: Sage.

———. 1981b. "Resource Scarcity and the Reform Model: The Management of Retrenchment in Cincinnati and Oakland." *Public Administration Review* 41, no. 6 (November/December): 619–28.

———. 1982. "Managing Organizational Retrenchment: Preconditions, Deficiencies, and Adaptations in the Public Sector." *Administration and Society* 14, no. 1 (May): 101–36.

Lewis, Carol W., and Logalbo, Anthony T. 1980. "Cutback Principles and Practices: A Checklist for Managers." *Public Administration Review* 40, no. 2 (March/April): 184–88.

Light, Paul C. 1997a. "The Tides of Reinvention." *Government Executive* 29, no. 1 (January): 23–24.

———. 1997b. *The Tides of Reform: Making Government Work.* New Haven, CT: Yale University Press.

Lynn, Laurence E. Jr. 1994. "Public Management Research: The Triumph of Art over Science." *Journal of Policy Analysis and Management* 13, no. 2 (Spring): 231–59.

March, James G., and Olsen, Johan P. 1983. "Organizing Political Life: What Administrative Reorganization Tells Us About Government." *American Political Science Review* 77, no. 2 (June): 281–96.

———. 1989. "Institutional Reform as an Ad Hoc Activity." In *Rediscovering Institutions: The Organizational Basis of Politics,* 69–94. New York: Free Press.

Marshall, Catherine, and Rossman, Gretchen B. 1989. *Designing Qualitative Research.* Newbury Park, CA: Sage.

Maynard-Moody, Steven; Stull, Donald D.; and Mitchell, Jerry. 1986. "Reorganization as Status Drama: Building, Maintaining, and Displacing Dominant Subcultures." *Public Administration Review* 46, no. 4 (July/August): 301–10.

McCarthy, Eugene Michael. 1994. "The Elusive 252,000, or, A Layman's Guide to Government Downsizing." *Classifiers' Column* 25, nos. 3–4 (March/April): 2–6.

McClelland, David C. 1951. *Personality.* New York: Holt, Rinehart & Winston.

———. 1973. "Testing for Competence Rather Than for 'Intelligence.'" *American Psychologist* 28, no. 1 (January): 1–14.

———. 1976. *A Guide to Job Competency Assessment.* Boston: McBer and Company.

McCune, Joseph T.; Beatty, Richard W.; and Montagno, Raymond V. 1988. "Downsizing: Practices in Manufacturing Firms." *Human Resource Management* 27, no. 2 (Summer): 145–61.

McKelvey, Bill. 1982. *Organizational Systematics: Taxonomy, Evolution, Classification.* Berkeley, CA: University of California Press.

McKinley, William. 1984. "Organizational Decline and Innovation in Manufacturing." In *Strategic Management of Industrial R&D,* ed. Barry Bozeman, Michael Crow, and Albert Link, 147–59. Lexington, MA: Lexington Books.

———. 1993. "Organizational Decline and Adaptation: Theoretical Controversies." *Organization Science* 4, no. 1 (February): 1–9.

McTighe, John J. 1979. "Management Strategies to Deal with Shrinking Resources." *Public Administration Review* 39, no. 1 (January/February): 86–90.

Meyer, Alan D. 1982. "Adapting to Environmental Jolts." *Administrative Science Quarterly* 27, no. 4 (December): 515–37.

Meyer, Marshall W. 1979. *Change in Public Bureaucracies.* Cambridge: Cambridge University Press.

Miles, Matthew B., and Huberman, A. Michael. 1994. *Qualitative Data Analysis.* 2d ed. Thousand Oaks, CA: Sage.

Miles, Robert H., and Cameron, Kim S. 1982. *Coffin Nails and Corporate Strategies.* Englewood Cliffs, NJ: Prentice-Hall.

Miller, Danny, and Friesen, Peter H. 1980. "Momentum and Revolution in Organizational Adaptation." *Academy of Management Journal* 23, no. 4 (December): 591–614.

Milward, H. Brinton. 1994. "Implications of Contracting Out: New Roles for the Hollow State." In *New Paradigms for Government: Issues for the Changing Public Service,* ed. Patricia W. Ingraham, Barbara S. Romzek, and Associates, 41–62. San Francisco: Jossey-Bass.

Milward, H. Brinton; Provan, Keith G.; and Else, Barbara A. 1993. "What Does the 'Hollow State' Look Like?" In *Public Management: The State of the Art*, ed. Barry Bozeman, 309–22. San Francisco: Jossey-Bass.

Mintzberg, Henry. 1973. *The Nature of Managerial Work*. Englewood Cliffs, NJ: Prentice-Hall.

———. 1979. "An Emerging Strategy of 'Direct' Research." *Administrative Science Quarterly* 24, no. 4 (December): 582–89.

Moe, Ronald C. 1992. *Reorganizing the Executive Branch in the Twentieth Century: Landmark Commissions*. CRS Report for Congress, 92–293 GOV, Congressional Research Service, March. Washington, DC: Library of Congress.

———. 1993. "Let's Rediscover Government, Not Reinvent It." *Government Executive* 25, no. 6 (June): 46–49.

———. 1994. "The 'Reinventing Government' Exercise: Misinterpreting the Problem, Misjudging the Consequences." *Public Administration Review* 54, no. 2 (March/April): 111–22.

Mohrman, Susan Albers, and Mohrman, Allan M. Jr. 1989. "The Environment as an Agent of Change." In *Large-Scale Organizational Change*, ed. Allan M. Mohrman Jr., Susan Albers Mohrman, Gerald E. Ledford Jr., Thomas G. Cummings, Edward E. Lawler III, and Associates, 35–47. San Francisco: Jossey-Bass.

Morgan, Gareth. 1988. *Riding the Waves of Change: Developing Managerial Competencies for a Turbulent World*. San Francisco: Jossey-Bass.

Nadler, David A., and Tushman, Michael L. 1989. "Leadership for Organizational Change." In *Large-Scale Organizational Change*, ed. Allan M. Mohrman Jr., Susan Albers Mohrman, Gerald E. Ledford Jr., Thomas G. Cummings, and Edward E. Lawler III, and Associates, 100–119. San Francisco: Jossey-Bass.

———. 1990. "Beyond the Charismatic Leader: Leadership and Organizational Change." *California Management Review* 32, no. 2 (Winter): 77–97.

National Academy of Public Administration. 1995. *Effective Downsizing: A Compendium of Lessons Learned for Government Organizations*. Washington, DC: National Academy of Public Administration.

National Performance Review. 1993a. *From Red Tape to Results: Creating a Government That Works Better and Costs Less*. Report of the National Performance Review Led by Vice President Al Gore, 7 September. Washington, DC: U.S. Government Printing Office.

National Performance Review. 1993b. *From Red Tape to Results: Creating a Government That Works Better and Costs Less, Department of the Interior*. Accompanying Report of the National Performance Review Led by Vice President Al Gore, September. Washington, DC: U.S. Government Printing Office.

National Performance Review. 1994. *Creating a Government That Works Better and Costs Less: Status Report*. Report of the National Performance Review Led by Vice President Al Gore, September. Washington, DC: U.S. Government Printing Office.

National Performance Review. 1995. *Common Sense Government: Works Better and Costs Less*. Third Report of the National Performance Review, Vice President Al Gore, September. Washington, DC: U.S. Government Printing Office.

National Performance Review. 1996. *A Report to President Bill Clinton: The Best Kept Secrets in Government*. Fourth Report of the National Performance Review, Vice President Al Gore, September. Washington, DC: U.S. Government Printing Office.

National Performance Review. 1997. *Blair House Papers*. President Bill Clinton and Vice President Al Gore, January. Washington, DC: U.S. Government Printing Office.

Nichols, Earl. 1991. "Roots: How the Defense Logistics Agency Began and How It Grew." *Dimensions Defense Logistics Agency* 12, no. 11 (October): 3–5.

Noer, David M. 1993. *Healing the Wounds: Overcoming the Trauma of Layoffs and Revitalizing Downsized Organizations*. San Francisco: Jossey-Bass.

Nutt, Paul C., and Backoff, Robert W. 1993. "Transforming Public Organizations with Strategic Management and Strategic Leadership." *Journal of Management* 19, no. 2 (Summer): 299–347.

Orum, Anthony M.; Feagin, Joe R.; and Sjoberg, Gideon. 1991. "Introduction." In *A Case for the Case Study*, ed. Joe R. Feagin, Anthony M. Orum, and Gideon Sjoberg, 1–26. Chapel Hill, NC: The University of North Carolina Press.

Osborne, David. 1993. "Reinventing Government." *Public Productivity and Management Review* 16, no. 4 (Summer): 349–56.

Osborne, David, and Gaebler, Ted. 1992. *Reinventing Government: How the Entrepreneurial Spirit Is Transforming the Public Sector*. New York: Penguin Books USA.

Overman, E. Sam, and Boyd, Kathy J. 1994. "Best Practice Research and Postbureaucratic Reform." *Journal of Public Administration Research and Theory* 4, no. 1 (January): 67–83.

Perrow, Charles. 1973. "A Framework for the Comparative Analysis of Organizations." In *Contingency Views of Organization and Management*, ed. Fremont E. Kast and James E. Rosenzweig, 138–59. Chicago: Science Research Associates.

Peters, B. Guy. 1981. "The Problem of Bureaucratic Government." *Journal of Politics* 43, no. 1 (February): 56–82.

Peters, B. Guy, and Savoie, Donald J. 1996. "Managing Incoherence: The Coordination and Empowerment Conundrum." *Public Administration Review* 56, no. 3 (May/June): 281–90.

Peters, Katherine McIntire. 1996. "The Drawdown Drags On." *Government Executive* 28, no. 3 (March): 20–25.

Petrie, Hugh G., and Alpert, Daniel. 1983. "What Is the Problem of Retrenchment in Higher Education?" *Journal of Management Studies* 20, no. 1 (January): 97–119.

Pettigrew, Andrew M. 1985. *The Awakening Giant: Continuity and Change at ICI*. Oxford: Basil Blackwell.

Pfeffer, Jeffrey, and Salancik, Gerald R. 1978. *The External Control of Organizations: A Resource Dependence Perspective*. New York: Harper & Row.

Pfiffner, James P. 1997. "The National Performance Review in Perspective." *International Journal of Public Administration* 20, no. 1 (January): 41–70.

Poister, Theodore H. 1988. "Crosscutting Themes in Public Sector Agency Revitalization." *Public Productivity Review* 11, no. 3 (Spring): 29–36.

Pugh, Derek S.; Hickson, David J.; and Hinings, C. R. 1969. "An Empirical Taxonomy of Work Organizations." *Administrative Science Quarterly* 14, no. 1 (March): 115–26.

Quinn, Robert E. 1988. *Beyond Rational Management: Mastering the Paradoxes and Competing Demands of High Performance*. San Francisco: Jossey-Bass.

Quinn, Robert E.; Faerman, Sue R.; Thompson, Michael P.; and McGrath, Michael R. 1990. *Becoming A Master Manager: A Competency Framework*. New York: John Wiley & Sons.

Quinn, Robert E., and Rohrbaugh, John. 1983. "A Spatial Model of Effectiveness Criteria: Towards a Competing Values Approach to Organizational Analysis." *Management Science* 29, no. 3 (March): 363–77.

Radin, Beryl A. 1995. "Varieties of Reinvention: Six NPR 'Success Stories.' " In *Inside the Reinvention Machine: Appraising Governmental Reform*, ed. Donald F. Kettl and John J. DiIulio Jr., 107–30. Washington, DC: Brookings Institution.

Rainey, Hal G. 1991. *Understanding and Managing Public Organizations*. San Francisco: Jossey-Bass.

————. 1997. *Understanding and Managing Public Organizations*. 2d ed. San Francisco: Jossey-Bass.

Reisner, Marc. 1986. *Cadillac Desert: The American West and Its Disappearing Water*. New York: Viking Penguin.

Relyea, Harold C. 1993. *Reinventing Government and the 103d Congress: A Brief Overview*. CRS Report for Congress, 93-859 GOV, Congressional Research Service, 6 October. Washington, DC: Library of Congress.

Relyea, Harold C., and Galemore, Gary L. 1993. *Reforming Government: The Grace Commission and the National Performance Review*. CRS Report for Congress, 93-933 GOV, Congressional Research Service, 27 October. Washington, DC: Library of Congress.

Robinson, Michael C. 1979. *Water for the West: The Bureau of Reclamation, 1902–1977*. Chicago: Public Works Historical Society.

Roland, Alex. 1983. "National Aeronautics and Space Administration." In *The Greenwood Encyclopedia of American Institutions: Government Agencies*, ed. Donald R. Whitnah, 306–7. Westport, CT: Greenwood Press.

————. 1989. "Barnstorming in Space: The Rise and Fall of the Romantic Era of Spaceflight, 1957–1986." In *Space Policy Reconsidered*, ed. Radford Byerly Jr., 33–52. Boulder, CO: Westview Press.

Rosenblatt, Zehava; Rogers, Kathryn S.; and Nord, Walter R. 1993. "Toward a Political Framework for Flexible Management of Decline." *Organization Science* 4, no. 1 (February): 76–91.

Rosenbloom, David H. 1993. "Editorial: Have an Administrative Rx? Don't Forget the Politics!" *Public Administration Review* 53, no. 6 (November/December): 503–7.

Rubin, Irene S. 1979. "Retrenchment, Loose Structure and Adaptability in the University." *Sociology of Education* 52, no. 4 (October): 211–22.

————. 1980a. "Preventing or Eliminating Planned Deficits: Restructuring Political Incentives." *Public Administration Review* 40, no. 6 (November/December): 621–26.

————. 1980b. "Retrenchment and Flexibility in Public Organizations." In *Fiscal Stress and Public Policy*, ed. Charles H. Levine and Irene S. Rubin, 159–78. Newbury Park, CA: Sage.

————. 1985. *Shrinking the Federal Government: The Effects of Cutbacks on Five Federal Agencies*. New York: Longman.

Salamon, Lester M. 1981. "The Question of Goals." In *Federal Reorganization: What Have We Learned?* ed. Peter Szanton, 58–84. Chatham, NJ: Chatham House.

Sanders, Ronald P. 1994. "Reinventing the Senior Executive Service." In *New Paradigms for Government: Issues for the Changing Public Service*, ed. Patricia W. Ingraham, Barbara S. Romzek, and Associates, 215–38. San Francisco: Jossey-Bass.

————. 1996. "Reinvention: Back to the Future." *Government Executive* 28, no. 12 (December): 47–48.

Sanders, Ronald, and Thompson, James. 1996. "Laboratories of Reinvention: A Special Report." *Government Executive* 28, no. 3 (March): 1A-12A.

————. 1997. "Beyond Reinvention: To Boldly Go . . . ." *Government Executive* 29, no. 4 (April): 45–58.

Schein, Edgar H. 1992. *Organizational Culture and Leadership*. 2d ed. San Francisco: Jossey-Bass.

Schroder, Harold M. 1989. *Managerial Competence: The Key to Excellence*. Dubuque, IA: Kendall/Hunt.

Schroder, Harold M.; Driver, M.J.; and Streufert, S. 1967. *Human Information Processing*. New York: Holt, Rinehart & Winston.

Seidman, Harold, and Gilmour, Robert. 1986. *Politics, Position, and Power: From the Positive to the Regulatory State*. 4th ed. New York: Oxford University Press.

Selznick, Philip. 1957. *Leadership in Administration: A Sociological Interpretation*. White Plains, NY: Row, Peterson.

Shefter, Martin. 1977. "New York City's Fiscal Crisis: The Politics of Inflation and Retrenchment." *Public Interest*, no. 48 (Summer): 98–127.

Shoop, Tom. 1993. "The Executive Transition." *Government Executive* 25, no. 9 (September): 22–25.

————. 1994a. "Targeting Middle Managers." *Government Executive* 26, no. 1 (January): 10–15.

————. 1994b. "True Believer." *Government Executive* 26, no. 9 (September): 16–23.

Singh, Jitendra V. 1986. "Performance, Slack, and Risk Taking in Organizational Decision Making." *Academy of Management Journal* 29, no. 3 (September): 562–85.

Sonnenfeld, Jeffrey A., and Peiperl, Maury A. 1988. "Staffing Policy as a Strategic Response: A Typology of Career Systems." *Academy of Management Review* 13, no. 4 (October): 588–600.

Spencer, Lyle M., and Spencer, Signe M. 1993. *Competence at Work: Models for Superior Performance*. New York: John Wiley & Sons.

Sperry, Roger. 1996. "Reinvention: An Assessment." *Government Executive* 28, no. 11 (November): 65–66.

Starbuck, William H.; Greve, Arent; and Hedberg, Bo L.T. 1978. "Responding to Crisis." In *Studies in Crisis Management*, ed. C.F. Smart and W.T. Stanbury, 111–36. Toronto: Butterworth.

Staw, Barry M.; Sandelands, Lance E.; and Dutton, Jane E. 1981. "Threat-Rigidity Effects in Organizational Behavior: A Multilevel Analysis." *Administrative Science Quarterly* 26, no. 4 (December): 501–24.

Stillman, Richard J. II. 1987. *The American Bureaucracy*. Chicago: Nelson-Hall.

————. 1996. *The American Bureaucracy: The Core of Modern Government*. 2d ed. Chicago: Nelson-Hall.

Strauss, Anselm L. 1987. *Qualitative Analysis for Social Scientists*. Cambridge: Cambridge University Press.

Strauss, Anselm L., and Corbin, Juliet. 1990. *Basics of Qualitative Research: Grounded Theory Procedures and Techniques*. Newbury Park, CA: Sage.

Streufert, Siegfried, and Swezey, R.W. 1986. *Complexity, Managers and Organizations*. Orlando, FL: Academic Press.

Sundquist, James L. 1995. "The Concept of Governmental Management; Or, What's Missing in the Gore Report." *Public Administration Review* 55, no. 4 (July/August): 398–99.

Sutton, Robert I., and D'Aunno, Thomas. 1989. "Decreasing Organizational Size: Untangling the Effects of Money and People." *Academy of Management Review* 14, no. 2 (April): 194–212.

Szanton, Peter. 1981. "So You Want to Reorganize the Government?" In *Federal Reorganization: What Have We Learned?*, ed. Peter Szanton, 1–24. Chatham, NJ: Chatham House.

Taylor, M. Susan, and Giannantonio, Cristina M. 1993. "Forming, Adapting, and Terminating the Employment Relationship: A Review of the Literature from Individual, Organizational, and Interactionist Perspectives." *Journal of Management* 19, no. 2 (Summer): 461–515.

Thompson, James D. 1967. *Organizations in Action*. New York: McGraw-Hill.

Thompson, James R., and Jones, Vernon D. 1995. "Reinventing the Federal Government: The Role of Theory in Reform Implementation." *American Review of Public Administration* 25, no. 2 (June): 183–99.

Thompson, James R., and Ingraham, Patricia W. 1996. "The Reinvention Game." *Public Administration Review* 56, no. 3 (May/June): 291–98.

Tomasko, Robert M. 1990. *Downsizing: Reshaping the Corporation for the Future.* Rev. ed. New York: AMACOM.

Tushman, Michael L.; Newman, William H.; and Romanelli, Elaine. 1986. "Convergence and Upheaval: Managing the Unsteady Pace of Organizational Evolution." *California Management Review* 29, no. 1 (Fall): 29–44.

Tushman, Michael L., and Romanelli, Elaine. 1985. "Organizational Evolution: A Metamorphosis Model of Convergence and Reorientation." In *Research in Organizational Behavior,* vol. 7, ed. L.L. Cummings and Barry M. Staw, 171–222. Greenwich, CT: JAI Press.

U.S. Congress. House. Committee on Government Operations. 1992. *Managing the Federal Government: A Decade of Decline.* A Majority Staff Report to the Committee on Government Operations, Committee Print, December. 102d Cong., 2d sess. Washington, DC: U.S. Government Printing Office.

U.S. Congress. Senate. Committee on Governmental Affairs. 1993. *Organization of Federal Executive Departments and Agencies.* Senate Print 103–26, Part 1, 1 January. 103d Cong., 1st sess. Washington, DC: U.S. Government Printing Office.

U.S. Congress. House. Committee on Government Reform and Oversight. 1995. *Making Government Work: Fulfilling the Mandate for Change.* Third Report by the Committee on Government Reform and Oversight together with Additional Views. House Report 104-435, 21 December. 104th Cong., 1st sess. Washington, DC: U.S. Government Printing Office.

U.S. Congress. House. Committee on Government Reform and Oversight. 1996. *Federal Government Management: Examining Government Performance As We Near the Next Century.* Eighteenth Report by the Committee on Government Reform and Oversight together with Additional and Minority Views. House Report 104-861, 28 September. 104th Cong., 2d sess. Washington, DC: U.S. Government Printing Office.

U.S. Department of Defense. 1997. *Report of the Quadrennial Defense Review.* William S. Cohen, Secretary of Defense, May. Washington, DC: U.S. Department of Defense.

U.S. General Accounting Office. 1993a. *Department of Education: Long-Standing Management Problems Hamper Reforms.* Report GAO/HRD-93-47, May. Washington, DC: U.S. General Accounting Office.

U.S. General Accounting Office. 1993b. *Management Reform: GAO's Comments on the National Performance Review's Recommendations.* Report GAO/OCG-94-1, December. Washington, DC: U.S. General Accounting Office.

U.S. General Accounting Office. 1993c. *Military Downsizing: Balancing Accessions and Losses Is Key to Shaping the Future Force.* Report GAO/NSIAD-93-241, September. Washington, DC: U.S. General Accounting Office.

U.S. General Accounting Office. 1994a. *FDA User Fees: Current Measures Not Sufficient for Evaluating Effect on Public Health.* Report GAO/PEMD-94-26, July. Washington, DC: U.S. General Accounting Office.

U.S. General Accounting Office. 1994b. *Management Reform: Implementation of the National Performance Review's Recommendations.* Report GAO/OCG-95-1, December. Washington, DC: U.S. General Accounting Office.

U.S. General Accounting Office. 1995. *Workforce Reductions: Downsizing Strategies Used in Selected Organizations.* Report GAO/GGD-95-54, March. Washington, DC: U.S. General Accounting Office.

U.S. General Accounting Office. 1996a. *Management Reform: Status of Agency Reinvention Lab Efforts.* Report GAO/GGD-96-69, March. Washington, DC: U.S. General Accounting Office.

U.S. General Accounting Office. 1996b. *Executive Guide: Effectively Implementing the Government Performance and Results Act.* Report GAO/GGD-96-118, June. Washington, DC: U.S. General Accounting Office.

U.S. Office of Personnel Management. 1992. *Occupational Study of Federal Executives, Managers, and Supervisors: An Application of the Multipurpose Occupational Systems Analysis Inventory—Closed Ended (MOSAIC).* Report No. PRD 92-21. Washington, DC: U.S. Office of Personnel Management.

U.S. Office of Personnel Management. 1993. *The Senior Executive Service.* SES-93-1, October. Washington, DC: U.S. Office of Personnel Management.

U.S. Office of Personnel Management. 1994. *Guide to SES Qualifications.* SES-94-01, August. Washington, DC: U.S. Office of Personnel Management.

U.S. Office of Personnel Management. 1995. *The Status of the Senior Executive Service 1994.* SES-95-07, September. Washington, DC: U.S. Office of Personnel Management.

U.S. Office of Personnel Management. 1996. *Guide to Implementing Voluntary Separation Incentive Programs under Public Law 104-208.* 2 December. Washington, DC: U.S. Office of Personnel Management.

Van Wart, Montgomery. 1995. "The First Step in the Reinvention Process: Assessment." *Public Administration Review* 55, no. 5 (September/October): 429–38.

Volcker Commission Report. 1990. *Leadership for America: Rebuilding the Public Service.* Report of the National Commission on the Public Service and the Task Force Reports to the National Commission on the Public Service, Paul A. Volcker, Chairman. Lexington, MA: Lexington Books.

Wamsley, Garry L., and Zald, Mayer N. 1973. *The Political Economy of Public Organizations.* Lexington, MA: D.C. Heath.

Warne, William E. 1973. *The Bureau of Reclamation.* New York: Praeger.

Warwick, Donald P. 1975. *A Theory of Public Bureaucracy: Politics, Personality, and Organization in the State Department.* Cambridge, MA: Harvard University Press.

Whetten, David A. 1980a. "Organizational Decline: A Neglected Topic in the Organizational Science." *Academy of Management Review* 5, no. 4 (October): 577–88.

———. 1980b. "Sources, Responses, and Effects of Organizational Decline." In *The Organizational Life Cycle*, ed. John R. Kimberly, Robert H. Miles, and Associates, 342–74. San Francisco: Jossey-Bass.

———. 1981. "Organizational Responses to Scarcity: Exploring the Obstacles to Innovative Approaches to Retrenchment in Education." *Educational Administration Quarterly* 17, no. 3 (Summer): 80–97.

———. 1987. "Organizational Growth and Decline Processes." In *Annual Review of Sociology*, vol. 13, ed. W. Richard Scott and James F. Short Jr., 335–58. Palo Alto, CA: Annual Reviews.

Whittaker, James B. 1995. *The Government Performance and Results Act of 1993: A Mandate for Strategic Planning and Performance Measurement.* Arlington, VA: Educational Services Institute.

Wilkinson, Charles F. 1992. *Crossing the Next Meridian: Land, Water, and the Future of the West.* Washington, DC: Island Press.

Williams, Walter. 1990. *Mismanaging America: The Rise of the Anti-Analytic Presidency.* Lawrence, KS: University Press of Kansas.

Wolman, Harold. 1980. "Local Government Strategies to Cope With Fiscal Pressure." In *Fiscal Stress and Public Policy*, ed. Charles H. Levine and Irene Rubin, 231–48. Beverly Hills, CA: Sage.

Worster, Donald. 1985. *Rivers of Empire: Water, Aridity, and the Growth of the American West.* New York: Pantheon Books.

Wyatt. 1993. *Best Practices in Corporate Restructuring: Wyatt's 1993 Survey of Corporate Restructuring*. Chicago: Wyatt Company.

Yin, Robert K. 1994. *Case Study Research: Design and Methods*. 2d ed. Thousand Oaks, CA: Sage.

Young, James Harvey. 1983. "Food and Drug Administration." In *The Greenwood Encyclopedia of American Institutions: Government Agencies*, ed. Donald R. Whitnah, 251–57. Westport, CT: Greenwood Press.

Zammuto, Raymond F., and Cameron, Kim S. 1985. "Environmental Decline and Organizational Response." In *Research in Organizational Behavior*, vol. 7, ed. Larry L. Cummings and Barry M. Staw, 223–62. Greenwich, CT: JAI Press.

Index

255